"Wilhelm and Steketee have produced a step-by-step manual that is eminently practical and well grounded in theory and research. This book provides an evidence-based alternative to traditional behavioral treatments for OCD. It will be required reading for all of my students who treat OCD, and it should be read by anyone who works with this complex problem. It will certainly influence the way I approach OCD in my own practice."

— *Martin M. Antony, Ph.D., ABPP, director of the Anxiety Treatment and Research Centre at St. Joseph's Healthcare in Hamilton, ON, and author of* When Perfect Isn't Good Enough *and several other books*

Cognitive Therapy
for Obsessive-Compulsive Disorder

A Guide for Professionals

SABINE WILHELM, PH.D.
GAIL S. STEKETEE, PH.D.

New Harbinger Publications, Inc.

Publisher's Note

This publication is designed to provide accurate and authoritative information in regard to the subject matter covered. It is sold with the understanding that the publisher is not engaged in rendering psychological, financial, legal, or other professional services. If expert assistance or counseling is needed, the services of a competent professional should be sought.

Distributed in Canada by Raincoast Books

Cover design by Amy Shoup; Acquired by Tesilya Hanauer
Edited by Brady Kahn; Text design by Tracy Marie Carlson

Library of Congress Cataloging-in-Publication Data

Wilhelm, Sabine.
  Cognitive therapy for obsessive compulsive disorder : a guide for professionals / Sabine Wilhelm and Gail S. Steketee.
        p. cm.
  Includes bibliographical references.
  ISBN 1-57224-429-1
  1. Obsessive-compulsive disorder—Treatment. 2. Cognitive therapy. I. Steketee, Gail. II. Title.
  RC533.W477 2005
  616.85'22706—dc22
                                                              2005030447

New Harbinger Publications' Web site address: www.newharbinger.com

12   11   10

10   9   8   7   6   5   4   3   2

To Richard and Paula.
—S.W.

To Brian.
—G.S.

Contents

Foreword

It is a pleasure to introduce Drs. Wilhelm and Steketee's cognitive treatment manual for obsessive compulsive disorder (OCD). The authors, both clinical researchers funded by the National Institute of Mental Health and Beck Institute Scholars, have drawn from cognitive theory, cutting-edge empirical research, and their extensive clinical experience to develop the empirically supported treatment presented in this thoughtful, informative, and practical treatment manual.

Drs. Wilhelm and Steketee provide a thorough explanation of the cognitive model of OCD, whereby obsessive anxiety and compulsions are conceptualized as the consequences of problematic *beliefs* about intrusions (thoughts, images, or impulses) that trigger negative emotions and avoidance behavior. In an extension of this model, the authors delineate eight categories or "domains" of beliefs identified by international OCD experts as highly germane to the development and maintenance of OCD. A convenient assessment form enables clinicians to identify the belief domains of greatest clinical relevance for their individual patients with OCD.

Organized according to the eight belief domains, this manual includes detailed descriptions of a variety of cognitive therapy techniques that effectively assist patients in modifying their pathogenic beliefs. Also included are detailed cognitive strategies useful in modifying core beliefs associated with OCD, and with related depressive and anxiety symptoms.

The manual concludes with a chapter on relapse prevention strategies designed to help transfer "therapeutic responsibility" from the therapist to the OCD patient who may be especially hesitant to assume personal responsibility. Unlike treatments that derive predominantly from behavioral theory, the cognitive treatment described in this manual does not require the use of prolonged, in-vivo exposure and response-prevention techniques. Instead, it engages patients in testing their beliefs in brief behavioral experiments, once the original obsessive hypothesis and new alternative hypothesis have been clarified. Thus, this treatment is a pragmatic alternative for clinicians who are unable to conduct lengthy, out-of-office sessions and for patients who refuse to undergo distressing exposures. It is also likely to be especially helpful for patients with mainly mental compulsions (for example, patients who suffer predominantly from sexual, harming, or religious obsessions) for which cognitive methods are uniquely suited.

Drs. Wilhelm and Steketee do a great service in recognizing the heterogeneity of OCD symptom presentations. Their manual provides concrete instructions on how to design a treatment plan so that it is individually tailored to meet the needs of patients who may differ in their particular beliefs. Homework and in-session exercises are clearly described for each treatment module, and reproducible handouts and therapist forms guide the treatment in a step-by-step fashion. The result is a highly readable, comprehensive manual that will benefit the novice as well as experienced clinicians and a wide range of patients with OCD symptoms.

—Aaron T. Beck
   University Professor of Psychiatry
   University of Pennsylvania
   Department of Psychiatry

Preface

People with obsessive-compulsive disorder (OCD) suffer from obsessions and compulsions that interfere with their functioning and cause them considerable emotional distress. These symptoms are the primary target for those who seek treatment because they want relief from their distress and from the constant pressure of coping with unpleasant and time-consuming intrusive thoughts and compulsive behaviors. In this manual we will focus intensively on the OCD thoughts and beliefs that produce negative emotions and drive compulsive behaviors. We describe a method of treatment called cognitive therapy (CT) modified specifically for use with OCD problems. This treatment has several important features that make it particularly attractive for use in clinical settings:

- CT does not require the use of prolonged exposure and response prevention (ERP), which provokes high levels of discomfort, as described in previous manuals (e.g., Kozak & Foa, 1997; Steketee, 1999).

- CT can be conducted entirely in the therapist's office. The protocol is provided in a modular format that is flexible and readily tailored to each client's specific symptoms.

- CT is especially useful for patients with mental rituals and neutralizing strategies.

- The treatment is based on NIMH-funded research and is empirically supported.

This manual is intended to provide a solid basis for conducting cognitive therapy (CT) with limited use of behavioral exposure methods. It provides reproducible handouts and therapist forms that guide the treatment in a step-by-step fashion. Homework and in-session exercises are clearly described for each treatment module. We focus on cognitive therapy alone to enable you to provide effective treatment for patients who are frightened of and unwilling to do the exposures and blocking of rituals. Instead of prolonged exposure, CT uses behavioral experiments designed to test hypotheses about patients' thinking, emotions, and behavior. We believe that competent delivery of this method will enable the large majority of OCD patients to resolve their symptoms and lead more productive lives. Of course, the proof is in the research evidence which strongly supports the benefits of cognitive therapy in OCD and many other disorders.

We would like to acknowledge our sources for this manual, which derives from our own research and clinical practice and is also based on adaptations of previous writings, including manuals and descriptions by Lee Baer (1992), Judith Beck (1995), Mark Freeston, Josée Rhéaume, and Robert Ladouceur (1996), Ingrid Söchting, Maureen Whittal, and Peter McLean (1996), and Patricia van Oppen and Arnaud Arntz (1994). We are especially grateful to Judith Beck and Leslie Sokol of the Beck Institute who provided feedback on portions of an earlier draft of this manual. We are also very grateful for consultation from the following colleagues who have provided specific suggestions for the development of our treatment: Mark Freeston of the University of Newcastle on Tyne; Dianne Chambless of the University of Pennsylvania; Paul Salkovskis at the Maudsley Institute of Psychiatry; and Michael Otto of Boston University. Our work on this manual was greatly assisted by input from the following colleagues who provided direct treatment to patients using an earlier version of this manual: Ulrike Buhlmann, Anne Chosak, Jeanne Fama, and Noreen Reilly-Harrington of Massachusetts General Hospital and Harvard Medical School; Bethany Teachman of the University of Virginia; and Kimberly Wilson at Stanford University. Thanks also to Laura Cook and Kara Watts, from Massachusetts General Hospital, who helped us by reading an earlier draft. We would also like to thank our editor Tesilya Hanauer for her patience and her helpful comments. Without the support from the National Institute of Mental Health, the development of our treatment would not have been possible. Finally, we are both extremely blessed to have kind and thoughtful husbands (Arun Hiranandani and Brian McCorkle) without whose help we would never have been able to find the time and energy to write this manual and conduct the research that supports it.

Chapter 1

Cognitive Features, Theories, and Treatments for OCD

The purpose of this introductory chapter is to familiarize mental health clinicians with the clinical features of OCD that pertain to cognitive treatment, as well as the theoretical model that is the basis for this therapy. The latter part of the chapter reviews research on cognitive treatments for OCD. We do not focus here on behavioral treatments or on the integrative combination of cognitive and behavioral methods because excellent manuals for these methods are already available (see Kozak & Foa, 1997; Steketee, 1999). Because patients with OCD are often very intelligent and well read, clinicians like yourself must be credible experts, fully familiar with the research literature on OCD symptoms and treatment. Without this knowledge, your responses to patients' questions may be inadequate or inaccurate, causing them to question your expertise. So, please read on to make sure you feel well informed before starting this therapy.

SYMPTOMS AND CHARACTERISTICS OF OCD

Obsessions are intrusive and repetitive thoughts, impulses, and/or images that are upsetting and lead people to do compulsive mental or physical actions in order to reduce the discomfort. These compulsions or rituals (we use these words interchangeably) can be overt behaviors or mental manipulations. For example, patients wash their hands, clean things, arrange or put things in order, check (lights, stoves, faucets, locks, papers, etc.), and ask others for reassurance. They also pray, count, form a good image to fix a bad one, do mental checking, repeat words silently, and try to reassure themselves. Freeston and Ladouceur (1997) studied the many forms of what are commonly called *neutralizing* thoughts and behaviors. These include replacing one thought with another, saying "stop," trying to magically undo something, and simply thinking something through carefully. These could be called coping strategies but are often difficult to differentiate from mental rituals. For our purposes in doing therapy, any thought or action that reduces patients' obsessive discomfort can be considered a ritual that you will help them reduce or eliminate altogether via cognitive therapy. As you will see, the cognitive therapy described in this book is especially appropriate for patients with mental rituals and neutralizing coping strategies.

Patients do their compulsive rituals until the discomfort from the obsession subsides. Occasionally, some patients can delay rituals, but rarely can they forego them altogether. Most compulsions are aimed at preventing harm or correcting mistakes, and they are nearly always excessive in comparison to the actual threat. However, most obsessions and compulsions have elements of truth to them; they pertain to "gray" areas in which certainty about harm is difficult to achieve. For example, checking stoves to prevent fire is wise in some situations on a limited basis—but not repeatedly or in all cases. It is true that the use of pesticides or toxic chemicals is problematic, but most people tolerate some exposure to these compounds and even the U.S. Environmental Protection Agency sets tolerance levels for these chemicals that permit very limited exposure. In contrast, patients with chemical contamination fears try to prevent *all* contact, however minute.

In the *Diagnostic and Statistical Manual of Mental Disorders* (DSM-IV; American Psychiatric Association, 1994), OCD is considered an anxiety disorder. Certainly anxiety is a central feature of this condition, along with other emotions such as guilt and shame. OCD is diagnosed when it is time-consuming (more than one hour per day), distressing, and interferes noticeably with functioning in home, social, and work situations. Obsessions are considered to be different from worries about real-life problems evident in generalized anxiety disorder (GAD), problems such as work performance, financial security, and health. However, these two anxiety disorders are similar in the use of mental and behavioral strategies to reduce anxiety. Likewise, psychiatric problems such as hypochondriasis, body dysmorphic disorder (BDD), anorexia, and bulimia have similarities in the type of mental, emotional, and behavioral (ritualized coping strategies) symptoms, although the content of patients' fears is specific to somatic symptoms and appearance concerns. Given the structural similarities of these disorders to OCD, it is not surprising that many of the CT treatment methods described here also work well for these other disorders.

INSIGHT/RECOGNITION OF THE PROBLEM

Most people with OCD consider their behavior unreasonable, although this may not be true of children with this disorder who are not yet fully cognizant of "normal" behavior in the world. Adults may vary in their degree of insight (Foa & Kozak, 1993), and most do not consider their obsessions entirely senseless (Rachman & de Silva, 1978). This is especially true in the middle of an obsessive thought, when discomfort is very high (Kozak & Foa, 1994). Even patients who present with atypical intrusive thoughts (such as climbing up a telephone pole and becoming contaminated with chemicals and then putting these into others' drinks) would be diagnosed with OCD if they considered the event very unlikely but were still quite distressed about it. However, OCD and schizophrenia do sometimes co-occur, and some obsessions can seem frankly delusional when patients lose their perspective and cease to resist them (see the excellent paper by Kozak & Foa [1994] for a discussion). Poor insight can be associated with more severe symptoms, especially if psychotic features are present (Eisen & Rasmussen, 1993; Minichiello, Baer, & Jenike, 1987). However, low insight is not always a predictor of poor therapeutic response (Basoglu, Lax, Kasvikis, & Marks, 1988; Foa, 1979). We do not yet know whether cognitive therapy methods that try to increase patients' rational thinking will be helpful for patients with poor insight. Nonetheless, given the effectiveness of cognitive therapy methods for schizophrenia, it seems reasonable to at least apply CT to OCD patients with low insight to see if they benefit.

TYPES OF OCD SYMPTOMS

Obsessions and compulsions take many forms. Many investigators have tried to classify them into symptom subtypes using various statistical methods (Abramowitz, Franklin, Schwartz, & Furr, 2003; Baer, 1994; Calamari, Wiegartz, & Janeck, 1999; Leckman, Grice, Boardman, & Zhang, 1997; Mataix-Cols, Rauch, Manzo, Jenike, & Baer, 1999; Summerfeldt, Richter, Antony, & Swinson, 1999). Using the Symptom Checklist from the Yale-Brown Obsessive Compulsive Scale (YBOCS) to classify OCD symptoms, these studies identified the following general subtypes:

- harming, religious, and/or sexual obsessions with mental or checking rituals
- contamination obsessions with washing or cleaning rituals
- symmetry and obsessions about certainty, accompanied by ordering rituals
- counting/repeating/checking compulsions
- hoarding

It is important to realize that many patients have more than one type of obsession and compulsion, so the list of subtypes does not translate neatly into types of patients. That is, you will rarely be able to categorize your patients as a "checker" or "washer" because many will have more than one symptom, although one symptom may predominate. We should note here that we are reasonably confident that this manual will apply well to all of the OCD subtypes listed above *except* for compulsive hoarding. For this problem, we refer you to another treatment manual developed by Gail Steketee and Randy Frost (in press).

You may have already realized that knowing what type of symptom a patient has does not necessarily help clinicians know what treatment to provide. Pharmacological, behavioral, and cognitive interventions are similar for most types of symptoms, although we have preliminary indications that hoarding (Abramowitz et al., 2003; Black et al., 1998; Mataix-Cols et al., 1999) is less responsive than other forms of OCD to pharmacological and behavioral intervention. However, behavioral researchers like Foa and Rachman have shown that distinguishing obsessions from rituals, especially mental rituals, is essential in designing treatment using exposure and response prevention. At this point, we still know very little about how specific OCD subtypes affect the outcome of the cognitive therapy you will learn here. We suspect that CT may be slightly less effective than exposure treatment for patients with contamination/washing problems and more effective for those with mental rituals, but it is still too early to tell.

PREVALENCE

About 2 percent of the population have experienced OCD during their lifetime (e.g., Weissman et al., 1994). OCD can begin during early childhood, but onset is most common during adolescence and early adulthood and rarely occurs after age fifty (Rachman & Hodgson, 1980; Rasmussen & Tsuang, 1986). Boys usually develop symptoms earlier than girls, usually in mid-adolescence compared to the early twenties, and women with OCD slightly outnumber men (Bellodi, Sciuto, Diaferia, Ronchi, & Smeraldi, 1992; Rasmussen & Eisen, 1990). Onset usually follows stressful life events (Kolada, Bland, & Newman, 1994; Rachman, 1997) and sometimes actual traumatic experiences (de Silva & Marks, 1999; Rhéaume, Freeston, Léger, & Ladouceur, 1998). However, for up to 40 percent of cases, no precipitant could be identified. Pregnancy, childbirth, and related stressors can play a role, such as new mothers and fathers who begin obsessing about harming their child (Wisner, Peindl, Gigliotti, & Hanusa, 1999). A relatively recent prospective study from Swedish investigators (Skoog & Skoog, 1999) has indicated that most people (80 percent) improve during the forty years after OCD onset. About half had recovered during this time, though many still had subthreshold symptoms, and one-third recovered within the first ten years.

This information is useful to clinicians in suggesting that late onset is unusual and should provoke careful questioning to determine whether unusual events may be at least partly responsible. New parents can be reassured that their intrusive thoughts, no matter how sexual or aggressive, are really *very* common and do not set them apart from other parents of new babies. You can also suggest that OCD is unlikely to resolve by itself without treatment.

COMORBIDITY

Many OCD patients have another diagnosable psychiatric problem, mainly depression and anxiety disorders (e.g., Lucey, Butcher, Clare, & Dinan, 1994; Rasmussen & Eisen, 1990). The most common among these are social phobia, generalized anxiety disorder, and panic disorder for a quarter to half of patients (Eisen et al., 1999). The risk of OCD increases considerably for patients with post-traumatic stress disorder (PTSD; Helzer, Robins, & McEvoy, 1987). Therefore, if trauma is the precipitating factor in your patient's OCD symptoms, determine whether the person also has PTSD symptoms and what you may need to do to address these during or before initiating cognitive therapy for OCD. When OCD co-occurs with GAD, this may indicate stronger beliefs about pathological responsibility and more indecisiveness (Abramowitz & Foa, 1998), both treatable with the CT methods described here. People with GAD tend to drop out of behavioral treatment (Chambless & Steketee, 1999), but this may not be problematic for cognitive therapy, which employs different techniques and probably different mechanisms to achieve change.

OCD and depressed mood co-occur at a very high rate, perhaps more than 75 percent. A serious form of depression called major depressive disorder (MDD) is present in 25 to 30 percent of patients with OCD (Steketee, Henninger, & Pollard, 2000), and lifetime rates for this condition are double these figures. Dysthymia accompanies OCD less frequently, at a rate of approximately 10 percent. The probability of developing a mood disorder after OCD begins is quite common and second only to the likelihood of developing another type of anxiety disorder (Yaryura-Tobias, Grunes, & Todaro, 2000). Because depression usually develops after OCD (Rasmussen & Eisen, 1992; Welner, Reich, Robins, Fishman, & van Doren, 1976), it is often considered a side effect of the poor functioning caused by the OCD symptoms. The fact that both pharmacological and behavioral and cognitive treatments also reduce depression (Cottraux et al., 2001; van Balkom et al., 1994) also suggests that depression is a secondary rather than a primary problem.

Thus, concurrent depression is *not* an indication that you should not proceed with cognitive therapy, and in fact, CT appears to be especially successful in reducing comorbid mood problems (see the upcoming section, Treatments for OCD). At the present time, we have relatively little information about whether other types of comorbid problems interfere with the benefits of cognitive therapy. For individual cases, it makes sense to evaluate concurrent psychiatric symptoms (for example, panic attacks) to determine if these play any role in the occurrence of obsessions and compulsions. If so, clinicians should consider how these might be treated in conjunction with the cognitive methods described here.

OBSESSIONS AND NORMAL INTRUSIONS

It is very important that you understand the cognitive models of OCD because they form the basis for developing a case formulation to help patients understand their symptoms and to guide your decisions about how to apply the cognitive therapy techniques in this manual. The following information can be especially useful in helping patients understand the natural process of intrusive mental phenomena.

Several investigators have studied whether intrusive thoughts, images, and impulses occur in ordinary people, not just in psychiatric patients. In 1978 in Britain, Rachman and de Silva asked 124 college students to complete a questionnaire about their mental experiences. Fully 80 percent of the sample reported intrusive thoughts and images whose content was quite similar to intrusive thoughts of people with OCD. Intrusions occurred more often when the participants were anxious or depressed, and these students tried to resist their unpleasant thoughts. The only differences were that the OCD patients experienced the intrusions for longer periods, felt more upset about them, and found them harder to dismiss. Two other studies have reported very similar findings, indicating that intrusive thoughts and images occur in about 90 percent of ordinary people from the community, who also use many ritual-like strategies to neutralize or fix the intrusions (Freeston, Ladouceur, Thibodeau, & Gagnon, 1991; Salkovskis & Harrison, 1984). The important conclusion from these studies is that people with and without OCD differ only in the quantity and severity of the intrusive thoughts, but not their presence, form, or content. These studies have led directly to the development of cognitive models proposing that how people interpret their intrusive thoughts determines whether they will develop OCD (e.g., Freeston et al., 1996; Rachman, 1997; Salkovskis, 1989; Wilhelm, 2000).

ETIOLOGY OF OCD

What might cause people's ordinary intrusive mental experiences to develop into OCD? We do not yet have a complete explanation, but the research literature points to several possibilities. As many researchers have suggested (e.g., Steketee & Barlow, 2002), both biological and psychological vulnerabilities are probably important determinants of whether OCD develops. In recent years, extensive findings from neuroimaging research indicate that particular neural pathways, especially the orbito-frontal region of the brain and possibly the basal ganglia, are involved in OCD. In addition, several studies indicate that both medication and behavioral interventions help normalize this type of brain activity (Baxter et al., 1992; Schwartz, Stoessel, Baxter, Martin, & Phelps, 1996).

Stressors and Mood

Psychological stress is probably also an important factor in the onset of OCD, because stressors prompt intrusive thoughts (e.g., Horowitz, 1975; Parkinson & Rachman, 1981). In addition, depressed and anxious mood can trigger intrusive thoughts. This may be because it is easier for people to think fearful and sad thoughts that match their mood and because it is harder for patients to dismiss intrusive thoughts when they are in a bad mood (Freeston et al., 1996; Rachman & Hodgson,

1980). Thus, stressful events may provide a direct pathway to intrusive thoughts via negative emotions (see Jones & Menzies, 1997). For clinical intervention purposes, these research findings suggest that you will want to understand clearly the patient's past and especially current sources of distress, so these can be considered during the case-formulation and treatment-planning stages for managing obsessive intrusions.

Pregnancy, Childbirth, and Responsibility

Previously we mentioned that pregnancy and childbirth were sometimes precipitants for OCD. Intrusive thoughts are very common among new parents, including fathers, often taking the form of fearing the child will be harmed or die. When such thoughts are misinterpreted to indicate bad parenting or an increased likelihood of harming a child, parents can develop OCD. These sorts of negative self-evaluations sometimes arise because the new parents were trained to feel responsible and guilty during their formative childhood years. As Salkovskis, Shafran, Rachman, and Freeston (1999) have proposed, early responsibility and rigid rules for conduct in school or at home could predispose some people to OCD. This sort of training may reinforce the notion that having certain thoughts is as bad as doing the action (thought-action fusion) and that simply thinking about harmful events increases their probability (magical thinking) (Rachman, 1993; Shafran, Thordarson, & Rachman, 1996). Both of these ideas are common in OCD and you can directly question your patients about these issues.

COGNITIVE MODELS OF OCD

Aaron T. Beck (1976) is widely credited with the development of cognitive theory, which was originally applied to depression. This theory provides the basis for understanding how intrusive thoughts could promote obsessive fears and rituals. Beck proposed that people hold strong beliefs about themselves, others, and the world around them and that these deep-seated or core beliefs determine their interpretation of everyday events, which in turn dictates their mood and actions. Fearful core beliefs ("I'm vulnerable," "The world is dangerous") will lead to interpretations about danger, anxious mood, and overly protective actions. People who hold strong positive beliefs about themselves and others usually attribute little importance to their intrusive thoughts, even if they were initially disturbing. As a result, they experience little discomfort and can easily ignore or dismiss the ideas (Guidano & Liotti, 1983). In contrast, those with negative basic beliefs will have much more difficulty ignoring intrusive unpleasant thoughts.

Role of Beliefs About Responsibility

For OCD in particular, Salkovskis (1985, 1989) suggested that distorted beliefs about personal responsibility for preventing harm is the major mechanism through which intrusive thoughts provoke anxiety. A thought that a fire might be caused by a toaster oven would be ignored by someone without OCD, who would merely remind himself that the toaster had never malfunctioned and that he was just upset because of a problem at work. However, if the intrusive thought activated general beliefs about being a responsible person and having a duty to prevent catastrophic events, the person vulnerable to OCD would engage in compulsive checking to make sure the duty was fulfilled.

Most intrusions probably produce distress only if they have special meaning for the person (Salkovskis, 1985, 1989). For example, a woman who grew up with parents who had high expectations and strongly criticized her mistakes might easily develop perfectionistic attitudes, guilt, or even shame, followed by over-responsible behavior. These experiences would be especially influential when she faced increased responsibilities and stress about leaving home, marriage, pregnancy and childbirth, or a job promotion. In this way, people who develop OCD may come to associate ordinary intrusive thoughts at times of stress with potential danger, for which they feel personally responsible.

Role of Harm Beliefs

OCD may also develop in people who overestimate the probability and severity of harm or danger, especially when they cannot tolerate ambiguity or uncertainty about the potential threat (e.g., Carr, 1974; Foa & Kozak, 1986; Obsessive Compulsive Cognitions Working Group [OCCWG], 1997). For example, Kozak, Foa, and McCarthy (1988) proposed that people with OCD have flawed reasoning when they assume that danger is present unless they can assure themselves the situation is safe. The doubting of one's personal experience seems to be a hallmark of OCD, and laboratory studies indicate that people with OCD have considerable difficulty making even simple decisions (e.g., Persons & Foa, 1984; Reed, 1985). They request more information to help them make decisions and frequently doubt their actions compared to others, perhaps because of perfectionistic attitudes and presumptions of danger rather than safety (Frost & Steketee, 1997). Doubting and seeking certainty in OCD may also reflect cognitive-information processing problems (trouble categorizing or organizing things, focusing on something new) in addition to responsibility and threat biases (Savage et al., 1999).

Below we describe several types of problematic beliefs that OCD patients are likely to have. We incorporated these beliefs into our own cognitive model of OCD, which is described later in this chapter. These beliefs will become the direct targets in cognitive therapy.

TYPES OF BELIEFS IN OCD

A large group of researchers who have studied OCD extensively outlined three types of thinking they considered important for the development and persistence of OCD. We have already discussed (1) intrusions—unwanted thoughts, impulses, or images, and

(2) interpretations or appraisals—the meaning given to events and intrusions. The third level is (3) beliefs—enduring assumptions held across situations (OCCWG, 1997). These researchers described six types of beliefs they considered important for the development and/or maintenance of OCD symptoms. Some of these are considered specific to OCD problems (importance given to thoughts, responsibility), whereas others are relevant to OCD but also occur in other disorders, such as anxiety disorders (overestimation of threat, perfectionism).

Overimportance of Thoughts

This refers to the idea that just having a thought means that the thought is important and requires special attention. Some people with OCD may mistakenly believe that thoughts signal actions, a phenomenon described as thought-action fusion (TAF; Rachman, 1993). This type of thinking has been divided into moral TAF and likelihood TAF. Moral TAF is evident in a mother who concludes that thinking about molesting a child means she is just as guilty as if she had actually done this. This belief leads her to try to protect children by avoiding being alone with them. Likelihood TAF is evident in a man who believes that thinking about stabbing someone makes him more likely to do it. These intrusions cause great anxiety because the person mistakenly concludes that the thoughts reveal their bad or dangerous nature, for example, "I'm a pervert; I'm a danger to others." Individuals with superstitious, sexual, religious, and harming obsessions usually have difficulty with overimportance of thoughts and with the belief that they can control their thoughts.

Control of Thoughts

Beliefs that intrusions are important are usually accompanied by efforts to control or suppress them. These represent "thinking about thinking," also called metacognition. People who believe they must control their thoughts usually employ mental rituals like replacing a good thought with a bad one. Efforts to control particular thoughts usually result in a rebound effect, so that trying to suppress or block thoughts actually makes them recur more frequently.

Overestimation of Danger

OCD sufferers often overestimate the likelihood of danger and of making mistakes, and they presume the worst outcomes. An example is "I am much more likely to be punished than others." In contrast to most people who presume they are safe unless there is clear evidence of danger, OCD patients appear to assume the reverse—a situation is dangerous unless proven safe. This is a difficult problem, since guarantees of safety are nearly impossible to obtain. Rituals to achieve this guarantee require extensive repetition because there is always room for error, even for the most careful people. Individuals with OCD may also employ unusual methods for estimating the likelihood of harm, relying more heavily on recent salient events (a newspaper article, something someone told them) to make predictions rather than taking into account the objective frequency of events over time. Overestimation of danger might be found, for example, in individuals with contamination fears, with concerns about getting an illness or disease, and with concerns about causing terrible outcomes (such as a fire, burglary, etc.).

Desire for Certainty

Sookman, Pinard, and Beck (2001) suggested that patients' distorted beliefs about the need for certainty are related to their perceived inability to cope with ambiguity, newness, and unpredictable change. OCD patients have difficulty tolerating ambiguous situations and tend to doubt the adequacy of their decisions and actions. Related to this problem are beliefs that it is important to be certain about things, and that he or she will not function in situations that are inherently ambiguous. An example is "If I'm not absolutely sure of something, I'm bound to make a mistake." Desire for certainty often motivates reassurance seeking, checking, and rereading. Of course, guarantees of safety can rarely be assured, and therefore the need for complete certainty to prevent mistakes and harm produces chronic anxiety in OCD patients and compensatory rituals (especially checking, mental reviewing, reassurance seeking).

Responsibility

As we have already suggested, people with OCD often consider themselves responsible for preventing danger. Responsibility refers to the belief that you possess pivotal power to cause or prevent particular unwanted outcomes, often with moral overtones. This can take the form of errors of commission (for example, "My thoughts about harming someone will cause me to commit an aggressive action") and errors of omission (for example, "If I don't pick up the nail on the road, someone will have an accident because of me"). Patients with these beliefs may view responsibility for feared outcomes as exclusively theirs rather than being shared with others. Assuming too much responsibility produces guilt and compulsions to relieve it. Not surprisingly, responsibility is often about protecting people from danger or harm, another component of OCD beliefs.

Perfectionism

Closely related to the need for certainty is perfectionism. We have already noted how the potential etiological significance of perfectionism for OCD and early experiences with rigid teachings might lead people to be more vulnerable to perfectionistic standards and fears of failing (Frost & Steketee, 1997; McFall & Wollersheim, 1979). Perfectionistic attitudes presume that it is both possible and desirable to find an exact solution to every problem. People may believe that even minor mistakes will have serious consequences. Examples are "Making a mistake is as bad as failing completely" and "If I don't do it perfectly, people won't respect me." Perfectionism has been linked to checking (Gershuny & Sher, 1995), rereading to understand something perfectly, repetitive washing to feel perfectly clean (Tallis, 1996), repeating and ordering rituals, and may be an important feature of obsessions and compulsions about needing to know.

In addition to the above six types of beliefs, two other cognitive domains not formally identified by the OCCWG (1997) are consequences of anxiety and fear of positive experiences. In our experience, these problems occur fairly commonly among OCD patients, although certainly they are not exclusive to this disorder.

Consequences of Anxiety

Irrational beliefs about being unable to tolerate anxiety or emotional discomfort may play a role in the development and maintenance of OCD. Extreme variants of these beliefs include fears that the person will lose control and "go crazy" or become mentally ill, although there is no evidence to support the fears. Other variants include fears that anxiety will render the person nonfunctional or cause him or her unusual embarrassment ("If I get too anxious, I'll fall apart"). Susceptible individuals may view rituals and avoidance as their only available coping strategy to prevent anxiety from causing one of these outcomes.

Fear of Positive Experiences

As they make progress in treatment, some people with OCD express concern that they do not deserve or will not be able to sustain the positive experiences they have briefly experienced. Although sometimes merely superstitious ("Good events will be followed by bad ones"), these doubts often take on a moral character, as people believe they are unworthy of simply enjoying life. People may actively shy away from positive experiences to avoid activating these anxiety- and guilt-provoking beliefs.

MOOD AND BELIEFS

Steketee and Barlow (2002) suggested that OCD patients' anxiety about internal cognitive cues (intrusions), as opposed to somatic events as in panic disorder, or external objects or situations as in specific and social phobia, has other implications. People with phobias can usually control their fears by avoiding events that cause them to panic. But people with OCD are continually buffeted with aversive mental intrusions that are not controllable, despite their best efforts. This has two effects. First, they strongly resist these mental experiences and develop overt and covert compulsions to neutralize them. Second, the rising anxiety sets off false alarms that become linked to the focus of their concern—the specific thoughts themselves. Some research evidence indicates that when ordinary people try to not think about unwanted thoughts, they paradoxically increase the salience of such ideas, making them even harder to dismiss (see Purdon,

1999; Wegner, 1989). When their efforts to suppress unwanted intrusions fail, they resort to rituals (Clark & Purdon, 1993).

Depressed mood also plays an important role in this process. Negative (obsessive) thoughts are more easily suppressed by other negative thoughts, but unfortunately, such depressing thoughts may further lower the mood of people with OCD (Salkovskis & Campbell, 1994; Wegner, 1989). Because intrusive thoughts are not controllable, people who experience strong unpleasant thoughts and images also feel helpless, an important precursor to the depression that so commonly accompanies OCD. People who have already experienced serious depression in stressful contexts may be especially prone to intrusive thoughts. This combination of depressed mood, obsessions, and compensatory compulsions produces an interactive downward spiral of more depression, more anxiety, and more OCD symptoms.

Like mood, comorbid conditions may also affect beliefs. For example, seriously depressed OCD patients may hold beliefs about being helpless to change events around them and may be hopeless about the future. Those with generalized anxiety disorder or post-traumatic stress disorder may interpret the world as a dangerous place that requires constant vigilance. A patient with social phobia may perceive rejection by others when there is little evidence to support this, thereby avoiding social situations necessary for testing OCD beliefs. Such beliefs are likely to impede progress in actively completing work regarding OCD beliefs. When interpretations and beliefs associated with comorbid conditions affect progress on OCD symptoms, they must be addressed in therapy, using the same cognitive therapy techniques described below for OCD. Although this manual is directed exclusively at OCD symptoms, some of the strategies may also have beneficial effects on other problems the patient is experiencing.

SUMMARY OF THE COGNITIVE MODEL FOR OCD

Figure 1 illustrates the elements of a cognitive model for OCD. To summarize, OCD probably begins following stress-related negative mood and neurobiological reactions that are triggered by negative life events and biological vulnerability. Like most people, people with OCD experience intrusive thoughts (images, impulses), but unfortunately they judge these ideas to be unacceptable and try to avoid or suppress them. When the thoughts invariably recur, this intensifies anxiety, depression, and guilt and reinforces the person's impression that the thoughts are unpredictable and uncontrollable. A pernicious negative feedback loop develops, as attention narrows onto the unacceptable thoughts that fail to respond to efforts to suppress them. Indeed, efforts to suppress the intrusions serve to increase their frequency. The type of obsession a person experiences often appears to be determined by previous learning that certain thoughts or images are unacceptable. Examples are blasphemous intrusions in someone raised with strict religious teachings and fears of mistakes in someone raised to strive for perfection. These mental intrusions become phobic triggers that provoke alarm and even panic. The relentlessness of this process often leads to hopelessness and depression that are

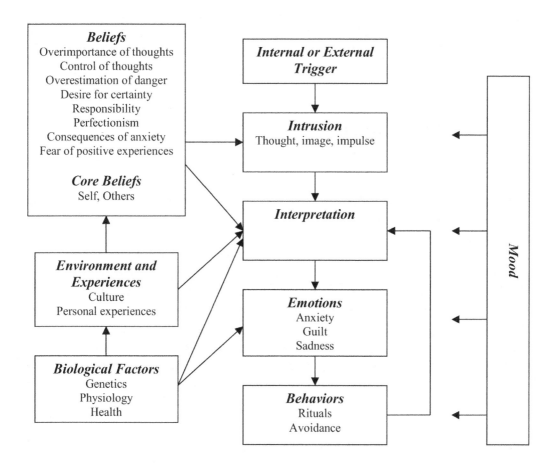

Figure 1: Cognitive Model of OCD

further exacerbated as the OCD symptoms interfere with usual effective functioning. The cognitive therapy described here directly targets patients' interpretations of intrusive thoughts and long-standing negative beliefs to interrupt the negative spiral of obsessions and compulsions that so disrupt functioning and contribute to depression and hopelessness.

TREATMENTS FOR OCD

Three types of treatment are known to be effective for OCD. Here we will briefly review findings about behavior therapy (exposure to feared situations and blocking of rituals) and pharmacological treatments (serotonergic medications) to provide you with summary information in case patients have questions about these methods compared to cognitive therapy. The findings for cognitive therapy for OCD follow in greater detail to substantiate the techniques we describe in this manual. Although compared to the number of studies of behavioral and medication treatments, fewer studies have examined the effects of cognitive therapy, research support for CT is strong and rapidly increasing.

Behavioral Treatment

Behavioral treatment uses prolonged exposure to feared situations that are linked to obsessions and response prevention or blocking of mental and overt rituals. This treatment is based on early findings that obsessions provoke anxiety or discomfort and compulsions reduce this (e.g., Rachman & Hodgson, 1980). Researchers also determined that extended and repeated periods of exposure to feared situations leads to reduction in emotional arousal (habituation) so that the triggers for obsessions no longer provoke discomfort. The major goal in exposure and response prevention (ERP) treatment is to provide sufficient exposure without interruption from rituals, so obsessive discomfort can habituate. Exposure also seems to change patients' attitudes toward their obsessions (they become less disturbing), toward anticipated danger (it seems less likely), and toward their capacity to cope (patients feel more capable). Whether it also changes other types of beliefs, such as excessive responsibility or perfectionistic attitudes, is unclear. In any case, it seems likely that behavioral treatment may also promote changes in beliefs that aid habituation and progress in therapy.

Meta-analyses of thirty or more open trials and controlled studies using hundreds of patients have indicated that ERP is highly effective. Van Balkom et al. (1994) reported that behavior therapy produced a very large average effect size (ES=1.46) and was significantly more effective than placebo treatments. In another meta-analysis, Abramowitz (1997) confirmed these findings and reported that more sessions with longer exposures produced greater benefit. Studies using the YBOCS to assess outcomes have reported reductions from average scores indicating moderately severe symptoms (scores of about 25) before therapy to scores in the mild to moderate range (10 to 17) after fifteen to twenty sessions of ERP (Steketee & Frost, 1998). Most patients (75 to 80 percent) who entered treatment were likely to benefit.

These findings are impressive, but it is important to remember that about 25 percent of patients refuse exposure treatment. Further, when drop-out, failure, and relapse rates are added together, only about 50 percent of patients actually benefit from ERP. Thus, there is room for improvement, especially by reducing the number of patients who refuse this therapy. Hiss, Foa, and Kozak (1994) helped improve the failure rate by demonstrating that including relapse strategies reduced relapse. Such methods are now commonly included in behavioral and cognitive therapies for OCD and other disorders.

Studies of predictors for behavioral treatment outcome provide some clues that encourage clinicians to consider using cognitive therapy techniques. Both poor insight and serious depression have been identified as potential problems for therapists using ERP (Foa, 1979; Steketee, Chambless, & Tran, 2001; Steketee & Shapiro, 1995). Cognitive techniques may prove especially useful for the problems posed by depression, as CT methods were originally developed for depressed patients (Beck, 1976) and recent research suggests that depressed mood in OCD patients responds well to CT

(Cottraux et al., 2001). Unfortunately, whether OCD patients with poor insight would respond to CT methods remains untested.

Pharmacological Treatment

Serotonergic reuptake inhibitors (SRIs; e.g., clomipramine) and selective serotonin reuptake inhibitors (SSRIs; e.g., fluoxetine, fluvoxamine, sertraline, paroxetine, citalopram, venlafaxine) have emerged as effective medications for reducing obsessions and compulsions. Although clomipramine has been the most extensively studied drug for OCD, meta-analyses do not indicate that it is better than other serotonergic medications (Abramowitz, 1997; Pigott & Seay, 1999), and the newer SSRIs are generally better tolerated. These medications reduce OCD symptoms by about 50 percent on average, according to the YBOCS, and most patients scored below 16, the cutoff for entry into OCD clinical trials, after about ten weeks on medications.

Most reviews indicate that serotonergic drugs do not differ in their relative effectiveness. The mechanism by which they work to reduce OCD symptoms remains poorly understood. These drugs do not perform better than ERP (e.g., Kozak, Liebowitz, & Foa, 2000), nor have they increased the benefits of ERP, according to several studies (Cottraux et al., 1990; Kozak et al., 2000; van Balkom et al., 1998). However, in routine clinical practice, medications and behavioral therapy are commonly combined (March, Frances, Carpenter, & Kahn, 1997). When medications are discontinued, relapse often follows (O'Sullivan, Noshirvani, Marks, Monteiro, & Lelliott, 1991; Pato, Zohar-Kadouch, Zohar, & Murphy, 1988), rendering medications alone a less desirable therapy. Behavior therapy administered with medication seems to protect patients from relapse when medication is withdrawn (Kozak et al., 2000). So far, cognitive treatment has not been tested against or in combination with medications.

COGNITIVE THERAPY

If behavioral and pharmacological treatments work for OCD, why use cognitive therapy? There are several reasons for this, not the least of which is that research indicates that CT for OCD is highly effective. Below we review these findings.

Individual Cognitive Therapy

The first controlled study of cognitive therapy for OCD patients was conducted in the Netherlands by Emmelkamp, Visser, and Hoekstra (1988) using rational emotive therapy (Ellis, 1962). This study and a later one by the same group (Emmelkamp & Beens, 1991) found the cognitive method as effective as ERP. Combining cognitive methods with exposure techniques was no more effective than either treatment alone.

More recent studies have used a Beckian cognitive therapy method of identifying problematic thoughts and beliefs and helping patients determine their effects on negative mood and compulsive behaviors. This method uses Socratic dialogue to identify and challenge beliefs that support OCD behavior, as well as other cognitive strategies designed to evaluate and correct problematic beliefs of people with OCD. The techniques used in these treatments are included in this manual, along with additional ones we have employed in our own research described below. Van Oppen et al. (1995) published the first study to examine a pure form of CT that included only behavioral experiments but no pronged exposures. She and her colleagues compared this to self-controlled ERP that may have been a weaker form of treatment than employed in the ERP studies described earlier. CT methods were based on Beck's (1976) and Salkovskis' (1985) model. Both ERP and CT were equally effective. After session sixteen, patients receiving CT showed slightly more improvement on measures of anxiety and general irrational beliefs.

Cottraux et al. (2001) tested the effects of twenty sessions of CT given once or twice weekly, using similar methods to van Oppen's study, compared to a more intensive therapist-directed ERP. CT was quite effective and did not differ from ERP. At a one-year follow-up, 76 percent of CT patients and 87 percent of ERP patients remained at least 25 percent improved. Overall, both treatments performed well on most measures, with ERP showing slightly greater effects on OCD symptoms compared to CT's slightly greater effects on obsessive beliefs and depressed mood.

Freeston et al. (1997) combined CT techniques with ERP methods and compared these to a waitlist control condition for OCD patients who had severe obsessions and only mental rituals, traditionally considered hard to treat. Cognitive behavioral therapy (CBT) included education about the cognitive model, loop-taped exposure to obsessions, response prevention, a variety of CT techniques, and relapse prevention. CT techniques were targeted toward overimportance of intrusive thoughts, perfectionism, intolerance of uncertainty, need to control thoughts, inflated responsibility, and overestimation of threat. This type of CBT was highly effective for OCD symptoms, anxiety, and depression, and at six-month follow-up, 53 percent of patients maintained their improvement. Interestingly, most of the 22 percent who dropped out of therapy did so during the exposure phase.

Our own research group has studied the effects of the specific CT techniques described in this manual, which are intended to reduce common cognitive distortions among OCD patients (Wilhelm et al., in press). In an open trial of CT with fifteen OCD patients, we provided fourteen weekly one-hour sessions. Scores on the YBOCS reduced substantially from 23.3 to 13.5, well below the clinical cutoff of 16. Patients also improved significantly on depressed mood, anxiety, and on OCD beliefs. Unfortunately, five patients who had previously failed to benefit from ERP improved only marginally using cognitive methods, but those with no previous behavioral treatment improved greatly. Our study is preliminary and our sample size is small, so we are not yet sure whether CT will be an effective alternative therapy for patients who have not benefited from ERP. However, since there are few alternatives, clinicians may certainly wish to try CT with patients who fail ERP treatment.

We are currently completing the follow-up phase of another trial of CT compared to a waitlist control condition, using more extensive cognitive techniques plus brief behavioral experiments, but no ERP (Wilhelm, Steketee, Fama, & Golan, 2003). In this revised therapy, patients received twenty-two one-hour sessions of CT. Sessions were held weekly except for two final relapse prevention sessions which were spaced two weeks apart. The specific methods of treatment are detailed in this manual. Findings from fifteen patients in each group showed that CT patients' OCD symptoms reduced substantially on the YBOCS, whereas waitlisted patients' symptoms did not change. Depressed mood also reduced.

Group Cognitive Therapy

Cognitive methods delivered in a group therapy format for OCD patients have been less successful than individual treatment. Cordioli et al. (2003) combined cognitive and behavioral methods in twelve two-hour sessions and compared them to a waitlist condition. Although group CBT benefited sixteen of the twenty-three patients, who improved at least 35 percent after therapy, half of the treated patients continued to have significant symptoms, and many showed limited compliance because of fears of exposure.

McLean et al. (2001) used a very similar format to provide group ERP or group CT compared to waitlist control. Although both active treatments were more effective than waitlist, ERP was more effective for OCD symptoms after treatment and at three-month follow-up, despite the higher drop-out rate in this group. The poor showing of CT in this trial compared with previous studies was due to the group method, which may not have afforded sufficient time to evaluate and address individual OCD beliefs. In fact, only one of seven belief domains changed after CT in this study, in contrast to our findings in which all belief domains showed change after individual CT.

The same group of researchers then conducted another study of individually treated patients using CT and ERP (Whittal, Thordarson, & McLean, in press). The individual CT method produced lower YBOCS scores than did group methods; after treatment, 67 percent of individual CT participants were clinically significantly improved compared to only 16 percent of group CT members. Interestingly, both CT and ERP led to equal improvement on measures of OCD beliefs, with more improvement occurring in the individually treated patients.

In summary, research on the effectiveness of CT treatments indicates that these methods are quite effective in treating OCD, probably as effective as ERP. This treatment should be administered individually. CT appears to have broad therapeutic effects, decreasing not only OCD symptoms but also depression, general anxiety, and distorted beliefs. Nonetheless, more research is needed to fully establish the efficacy and mechanisms of change in CT.

Does CT Help with Refusal, Dropout, Failure, and Relapse?

Treatment acceptability and compliance is an important problem for therapists treating OCD patients. Refusal rates for ERP are in the range of 25 to 30 percent, about 15 to 20 percent who complete ERP do not respond, and another 20 percent relapse (Riggs & Foa, 1993). Combining these figures leaves a large number of treatment seekers without adequate benefit. Although our own study suggests that CT may not be helpful to patients who have already failed to benefit from ERP, it may help those who refuse ERP. When we asked fifteen treatment applicants who requested psychosocial treatment (not medication) whether they would prefer CT or ERP, thirteen (87 percent) chose CT, suggesting that it may be more acceptable to most patients than ERP. Because CT is a relatively new treatment for OCD, some prospective patients may have avoided contacting our OCD clinic, thinking that their only options were ERP and/or medications, neither of which may be acceptable to them. In our recent CT study, very few patients refused cognitive therapy (Wilhelm et al., 2003).

Drop-out rates as high as 20 percent have been observed in CT (van Oppen et al., 1995), but they generally appear to be in the 10 to 15 percent range for most CT studies. Our own open trial of CT contained only one of fifteen patients who discontinued and this was because she moved out of the area (Wilhelm et al., in press). Although much more research is needed to determine how acceptable CT is to prospective patients, it appears that CT's very limited use of exposure (behavioral experiments) renders this method less threatening and more acceptable to many patients.

Acceptability of CT to Clinicians

CT may be more comfortable than ERP for therapists as well. High quality ERP treatment requires more than one session per week, often out of the therapist's office, for periods of ninety minutes, if possible (Foa, Franklin, & Kozak, 1998). With most psychology training programs providing at least some training in cognitive therapy methods, CT methods may actually be more readily available to patients with OCD.

CT and Symptom Subtypes

Research on the use of CT for patients with different types of OCD symptoms is very limited at this point. Van Oppen et al. (1995) indicated that CT might be more effective than ERP for checking symptoms, but the difference was not large. We have recently analyzed treatment outcome data from nine different sites that used CT, ERP, and combined treatment. The findings suggest that patients *without* washing rituals may respond better to CT methods than those with washing rituals, and from our own clinical experience, we suspect that ERP may work better for these patients (Wilhelm, Steketee, & Yovel, 2004).

CT may be especially helpful for patients with *pure* obsessions, who have only mental and no behavioral rituals. Experienced ERP therapists can be effective for such patients (e.g., Abramowitz, 2001, 2002), but in general, primary obsessive thoughts have predicted worse outcome with ERP (Christensen, Hadzi-Pavlovic, Andrews, & Mattick, 1987; Mataix-Cols, Marks, Greist, Kobak, & Baer, 2002), perhaps because it is sometimes difficult to identify appropriate exposures and methods for preventing mental rituals. Freeston and colleagues (1997) obtained excellent results for these patients by using cognitive methods combined with loop-tape exposures. This suggests that CT may work well for this group. Our own experience with CT methods has shown good benefits for patients with sexual, religious, and harming obsessions (Wilhelm et al., 2003; Wilhelm et al., in press).

Patients with primary hoarding symptoms fare relatively poorly compared to those with other forms of OCD (Abramowitz et al., 2003; Black et al., 1998; Mataix-Cols et al., 2002). Although there are no controlled trials, case studies indicate that hoarding symptoms may respond to multifaceted treatments that combine psychoeducation, training in decision-making and organizational skills, exposure to not acquiring and to discarding, and cognitive restructuring of beliefs about possessions (e.g., Hartl & Frost, 1999; Steketee, Frost, Wincze, Green, & Douglas, 2000). Thus, inclusion of CT methods for this difficult-to-treat group seems advisable, but CT alone is likely to be insufficient.

CONCLUSIONS

Research findings support the conclusion that specialized cognitive therapy for OCD delivered individually is very effective. Most likely, CT will not prove to be more effective than ERP, but it may work especially well for particular forms of OCD symptoms, such as harming, sexual, and religious obsessions, and for patients with mainly mental rituals. ERP and CT may reduce OCD symptoms through different mechanisms. CT is thought to work by altering distorted beliefs about intrusions and helping patients test their predictions via behavioral experiments. In contrast, ERP is believed to work because it produces habituation of obsessive fears during exposure and prevents rituals from negatively reinforcing obsessions. But it is not yet clear whether these are, in fact, the mechanisms by which CT and ERP are effective. For example, ERP also reduces mistaken beliefs and CT also reduces obsessive anxiety. Ongoing research on the mechanisms responsible for change in OCD will likely shed more light on this issue and may influence how we deliver these treatments. But for now, we know that CT is very acceptable to patients and might reduce drop out from therapy. Overall, cognitive therapy is a very promising method of treatment for OCD, which provides an effective alternative to both ERP and medications.

Chapter 2

Structure and Application of Cognitive Therapy

This manual is designed for use with patients seeking treatment for obsessive-compulsive disorder as their primary psychiatric problem. We don't recommend this manual for use with patients who suffer from comorbid developmental disabilities (e.g. autism), Tourette's syndrome and tic disorders, or personality traits or disorders that interfere significantly with engaging in the treatment process or completing homework. This chapter will familiarize you with the components of cognitive therapy to provide an overview of the entire treatment before you begin to use specific sections of the manual. In arranging treatment for your patients, you will need to consider several elements, including setting goals, deciding on the number and timing of sessions, and selecting the type and sequencing of cognitive strategies. Below we discuss these issues briefly as they apply to most patients and also indicate where more detail on implementing the strategies can be found within this manual.

PRETREATMENT ASSESSMENT

If you don't have an intake interviewer at your clinic, we strongly recommend that you meet with your patient once to determine whether your patient meets criteria for OCD and appears to be a good candidate and interested in CT. We recommend the following measures to determine diagnosis and assess the type and severity of symptoms.

Diagnosing OCD and Comorbid Conditions

To determine whether your patient indeed meets criteria for OCD or has any comorbid conditions that might interfere with treatment outcome, ideally you will conduct a diagnostic interview. The *Structured Clinical Interview for DSM-IV Axis I Disorders—Patient Edition* (SCID-P; First, Spitzer, Gibbon, & Williams, 1995) or the *Anxiety Disorders Interview Schedule* (ADIS; DiNardo, Brown, & Barlow, 1994) may be used for this purpose. You should also ask about tics and other repetitive habits that may have a neurological substrate that is not cognitively mediated. Because CT focuses on interpretations and beliefs, it is unlikely to be useful for tic-like symptoms or repetitive habits.

We have found that CT works well for patients with repugnant (e.g., sexual, religious, or harming) obsessions. While the large majority of patients who sought treatment in our clinic indeed met criteria for OCD, you need to be careful when diagnosing patients who present for treatment for repugnant thoughts. For example, if your patient suffers from postpartum psychosis, some of her negative thoughts (e.g., about harming her baby) might look quite similar to what you'd expect in an OCD patient. Moreover, a patient who suffers from antisocial personality disorder or pedophilia might express thoughts that initially look like OCD (e.g., thoughts about harming or sexually molesting others) but are substantially different. You should consider a diagnosis other than OCD if your patient

- Does not feel distressed by repugnant thoughts but instead finds them logical or pleasurable

- Has acted on violent or inappropriate sexual thoughts or impulses in the past

- Expresses paranoid or delusional ideas or has other psychotic symptoms

- Has a history of angry outbursts and difficulty controlling angry emotions

In such cases, referral to a higher level of care is appropriate to ensure behavioral control.

Optimally, OCD should be the patients' most severe problem and main reason for seeking treatment. Complicating factors that could interfere with full engagement in the treatment process should be identified early for appropriate intervention. It's also important to determine how comorbid problems might influence OCD beliefs and attitudes relevant to cognitive therapy. While comorbid major depression is usually not a problem, symptoms associated with suicidality or severe depression will necessitate a conversation about safety and determination of the potential need for immediate treatment of the mood problem before treating the OCD. Likewise, if domestic violence or self-harming is a current problem, you should determine whether immediate referral is needed to maintain safety, or if not, whether some attention may be needed during treatment to patient attitudes about what they deserve (see chapter 12). Current substance abuse or dependence should be explored to ensure that this will not interfere with motivation and capacity to engage in treatment procedures.

If your patients present with OCD spectrum disorders, such as hypochondriasis or body dysmorphic disorder (BDD), many of the techniques contained in this manual will be helpful. However, you will also need to incorporate disorder-specific interventions into your treatment plan.

Reviewing Current Treatments and Treatment History

Ask your patient if he or she is taking any medications currently. Inquire about all medications, not just psychotropic ones, in case others have psychological side effects. Determine the kind and dosage, and how helpful the medications are for OCD symptoms. Also obtain a history of psychotropic medications if your patient has taken any in the past, including dosages to determine whether these were adequate. Ask your patient about their benefits and problems. If your patient is taking medications currently, discuss how to stabilize the medications prior to starting CT. This way, your patient can determine the direct benefits of the cognitive treatment without confusion about how much improvement might be related to medication changes. This will ensure that your patient appropriately attributes any observed changes to the benefits of their work using cognitive therapy skills.

Determine whether your patient is currently in any other psychological treatments and how helpful this has been. In general, it's not a problem for a patient to also participate in concurrent couples therapy or support groups, so long as the messages learned in those treatments do not conflict with the strategies learned in CT. Concurrent ERP also should not pose a problem and is likely to be very beneficial. However, if your patient wants both treatments, in our clinical experience, it's usually best to start with the CT techniques and introduce exposures and blocking of rituals later on, perhaps around session six or eight. Also inquire about your patient's treatment history, as this will help you determine whether your patient is a good candidate for CT. If your patient didn't benefit from or relapse after a similar treatment in the past, discuss the potential reasons for this (e.g., lack of homework compliance) before agreeing to a course of CT.

Assessing the Severity of OCD and Related Symptoms

We recommend that you ask your patients to complete a small battery of assessment forms before entering treatment. These will assess the severity of OCD symptoms and cognitive aspects pertinent to OCD and mood.

Yale-Brown Obsessive Compulsive Scale (YBOCS; Goodman et al., 1989). This ten-item scale rates the severity of obsessions and compulsions with respect to time spent, interference, distress, resistance against obsessions and compulsions, and control over OCD symptoms. See Steketee (1999) for a copy of this instrument.

Obsessive Compulsive Symptoms Rating Scale (OCSRS; Wilhelm et al., 2005; see the appendix). This measure rates the severity of specific types of obsessions (contamination, harming, sexual, hoarding, religious, symmetry, miscellaneous) and compulsions (cleaning, checking, repeating/counting, ordering/arranging, hoarding, miscellaneous). Although you can determine a total score, the main purpose of this measure is to identify the most severe OCD symptoms.

Obsessive Beliefs Questionnaire—Extended (OBQ-Ext; OCCWG, 1997; see the appendix). The original version of the OBQ self-report instrument assesses general beliefs and attitudes in the cognitive domains that are the subject of this treatment manual: overimportance of thoughts, control of thoughts, overestimation of danger, desire for certainty, responsibility, and perfectionism. Because we have encountered many patients who also exhibit fears of positive experiences and have exaggerated concerns about consequences of anxiety, we have extended the original OBQ by adding questions pertaining to those two domains as well.

You can use the questionnaire to determine any domain's severity. Simply add the scores for statements pertaining to that domain. Note: At the beginning of the questionnaire, the first six belief domains are mixed together, so we've included a scoring key to help you determine which statements reflect which domain. The final two domains are listed separately, so these should be relatively easy to score. This instrument will help you determine what content areas to focus on during CT. While cutoff scores are not available, the following mean scores have been calculated for OCD patients and community participants for the first six domains. To get a sense of the severity of your patient's OCD beliefs, you can compare your patient's score to the scores below (higher scores indicate stronger beliefs).

Normative Scores on the Obsessive Beliefs Questionnaire		
	OCD	Community Participants
Overimportance of thoughts	44.0	21.7
Control of thoughts	60.7	29.1
Overestimation of danger	54.1	24.9
Desire for certainty	54.3	30.2
Responsibility	65.7	37.3
Perfectionism	63.6	36.8
Fear of positive experiences	44.6	not available
Consequences of anxiety	64.4	not available

Beck Depression Inventory—II (BDI-II; Beck, Steer, & Brown, 1996). The BDI-II is a twenty-one-item self-report inventory that measures the severity of depression. This scale is available from Hartcourt Assessment at http://harcourtassessment.com or 1-800-228-0752.

TREATMENT SCHEDULE

This manual was designed for approximately eighteen to twenty-two sessions of cognitive therapy spaced over twenty to twenty-four weeks. Assessment and treatment sessions are scheduled weekly, and the final two relapse prevention sessions are held every other week. If feasible, you can extend the initial assessment sessions (see chapter 4) to allow extra time to collect information, explain the CT model, and formulate the case. Later sessions, in which you are applying specific CT strategies, are typically fifty to sixty minutes long. However, the duration and number of sessions can be flexible, depending on the protocol you and your patient establish for the cognitive therapy. We do recommend a time-limited treatment to assist both you and your patient in remaining focused on CT methods aimed at changing problematic interpretations and beliefs (obsessions), as well as OCD behaviors (avoidance and rituals).

ASSESSMENT AND EDUCATION

Treatment always begins with assessment and education (described in detail in chapter 4), during which you provide information about the nature of OCD and the cognitive model for OCD. Your patient learns about alternative interpretations of intrusions from your description of them as ordinary thoughts that nearly everyone experiences. Here you will need to assist your patient in heightening his or her awareness of factors that may have influenced maladaptive interpretations (past family experience, recent stressors, current mood, etc.). It's also important to help your patient understand the role of avoidance and mental rituals in the maintenance of obsessions. Of course, in this first phase of treatment, you also work on developing rapport and on socializing your patient to cognitive therapy.

After explaining the cognitive model, you will establish a treatment contract (see appendix). Before agreeing to proceed with treatment, it's critical that your patient understands the rationale for cognitive therapy and the content of the treatment. Thus, your patient agrees to learn to identify interpretations of intrusions, and to examine these carefully to determine whether his or her assumptions are reasonable. Moreover, he or she agrees to complete homework assignments. Subsequent sessions focus on learning basic cognitive strategies to identify maladaptive interpretations of intrusive thoughts and to generate possible alternative interpretations. You will learn to use Socratic questioning as well as other cognitive methods to help your patient think of rational alternatives. For example, you might ask, "What is the evidence for and against your specific interpretation? Is your interpretation realistic? What would a friend say about this?" Patients learn to complete thought records in which they record their intrusions and their interpretations and respond in writing to maladaptive interpretations. These cognitive assessment strategies are conducted during office sessions and as homework assignments.

Many of the basic cognitive therapy skills that are useful for all patients are introduced in sessions 1 to 4. They are described in detail in chapter 4. After learning the basics, you and your patient will move on to the modular treatment plan described below.

SELECTING COGNITIVE THERAPY MODULES

Cognitive therapy will proceed differently for different patients, depending on their particular types of obsessions and associated belief domains. Selection of which modules to implement is made during the assessment and education phase of treatment. Usually, this will be decided based on pretreatment scores on the subscales of the Obsessive Beliefs Questionnaire—Extended and on the thoughts recorded on the thought record forms (see appendix). After reviewing these forms, you and your patient together make an educated guess as to which types of domains are most problematic for the person and what order to work on these. Chapters 5 through 12 each cover a different module. The first module selected should be the one that seems responsible for the most prominent and problematic beliefs reflected in interpretations of intrusions and obsessive concerns. So, for example, if your patient's most severe problems are in the realm of overestimating danger (e.g., overestimating the harm that germs can do followed by excessive washing rituals), you would start your treatment with that module (chapter 7). Most patients have problems in more than one domain, so as soon as you have made some headway in the first belief type, usually after about four sessions, move on to the next module. For example, if your patient also has concerns about responsibility, go to chapter 9 next.

You and your patient will typically spend two to four sessions on any given module, with homework assigned for each session, before moving to a new module. You can spend more sessions within a given module in the rare cases where few other modules are pertinent to your patient's obsessions. In these cases, entrenched beliefs may require more sessions for the techniques within the module to be effective. Otherwise, you and your patient will move from one module to the next based on evidence of progress according to homework assignments (including thought records, behavioral experiments, and other tasks assigned) and change in the relevant subscale of the OBQ-Ext. In some cases, you may decide that it's better to assign tasks from two modules at once because both modules are integrally tied to your patient's symptoms. For example, most patients who overestimate the importance of their thoughts also try to control them, making the strategies from both chapters 5 and 6 helpful. If four sessions are insufficient to produce change in beliefs and symptoms within a particular module, and other pertinent modules are applicable, you should move on to a different module in order to produce some change, possibly returning to the problematic domain thereafter.

APPLYING COGNITIVE THERAPY TECHNIQUES

After deciding on the basic plan for which beliefs to address and in what order, you will need to use a wide variety of cognitive therapy techniques, many of which are appropriate across several belief domains (see chapters 5 through 12). For example, listing the advantages and disadvantages of particular beliefs or actions may apply for patients who need certainty, who overestimate their responsibility, and who hold perfectionistic beliefs. Behavioral experiments can be used for most cognitive domains to test the empirical basis of dysfunctional thoughts and beliefs.

Negative core beliefs are likely to surface during the process of investigating automatic thoughts and beliefs about intrusions. You and your patient can begin to identify these core beliefs, especially after the first few sessions when your patient has learned to identify the interpretations (also called automatic thoughts) more easily and has begun to practice challenging these. Because negative core beliefs are often highly distressing, they should be addressed gradually during the course of treatment, as your patient gains skills in using the cognitive methods and gains confidence in you and in the effectiveness of the therapy. After the first eight to ten sessions, you can begin to focus on deeper level beliefs. Chapter 13 provides several cognitive techniques for helping patients revise their core beliefs about themselves and others. These methods can be used throughout the middle and later sessions of treatment, interspersed with work on interpretations and intermediate beliefs from the various domains identified during the assessment.

PREVENTING RELAPSE

The final two treatment sessions focus on relapse prevention (see chapter 14 for details). Use these sessions to review the most important aspects of the treatment and remind your patients of strategies that were helpful in the past. Encourage your patients to continue to practice their skills after the end of treatment. Discuss residual problems and fears about the end of treatment and identify overly optimistic or pessimistic thoughts about it. To facilitate your patient's feelings of self-efficacy, be sure to attribute progress during treatment to your patient's knowledge and skill. Prepare your patient for possible setbacks, especially when life circumstances are stressful. Present such setbacks as normal responses that can be readily corrected by using techniques just learned in therapy. Also help your patient to anticipate possible stressors and likely reactions during the coming months. This way you can solve problems in advance.

SUMMARY OF CT METHOD

Thus, the overall treatment method is to identify domains of cognitive interpretations and beliefs about intrusive thoughts and to teach patients techniques to modify these distortions. All interventions are guided by your conceptualization of your patient's symptoms in the context of immediate interpretations of intrusions, beliefs, and attitudes, and more firmly held core beliefs about themselves, the world, and others. The process of cognitive conceptualization is dynamic and requires constant refinement whenever you learn new information that might modify your understanding of your patient in context. You will want to share new insights about how beliefs, emotions, and behaviors interact with your patient. This helps you verify that your understanding is correct. It also teaches your patients about their own internal processing of emotional information. You will continue to refine your case formulation in consultation with your patient throughout treatment.

THERAPIST STYLE

The first few sessions are critical in building an alliance with your patient. During those sessions, you raise expectations regarding how you interact with your patient and your attitude toward treatment. When working with your patients, be respectful, understanding, interested, encouraging, challenging, and have clear expectations in terms of what you'd like them to do. A sense of humor can go a long way, so long as your patients don't feel you are making fun of them. As a cognitive therapist, you'll find yourself asking many questions, but don't grill your patient with too many questions in a row. Also, feel free to make direct comments if the situation calls for it. Always challenge your patients to do their best, as being too permissive and tolerant can backfire by conveying the message that low effort is acceptable. For example, if you and your patient agree on homework, expect your patient do it. If you let your patients get away with incomplete or no homework, you'll find that this will only reduce their motivation to do homework in the future.

Some OCD patients have a tendency to become dependent on their therapist. Encourage your patients to think and be as independent as possible. This means that over time, you shift more and more responsibility for the session and homework content to your patient. Gradually, encourage your patient to take on more responsibility for deciding on homework assignments and selecting the techniques to use in identifying and modifying maladaptive thoughts.

Some patients will have participated in an ineffective treatment before seeing you, or they may have a somewhat negative attitude toward treatment in general. If this is this case, explain how this treatment approach differs from their experience or expectations. These patients might also need more cheerleading than average.

Another important therapist characteristic is to notice and understand your patients' efforts and struggles. Be sure to pay attention to and reinforce their hard work. Try to be flexible; a rigid authoritarian style won't get you very far. The expectations you have for your patients should match their abilities. If a patient gives you feedback, be receptive, regardless of whether it's positive or negative. Your patients should feel good about their work with you, so they continue to work hard toward their own goals.

SETTING TREATMENT GOALS

Most patients come to treatment with the simple goal of getting rid of their OCD symptoms, or at least managing them better. Thus, the goal of cognitive therapy is symptom reduction. Be sure to explicitly state at the beginning of therapy that you will also help your patient address distorted thinking and beliefs that have led to the development of OCD or are responsible for maintaining it. Your aim is to help enable your patients to experience less discomfort when obsessions occur and to decrease their avoidance behaviors and compulsions.

If patients are prone to setting unrealistic goals because of perfectionism, you'll need to use strategies from the perfectionism module (see chapter 10) early in treatment to encourage a more flexible approach during the therapy process. You can also set secondary goals with your patient. For example, some patients may have less severe comorbid conditions, such as depression, BDD, or another anxiety disorder. (If the other disorders are more severe than OCD, they should be addressed first.) Many of the skills your patient learns as part of this treatment will apply to those disorders as well. However, at the beginning of treatment, you and your patient need to decide how these disorders will fit in the overall treatment plan (for example, that treatment for BDD will be started after the completion of OCD treatment).

Sometimes patients enter treatment only because their partner or family member is urging them to do so. Occasionally, spouses are frustrated and have threatened to leave if your patients' symptoms do not improve. If you suspect this, first explore your patient's motivation to resolve the OCD. Explain the requirements of cognitive therapy and also discuss the advantages and disadvantages (costs and benefits) of engaging in cognitive treatment. For example, if the OCD improves, a patient might no longer be eligible for disability payments and might be expected to get a job. Or, after successful treatment, a patient may lose privileges or might have to engage in more chores because he or she is no longer the "ill" family member. Severely ill patients might fear improvement because currently their OCD symptoms fill their entire day, and without the symptoms, they wouldn't know what to do with their time. Sometimes patients fear confronting failures in other areas of functioning (job, dating) that can be accounted for more comfortably by having OCD. Occasionally, they fear the treatment itself or they are afraid of your opinion. Once the advantages and disadvantages of engaging in cognitive treatment are established, the validity of the disadvantages (e.g., fears about getting better) should be evaluated. It's much better to deal with these problems as early as possible (without damaging your therapeutic alliance) than to waste time and effort on treatment that will fail because your patient is not really motivated to comply.

MANAGING PROBLEMS IN THERAPY

Patients sometimes exhibit behaviors that interfere with the cognitive therapy. If this happens, you need to address them right away. You will need to distinguish practical causes from dysfunctional beliefs and fears that may be interfering with therapy (e.g., "If I get better, my life will actually get worse"). You can view problematic behaviors as an opportunity to conceptualize your patient's situation further to better understand the case. Several examples are listed below.

Canceling Sessions Frequently

Your patient should be questioned directly about the reasons for frequent cancellations. Perhaps his or her life circumstances are very complicated and there are other more pressing problems, leaving little energy or time to devote to work on OCD. If so, it's better to reschedule the therapy to a later time frame, since irregular sessions are not conducive to steady progress and much effort will be wasted. You can also probe whether your patient would have something to lose by getting better.

Arriving Late

This may stem from the same source as canceling sessions if your patient is overwhelmed by other life responsibilities. Alternatively, your patient may arrive late to nearly all the appointments because he or she might get stuck in rituals or because of other problems planning effectively. Severe OCD symptoms can also result in last-minute cancellations, as your patient is not able to get out of the house. In this case, you and your patient might decide on a step-by-step plan to ensure he or she gets to treatment on time. For example, you may need to identify when they find their keys, put on their shoes and jacket, leave the house, etc. Alternatively, you might agree to schedule your session at an earlier time than it is really scheduled. In other words, patients write a 3 P.M. appointment on their calendar, but the actual appointment is not scheduled until 4 P.M. Over time, you can fade out the intermediate strategies and start putting your patient in your schedule at the correct time. If the problem occurs because of a wish to avoid sessions, possibly because of discomfort with the therapy or you, this should be discussed directly to determine how you can address the concerns.

Not Doing Homework

If patients are not engaging in homework productively, you can validate their emotional reluctance empathically with comments such as "I really understand that you feel _____ . I realize homework is sometimes unpleasant." However, you must directly address the importance of doing homework to practice the skills learned in treatment. Direct attention to this therapy-interfering behavior, perhaps by using problem-solving strategies, before moving on (e.g., "I am afraid we have to resolve this before we can make any progress"). For example, you could assess the pros and cons of completing homework. A metaphor may be useful here. For example, learning to ride a bicycle is difficult and not always pleasant in the beginning, but it becomes second nature after repeated practice. To acknowledge the emotional strain of letting go of usual methods of coping, you might compare cognitive therapy to using a life preserver. He or she must let go of the sinking boat to try a better option, but there is no way to know whether this life preserver will really work until your patient tries it.

Digressing to Other Topics

You and your patient must decide as early as possible whether OCD is the primary problem at this point in your patient's life. If not, treatment should be discontinued and your patient should be referred for help with the primary problem. If your patient is talkative and generally digresses from the agreed-on agenda, it's your job to remind your patient of the main subject. For example, you could say, "Sorry to interrupt, but I'd like to make sure that we cover the agenda we've set for today."

Making Suicidal Threats

If your patient has serious suicidal thoughts, OCD outpatient treatment may not provide sufficient protection, and your patient may need referral for more appropriate treatment options. If the risk does not seem imminent, determine whether suicidal thinking and/or threats are likely to interfere with treatment progress or may improve as your patient's OCD symptoms respond to cognitive treatment. Consider making a safety contract with your patient so that both of you feel comfortable engaging in CT for OCD.

Feeling Discouraged, Despite Progress

Some patients may not recognize progress or may discount it, especially if they are depressed. Some discounting may be linked to perfectionistic standards and dichotomous thinking, such as "If I am not completely better, a little progress is irrelevant." Such automatic thoughts may reflect core beliefs about being a failure. A useful strategy might be to identify and work on this belief using methods outlined in this manual (e.g., techniques from modules on perfectionism, fear of positive experiences). In addition, you may want to repeat one or more of the OCD assessment forms on a regular basis to actually show your patients that changes have occurred. Another possibility is that your patient might have superstitious fears and believe that acknowledging improvement will cause a relapse. This is a form of fear of positive experiences and can be addressed in that module.

Arguing

Occasionally patients are argumentative, challenging your statements or homework assignments. Engaging in argument will not be helpful, but discussion of your patient's concerns is essential since therapist and patient must work collaboratively. Arguing suggests that your patient disagrees with your views or goals, and this must be resolved.

Dealing with Religious Beliefs

When obsessions are tied to religious beliefs, it's important not to directly challenge or undermine such beliefs. As Salkovskis and colleagues (1999) note, clarification of the implications of religious beliefs may be important and helpful, but challenging a patient's religion is likely to provoke distrust in the therapy. Ask your patient to clarify what they believe and how they came to believe this over the course of their life. This line of questioning is designed to help them sort out their own beliefs and whether the obsessive concerns and associated interpretations are faithful representations of their true beliefs.

Wanting to Focus on the Etiology of OCD Symptoms

Patients often ask why the OCD developed. Don't spend too much time on this topic, since it will take away time from focusing on cognitive aspects of the symptoms. You can use the example of a patient who broke his leg. It's most important to repair the leg. Then it's good to determine why it might have happened to try to prevent a future recurrence. In the same way, for OCD, it's important to work to resolve the symptoms first. Understanding why the symptoms developed comes later. Of course, your work on intermediate and core beliefs is likely to at least partly address the causes of the problem.

DOS AND DON'TS IN COGNITIVE THERAPY

Based on our experience, the following basic principles may prove helpful in avoiding potential difficulties while conducting cognitive therapy for OCD.

Believe in the Model You Use

Don't weaken your position by introducing the model to your patient with hesitation, for example by using minimizing words like "a little" or "maybe." When some uncertainty about treatment method or efficacy must be noted, say, for example, "it appears to be" instead of "it could be that . . ."

Move On If You Get Stuck

If a technique is not working, tell your patient, "Why don't we move on. We can come back to this later." Then consult with colleagues or supervisors between sessions to determine the best course of action.

Consistently Link Symptoms and Interventions to the Underlying Model

Avoid jumping from problem to problem and intervention to intervention without relating them to the relevant theory and to a clear conceptualization of your patient's symptoms. To help you stick to the cognitive model as much as possible, repeatedly return to a diagram of the cognitive model from this manual (see chapter 1 and the appendix) or one created by yourself and your patient to illustrate the cognitive components and linkages of OCD symptoms to the model. Try to avoid doing this in terms that are too general or by going into a monologue, but instead link the model to concrete thoughts and situations that your patient mentions. Use the present situation as much as possible to clarify the connection between thoughts, emotions, and behavior.

Record Patients' Interpretations Literally

If your patient tells you that her intrusion was "I want to tear my husband's gut out," this is what you should write down. Do not soften it (e.g., "I thought I might hurt my husband"). If your patient interprets this to mean "I'm a lunatic," write this down as well. Also, be on the lookout for thoughts with absolute words, such as "always," "never," and "constantly," since these indicate cognitive errors your patient makes. Write down those thinking errors for discussion.

Work on Interpretations and Beliefs, Not Obsessive Intrusions

When a patient reports an intrusion that involves an overestimation of the probability or severity of danger, evaluating the intrusion directly can be helpful. For example, if you treat a woman who is concerned that she may get AIDS from an unlikely source, ask about her understanding of the actual probability of developing the illness as a result of that type of contact. You can also facilitate obtaining expert information if she is unclear on the facts.

Note that for other cognitive domains, challenging the intrusive thought, idea, image, or impulse can give it credibility in your patient's mind, and unfortunately can increase rather than decrease OCD symptoms (also see van Oppen & Arntz, 1994). For example, one of our OCD patients made consistent progress, but after the sixth session, the frequency of her sexual intrusions about incest began to increase. We uncovered the problem by discussing how the patient usually responded to intrusions. She reported that whenever they occurred, she told herself that there was no evidence of incest in her family (self-reassurance). By doing so, she was responding to the intrusion directly, instead of challenging her interpretation of it. In this case, cognitive restructuring was used incorrectly and had become a mental ritual. In reviewing her response and its effects, it became clear that challenging the intrusions made them seem even more important. We then reviewed the model of her symptoms and reminded her to not respond to the intrusions, but to just let them come and go without interference or special attention. This problem indicates the importance of understanding how cognitive techniques should be used. Therapists can avoid these problems by checking regularly on how patients are using interventions.

Be Flexible When Working with Perfectionistic Attitudes

Freeston and Ladouceur (1997) describe a patient who felt that she did not deserve to improve, because she was not as compliant as she thought she could have been. In such cases, don't encourage your patients to complete their homework assignments perfectly. Instead, they should complete only 80 to 90 percent of their homework and observe any intrusive thoughts that follow, so these can become the subject of upcoming sessions of cognitive therapy.

Focus Directly on Deeper Level Beliefs

Don't stop with interventions focused solely on modifying specific interpretations made in the context of OCD. Also identify and include challenges that address more core beliefs that patients have about themselves, their future, or the world around them. Link core beliefs to OCD symptoms. It's often best to begin this after your patient has some experience modifying interpretations.

Reinforce Patients

You must be authentic in making positive statements. For some patients, changing an apparently simple thought or behavior can be an enormous accomplishment and deserves special recognition.

Avoid Giving Reassurance

During initial assessment, it may be reasonable to provide some reassurance about your patient's likely success in therapy and other concerns. However, during active cognitive therapy, don't provide reassurance when patients already know the answers to their own questions. This would only serve to maintain or increase fears. Instead, ask why your patient is seeking reassurance and address the maladaptive beliefs that may have led to this by using the techniques described above.

As van Oppen and Arntz (1994) have noted, sometimes challenging interpretations can become a form of reassurance for patients and, in essence, serves as another ritual. That is, patients identify their problematic belief, then evaluate it as taught, and repeat the relevant Socratic question to provide self-reassurance. For example, the patient challenges the idea "I will drop my child down the stairs if I am not very careful" by asking himself, "What's the evidence for this?" and repeatedly answering the question in a ritualistic fashion, such as "I have never dropped my child before," over and over again until he feels better. This response to a Socratic question has become a ritual. Like van Oppen and Arntz, we recommend using a variety of different cognitive interventions, so patients don't ritualistically get stuck on only one.

Chapter 3

Summary of Cognitive Therapy Techniques

In this chapter, we summarize the assessment and treatment techniques that you will use in cognitive therapy to familiarize you with these methods before you begin to apply them in subsequent chapters.

THERAPY FORMS

The following assessment instruments and handouts for use by you and your patients are included in the appendix of this manual for photocopying. For each treatment module, the forms you will need are given at the top of the session description.

Symptom Measures

1. Obsessive Compulsive Symptoms Rating Scale (OCSRS)

2. Obsessive Beliefs Questionnaire—Extended (OBQ-Ext)

Therapist Forms

3. OCD Assessment Form

4. Cognitive Therapy Session Report

Handouts

5. What Is OCD?

6. Personal Session Form

7. Intrusions Reported by Ordinary People

8. Rituals and Neutralization Strategies

9. Cognitive Triangle

10. Cognitive Model of OCD

11. Graph of Progress in Therapy

12. Treatment Contract

13. Cognitive Model of OCD—Blank Form

14. Types of OCD Beliefs

15. List of Cognitive Errors

16. Thought Record and Guide—Five Column

17. Thought Record and Guide—Seven Column

18. States of Mind Diagram

19. Behavioral Experiment Form

20. Downward Arrow Form

21. Thought-Suppression Graph

22. Core Belief Filter

23. Core Beliefs Record

24. Self-Coaching Session Form

25. List of Cognitive Therapy Techniques

26. Problem-Solving Worksheet

TECHNIQUES FOR ASSESSING AND CONCEPTUALIZING OCD SYMPTOMS

A thorough understanding of your patient's cognitive makeup provides the framework for effective cognitive therapy and helps you choose interventions effectively (see Beck, 1995). You begin formulating a case during the first interaction with your patient and continue to refine this conceptualization throughout treatment in discussion with your patient. Chapter 4 guides you to formulate a case effectively, based on information gathered during initial sessions.

Assessment of OCD Symptoms

The OCD Assessment Form prompts you to collect information about your patient's current problems and their development, maladaptive thoughts and underlying beliefs, how these beliefs make your patient vulnerable to OCD, your patient's coping strategies, core beliefs, personal experiences that might have contributed to OCD, current stressors, and typical triggers for obsessions and rituals.

Education About the Cognitive Model

To socialize patients to cognitive therapy, you will be using your patients' own examples to develop the CT model in relation to their particular symptoms. Refer to this model repeatedly during therapy so patients understand the role of their own beliefs in determining their actions. Thus, it's not the situation itself but rather how the patient perceives it that affects how he or she feels. Most people simply accept their perceptions of situations or events as true, without even being aware that they are interpreting situations. Because these interpretations happen so quickly, most people simply notice the shift in emotion that follows. But why does one individual interpret the same situation differently from another? Different interpretations spring from different beliefs that two people may hold. We review these briefly in the next three sections to assist you in keeping the components of the model clearly in mind as you treat your patients with OCD.

Identifying Problematic Interpretations and Intermediate Beliefs

Identifying and modifying unreasonable interpretations of intrusions based on mistaken beliefs is the overarching goal of cognitive therapy for OCD. You will begin by working with your patients to find out what attitudes, rules, and assumptions feed their OCD. Typically, you will use the following methods to assess these:

- Thought records

- Subscale scores from the Obsessive Beliefs Questionnaire—Extended (OBQ-Ext.)

- Downward arrow technique (see discussion below) to determine the meaning patients attach to feared obsessive situations ("So if that happened, what would that mean to you?")

After identifying a maladaptive belief, you can help your patient evaluate it on the spot or later on, when the opportunity presents itself. More detail on how to decide when to evaluate the thinking is given throughout the manual.

Identifying Cognitive Errors

Another strategy for examining distorted interpretations of intrusions is to identify the patient's common thinking errors (see chapter 4 for how to do this). This is a widely used cognitive strategy. We adapted our list of cognitive errors from the books *Cognitive Therapy: Basics and Beyond* by Judith Beck (1995) and *Thoughts and Feelings* by Matthew McKay, Martha Davis, and Patrick Fanning (1997).

- Polarized or all-or-nothing thinking

- Labeling

- Overgeneralization

- Mental filter (filtering or selective abstraction)

- Discounting the positive

- Magnification

- Mind reading

- Fortune telling

- Emotional reasoning

- "Should" statements

You'll ask your patients to review the list and identify the ones they commonly use and give some examples. Patients who are familiar with the list usually find it easy to identify their own errors with a little practice. This strategy is useful throughout the modules, and some errors are particularly common in conjunction with particular types of beliefs. For example, emotional reasoning occurs most for overestimation of danger problems, whereas all-or-nothing or polarized thinking is often found when perfectionism is present.

Identifying Core Beliefs

Underlying the appraisals of situations and beliefs that support OCD symptoms are core beliefs, which are also called schemas or basic assumptions. Core beliefs are central ideas about the self, other people, and the world that develop beginning in childhood but extending throughout a person's life. Most people have relatively adaptive core beliefs, such as "I am basically a good person," "I am likeable," and "I am competent at many things." Note that these positive core beliefs are usually stated with some moderation, rather than in absolute terms, like "I am perfect," "Everyone loves me," or "I am competent at everything."

In contrast, negative core beliefs are often absolute, global, and overgeneralized. Examples are "I am weak," "I am vulnerable," "I am bad," and "I am dangerous." Patients may also have negative core beliefs about the world or others, like "The world is dangerous" or "No one could love me." When negative core beliefs are present, most people only process information that is consistent with their belief and ignore information that is inconsistent. The downward arrow technique is most useful for assessing core beliefs. In addition, whenever your patient shares thoughts, emotions, and behaviors, you can hypothesize the core belief that might have been activated and then decide when to raise this as a possibility for examination and eventual change. Chapter 13 provides strategies for modifying negative core beliefs and building positive alternative ones.

CT METHODS FOR CHANGING INTERPRETATIONS AND INTERMEDIATE BELIEFS

In treatment, you will use a wide variety of strategies to modify interpretations and beliefs that support the obsessive thinking. We describe these methods below, focusing most on the ones used commonly across belief domains and then briefly mentioning others that are more specialized. We detail these less commonly used methods within the modules where they are most commonly applied. The chapters that follow contain descriptions and examples of how to use these cognitive techniques for the several belief domains common to OCD.

Commonly Used Techniques

The methods described below are among the most common and widely used across types of belief domains.

Socratic Questioning

Central to the concept of testing hypotheses like a detective or a scientist is Socratic questioning, in which you ask a series of questions to help patients examine the logic behind their beliefs (see J. Beck, 1995). This is one of the most important methods to identify and evaluate dysfunctional thinking and is based on the assumption in cognitive therapy that patients will change their beliefs more quickly or more completely if they discover the faults in their reasoning themselves. Hence, the series of questions rather than statements that tell patients what they are doing wrong. Use this technique to help your patients determine the validity and usefulness of their thoughts. Typical questions are

"Is there any evidence to support the accuracy of this thought?"

"Is there any evidence that contradicts it?"

"Is there an alternative explanation?"

"What is the effect of believing this?"

"What could be the effect of changing your belief?"

Don't try to persuade your patients of your perspective, but rather, in a collaborative manner, encourage them to explore and review the available information. This technique is usually used throughout treatment, starting in the first session.

Patient As Detective or Scientist

In using Socratic methods and socializing your patient to the cognitive model of OCD, encourage him or her to take on a role that facilitates exploration of personal thoughts. Toward this end, encourage your patient to adopt the role of either a detective searching for clues or evidence or a scientist who is testing hypotheses. You can even suggest that, together, the two of you form a detective agency or a research team. In these roles, you and your patient identify specific predictions that are testable using various methods described below, especially behavioral experiments.

Review of the CT Model

The cognitive model should be introduced very early in treatment (see chapter 4) and referenced throughout the therapy. This model helps normalize the experience of intrusions as patients realize that nearly everyone has such thoughts. The benefit of understanding that everyone has intrusions is especially important for those who suffer from repugnant obsessions with sexual, aggressive, or religious content that they have previously believed to be unusual or bizarre. Periodic reviews of the CT model are helpful as patients put their own beliefs and behaviors in a larger context. Assist them in heightening their awareness of factors that may have influenced their maladaptive interpretations of intrusions (e.g., past family experience, recent stressors, mood state, etc.). If patients frequently ritualize or avoid situations, reviewing the model also teaches them that by doing those behaviors (e.g., washing), they cannot test whether their interpretations (for example, "If I don't wash after touching a doorknob, I will get sick") are accurate or not. Thus, the review will help patients understand the role of avoidance and mental rituals in the maintenance of obsessions, and it often motivates them to reduce those behaviors.

Identifying Cognitive Errors

As described previously, many, if not most, patients commonly make thinking errors. Such errors are defined in chapter 4 to help patients learn to identify erroneous patterns of thinking early in treatment. As listed above, they include all-or-nothing thinking, labeling, overgeneralization, mental filter, discounting the positive, jumping to conclusions (including mind reading and fortune-telling), magnification, emotional reasoning, and "should statements." Some of these errors correspond or overlap with types of problematic beliefs or with other cognitive techniques. For example, jumping to conclusions can be synonymous with overestimating danger in some patients, and emotional reasoning is closely linked to the technique of contrasting the rational and emotional mind.

Using Thought Records to Identify and Evaluate Beliefs

Like most forms of cognitive therapy, cognitive treatment for OCD relies heavily on having patients record their thoughts and evaluate them in situations when obsessions are provoking discomfort and strong urges to ritualize. Patients begin by using a simple five-column thought record to learn to identify thoughts and soon follow this with a seven-column thought record (both are given in the appendix) that includes additional columns to state alternative beliefs and rate the strength of these and the original beliefs. These forms are a mainstay of the treatment because they provide ready access to thinking as it is actually occurring and permit you to use Socratic questioning and other strategies to help patients restructure their thinking.

Metaphors, Stories, and Analogies

Metaphors, stories, and analogies are useful ways to communicate information in a format that is easily understood and retained. Hearing a story allows patients to get a new perspective on a situation and may sometimes be preferable to addressing a problem directly, as it decreases the likelihood for defensiveness. Like metaphors, analogies also help your patient take a step back and gain a new perspective. We often use analogies when treating patients who have a problem with overestimating danger (e.g., "If I feel tired, does this mean I am getting AIDS? If I cough, does this mean I have tuberculosis?"). We have borrowed several metaphors and analogies from works by Freeston and colleagues (1997) and from Michael Otto (2000), and describe some of our own in the chapters that follow.

Downward Arrow

This technique, derived from the work of Greenberger and Padesky (1995), is particularly useful to identify deeper level beliefs and/or catastrophic fears. In this method, you repeatedly ask for the meaning patients attach to feared obsessive situations, assuming that the initial thoughts were true ("So if that happened, what would that mean to you?" ... "What would that mean?" ... "What's the worst part about that?"). As described above, this technique can also be used to identify deeper level beliefs in the core beliefs module by asking, "What does this mean *about* you?" You will use the downward arrow method initially as an assessment tool to identify problematic beliefs and later on as a method to facilitate evaluation of the intermediate and/or core beliefs that emerge. This technique is appropriate for all modules (see appendix for Downward Arrow Form).

Behavioral Experiments

Behavioral experiments are useful when your patient's assumptions can readily be formulated into testable hypotheses. Therapist and patient formulate the hypothesis together, and the patient rates how strongly he/she believes it is true. You then help your patient think of a way to test the belief, usually as a homework assignment, although sometimes an experiment can be conducted in the office. Typically, you use Socratic questioning to design the experiment and decide what evidence is needed to support or refute the belief. For example, a patient who believes he's responsible for causing planes to crash just by thinking might test his prediction by deliberately thinking about one or more planes crashing.

Continuum Technique

The continuum technique (adapted from Beck, 1995) is useful to evaluate extreme or polarized thinking. We find it especially helpful for patients who overestimate the importance of thoughts (see chapter 5). Often this method uses a line representing some negative trait the patient has assumed (e.g., "badness") with a scale ranging from number 0 (none) to 100 (extreme). Considering where they lie on this continuum helps patients recognize the full range of human behavior and where their own behavior actually fits in this spectrum. This method is also applicable for other domains including the desire for certainty (chapter 8), responsibility (chapter 9), and perfectionism (chapter 10).

Advantages and Disadvantages

A frequently used cognitive strategy for patients who have difficulty making decisions (usually this means they have an excessive desire for certainty) is to encourage them to make a two-column list of the costs and benefits of a particular decision. Patients can then weigh the relative pros and cons. We often apply this technique for determining the advantages and disadvantages of holding on to certain beliefs or behaviors versus replacing them with new ones.

Courtroom Technique

The courtroom technique is a specialized version of role-play strategies (see Specialized Cognitive Strategies below). In the courtroom technique, you ask your patient to take the role of the prosecuting attorney to present the arguments and evidence implicating him or herself as the defendant (e.g., that she is a dangerous person because she dropped the jar). Initially, you play the defense attorney who provides the judge or jury with opposing arguments (for example, that it's normal to make mistakes). Eventually, you switch roles. Finally, you take all the arguments presented from both sides into account to take a guess at what the judge or jury might decide. There are multiple examples of these strategies throughout this manual. This is a very general technique that can be used for most types of obsessive beliefs.

Double-Standard Technique

This technique is particularly useful for those with excessive responsibility or high standards associated with perfectionism because it forces them to take another perspective. You can simply question patients about whether they would apply the same strict principles or attitudes they hold for themselves toward others who are like them. For example, when asked if she would presume that her sister was gay if she looked at another woman's legs, the patient says no, thereby providing an opportunity to ask about the reasons for applying two different standards.

Specialized Cognitive Strategies

The following more specialized cognitive methods are typically used to change one or two types of interpretations and beliefs and are therefore a little less broadly applicable than the methods described above.

Wise Mind = Rational + Emotional Thinking

Often patients say, "I know that my thinking is irrational, but it feels true." Whenever emotional reasoning (also a type of cognitive error) seems to be operating, it might be helpful to draw two large overlapping circles that represent rational thinking using facts and emotional thinking based on feelings (see States of Mind Diagram in the appendix). Patients write examples of rational and emotional thoughts within each circle to help clarify when they are attending more to emotions than thinking or evidence. Cognitive treatment aims to better integrate emotional and rational thinking into wise thinking which combines both and is illustrated by the overlap between the two circles (see Linehan, 1993). This technique is used mostly when working on overimportance of thoughts.

Consulting with Experts

One possible way to determine if the consequences of a feared outcome will be as devastating as expected is to have patients seek information from an expert. This requires prior consultation to be sure the strategy yields accurate knowledge about the range of outcomes, rather than worst-case scenarios. This method runs the risk of serving as reassurance seeking for your patient, and therefore consultants should never be used repetitively. Consulting with religious leaders can be helpful to address or modify the overimportance of thoughts (chapter 5). This technique is also used for overestimations of harm/danger (see chapter 7).

Thought-Suppression Experiment

A thought-suppression experiment can demonstrate how attempts to suppress obsessions can backfire and instead reinforce the very state of mind patients are trying so hard to avoid. In this method, patients first imagine a neutral image like a white elephant or a pink flamingo for three minutes and then try not to think about that image while engaged in conversation. Invariably, trying to suppress the image actually produces it, especially when the image is much more meaningful to the patient. This method is derived from work by Dr. Daniel Wegner (1989) in *White Bears and Other Unwanted Thoughts*. Patients who practice this begin to understand quickly that controlling thoughts is very difficult for everyone. This technique is used on control of thoughts (chapter 6).

Calculating the Probability of Harm

This technique is especially helpful for patients who overestimate the likelihood of negative outcomes (see chapter 7). The basic method is to first estimate the probability of a catastrophic outcome (house burning down) and then identify all of the events that would have to occur for that to happen. For example, a lampshade is too close to the bulb, the lampshade burns rather than melts, other items catch fire, no one notices the fire, etc. Patients assign a probability to each step and then multiply these together to obtain the actual likelihood. This is then compared to the patient's original probability estimate to demonstrate the magnitude of the overestimate.

Betting Money

Asking your patients whether they would bet a large sum of money on a feared outcome often helps them reconsider the likelihood of the feared event (M. Freeston, personal communication, 1997). For example, you can ask your patient whether he or she would like to bet $1,000 that the catastrophe has occurred (for example, the house burning down) or you can ask the patient to recommend that you bet for or against the outcome. We've used this technique most often for overestimation of danger (chapter 7).

Conducting a Survey

The survey method is particularly helpful if patients have lost touch with what kinds of precautions are necessary (e.g., washing hands after touching doorknobs) or whether others have similar experiences to their own. Patients conduct a poll of their friends or other relevant people to determine whether their assumptions are correct. This strategy is especially helpful for patients with problems overestimating danger (chapter 7), desire for certainty (chapter 8), and fear of positive experiences (chapter 12). It should not be used with patients who have a problem with reassurance seeking.

Fill in the Blanks

This strategy (by Freeston et al., 1996) is helpful for patients with an excessive need for certainty. Rather than focusing on each detail of every obsession, patients are encouraged to think of their various obsessions as one general obsession that always follows the same pattern but has interchangeable details so that patients can simply fill in the blanks. For example: "I think I might have seen _____ that might be a _____ and I might be held accountable for not saving _____ . I would feel guilty forever." For more details, see chapter 8 on desire for certainty.

Pie Chart

You can use a pie chart to help your patients determine their responsibility for situations for which they blame themselves unreasonably (chapter 9). This requires the patient to first estimate his or her own role in the negative outcome and then to list all persons or circumstances (e.g., the weather) that could affect the event in question. Assigning each of these a portion of the pie before adding the patient's own part last usually leaves little room left for personal responsibility.

Role-Plays and Taking Another's Perspective

Among our favorite techniques are role-plays in which you switch roles with your patient, so he or she takes the role of the therapist while you take the patient's part. This often allows your patient to assume a completely different perspective. For example, if your patient checks excessively to avoid potential errors, you could ask: "If I were your patient, and you were my therapist, what would you tell me about how important it is to do everything perfectly? How often would you recommend that I should check my work?" You'll also find that your patients are often surprisingly good at coming up with solutions to problems when they take the perspective of another person in scenarios pertinent to their obsessive fears. We use this for all domains, but most often for perfectionism (chapter 10).

Making Extreme Contrasts

Adapted from J. Beck (1995), this is similar to the continuum technique described above except that you now pick behaviors on the extreme ends of the continuum and compare them. It can be useful for a number of modules. For example, if your patient has an excessive desire for certainty, you could ask her to list facts that are more critical to be certain about (such as names of family members) and compare them to unimportant details that she would not need to be so sure of (name of a pet or distant relative). You can then discuss with your patient the importance of understanding the difference. We describe this method for consequences of anxiety (chapter 11) and core beliefs (chapter 13).

Retrospective Review of the Evidence

The behavioral experiments described earlier are designed to test prospective predictions. In addition, patients can also review their actual past experiences for supporting evidence about current beliefs, especially those related to the consequences of anxiety and fear of positive experiences. For example, for patients who are convinced that they could never enjoy a particular activity because intrusive thoughts might occur, you can ask if they have ever enjoyed anything despite the presence of intrusive thoughts. Encourage patients who answer affirmatively to consider these experiences in generating alternative predictions for the future.

Problem Solving

To prevent relapse, patients who describe real-life problems associated with their OCD symptoms may benefit from formal training in using problem-solving methods. First teach patients to specify or define the problem, determine the automatic thoughts or beliefs provoked, think of all possible solutions to the problem, and then consider which solution is most likely to be effective. After this, encourage your patient to implement the solution, evaluate the outcome, and if necessary, select another solution and try that one to see how well it works. We describe this method in chapter 14.

Modifying Core Beliefs

As noted earlier, core beliefs are entrenched convictions about oneself, others, and the future. A variety of strategies are available to help patients modify negative and overgeneralized core beliefs and strengthen positive core beliefs. These methods are detailed in chapter 13 and include making extreme contrasts described above. Another strategy from Judith Beck (1995) is the analogy of a core belief filter in which the person accepts negative information because it is consistent with negative beliefs about the self, while rejecting positive information that seems inconsistent with existing beliefs. Reframing the evidence is another strategy for considering information from a different viewpoint, and you can also use historical testing of core beliefs using memories from childhood. During treatment, you will likely work first on changing interpretations and intermediate beliefs, and as the patient gains skill at this, go on to work on core beliefs that undergird obsessive thinking.

Relapse Prevention

The final two sessions focus on relapse prevention. In this last phase of treatment, the focus is on reinforcing the patient's treatment gains, identifying the treatment strategies that were most useful, and planning how to minimize the recurrence of OCD symptoms in the future.

Chapter 4

Assessment and Education

The first few treatment sessions will focus on learning more about your patients' OCD symptoms and developing a cognitive conceptualization to guide the treatment. In this chapter, we provide general guidelines for the assessment sessions, beginning with what information to collect about your patient and how to interpret findings from standardized measures of OCD symptoms. This is followed by a session-by-session breakdown of the content of the first three to four assessment sessions. Of course, cognitive therapy actually begins during this process as you train your patients to closely observe their own thinking, emotions, and behaviors. We recommend you read this entire chapter to become very familiar with the content before proceeding with individual sessions. Don't memorize the material or read passages word for word, but instead put the content into your own words and adapt your style to the intellectual and emotional level of your patient. Whenever you cover new ground, ask your patient to summarize what he or she has learned to make sure that concepts are clearly understood.

GENERAL GUIDELINES

Allow one to one and a half hours for the first assessment session and thereafter approximately one hour for assessment and educational sessions. Assessing OCD symptoms and related problems and developing a working cognitive conceptualization of your patient's symptoms will likely take about three to four sessions, depending on the complexity of your patient's problems and your experience treating OCD patients. In some cases, you may need more time to understand how comorbid conditions like major depression and social phobia interact with a patient's OCD symptoms. If your patient is in crisis, you will need time to resolve this before proceeding with the planned OCD agenda. You may also need more time if your patient speaks very slowly or takes a long time to contemplate replies. Both of these problems may reflect current OCD symptoms—for example, a need to choose exactly the right words or to tell the story completely. In such cases, allow a little more time to complete the session agenda, until you can reduce the problematic interference using CT methods in therapy.

Goals for Assessment Sessions

Try to establish rapport with your patient at the first meeting. To set a respectful collegial alliance with your patient, convey expertise in treating OCD while providing empathy for the profound impact that the symptoms have on functioning. Since most patients feel anxious during their first few treatment sessions, assume an active role by providing structure and answering questions directly. Your goal is that your patient views you as respectful, interested, helpful, caring, understanding, and knowledgeable. This process should also activate a sense of hope and optimism about treatment, diminish anxiety, and create openness to intervention and change. Let your patients know that they are not to blame for their condition, that OCD is an illness, and that there are specific things they can learn to improve the symptoms. The first sessions should also socialize your patients to the process and structure of therapy, and educate them about the cognitive model for OCD and their disorder.

Session Structure and Content

The structure of each CT session is similar to the format outlined by J. Beck (1995):

1. Checking on your patient's recent symptoms and mood

2. Briefly reviewing content from the previous session

3. Setting the agenda

4. Reviewing the homework assignment

5. Working on the agenda items

6. Deciding on homework for the coming week

7. Asking for a summary and feedback about the session

Most patients soon learn to expect this and find it very comfortable.

Each week, you and your patient will set the current agenda collaboratively. Some agenda items are determined by the phase of treatment. Other agenda items should pertain to the specific cognitive domains pertinent to your patients' OCD problems and the CT techniques designed to address them.

The rest of this chapter outlines all the content that you will need to cover in the first three to four sessions of CT. We've suggested particular items in the sessions where we've most commonly introduced them. But because each patient is unique, you will have to use clinical judgment to decide the order in which you'll complete these activities, as well as how long you will spend on each one.

Remember, the handouts and therapist forms you will need in these sessions are in the appendix of this manual.

SESSION 1

This session is focused mainly on gathering information about the patient's OCD symptoms and other problems, defining OCD, and discussing the goals of the cognitive therapy. Review intake assessment information before meeting with the patient.

Handouts

What Is OCD?

Personal Session Form

Therapist Forms

OCD Assessment Form

Cognitive Therapy Session Report

Agenda

- Welcome and check on recent OCD symptoms and mood.

- Review intake assessment information with the patient.

- Set the agenda jointly with the patient.

- Provide patient with Personal Session Form and notebook to keep materials.

- Define and discuss OCD.

- Gather information about the patient's OCD symptoms and history using the OCD Assessment Form.

- Discuss treatment goals.

- Assign homework to read the What Is OCD? handout.

- Ask for summary and feedback about the session.

Welcome and Symptom/Mood Check

Start the first treatment session by welcoming your patient to treatment and asking about his/her current mood (depression, anxiety, anger, frustration, etc.) and subjective impression of the severity of obsessions and compulsions during the past week.

T: Hello, it's good to see you. Today we will start with your first CT session. How are you feeling this week? How were your OCD symptoms this week?

Thereafter, briefly summarize the results of the pretreatment assessment and ask your patient about his or her reactions to the assessment.

T: As you probably remember from your last visit, you've been diagnosed with OCD, and you also have mild depression. Do you have any question about the assessment? Was there anything that we didn't discuss and you feel I should know about?

Set the Agenda

Set the agenda collaboratively with your patient. In the first few sessions, you'll need to be directive to set the stage for the cognitive therapy. As treatment progresses, shift more responsibility for setting the agenda to your patient.

T: So let's set our agenda for today's session. What do you want to be sure we cover? ... Okay. Let me put that down. I want to make sure that I give you a notebook for your forms, and we talk about what OCD is, and gather some more specific information about your OCD symptoms. We also want to talk about your goals for treatment. How does that sound?

In future sessions you will review the homework your patient has completed for the current session prior to working on the agenda, but because no homework has been assigned yet, you can start with the agenda right away.

Provide Personal Session Form and Notebook

At the beginning of this first session, provide your patient with a notebook, and at every session, hand your patient a Personal Session Form.

T: Here's a notebook you can use to organize all your handouts from therapy. Please bring it to each session. This notebook will be especially important after therapy to help you remember the methods that were most useful to you during treatment to help prevent a relapse. Here's your first form for the notebook. This is a Personal Session Form you can use to take notes during the session and between sessions as well. It helps you keep track of the agenda, the most important points covered in the session, your homework assignment, and topics you'd like to discuss next time. This form will help you remember what you learned and what we need to focus on as we go along.

Define OCD

Acknowledge that your patient may already know a lot about OCD, but comment that it is important that you both have a shared understanding of what OCD is, so you can work together.

T: What's your understanding of what obsessions are? ... What about compulsions? ... What do you think compulsions do for you in the short term? ... What about the long run?

Provide corrective information and details about OCD symptoms, as necessary. Obviously, the less your patient knows, the more you'll have to explain.

T: People with OCD suffer from recurrent obsessions and/or compulsions that are severe enough to cause marked distress or interfere with work or educational activities, relationships, and everyday activities. Obsessions are intrusive thoughts, images, or impulses that repeatedly come to mind even though the person who has them doesn't really want them. Obsessions are senseless and unpleasant. Often they are distasteful. They can be triggered by many thoughts, feelings, or certain situations.

Keep in mind that patients are often ashamed of their OCD symptoms and might be concerned that you will think they are crazy or dangerous if they reveal the content of their obsessions. We've encountered patients who were reluctant to divulge their symptoms for fear the therapist would call the police to get them arrested. Therefore, tailor your description of OCD to your patient's specific problems, especially if your patient has repugnant (e.g., sexual, aggressive, or religious) obsessions. Note how the therapist in the example below incorporates a few examples of symptoms in the description of OCD. Using this strategy shows your patient that you are familiar with OCD and you won't be shocked when hearing about their symptoms.

T: Obsessions cause anxiety, guilt, disgust, or general discomfort. And since most people don't like feeling this way, they try to do something to reduce the anxiety. People avoid the situations that trigger the obsessions, for example, by not using sharp knives in the kitchen or not touching anything that looks dirty to them. People with OCD also engage in rituals or compulsions to reduce their negative feelings. Typical rituals are hand washing in response to fears about contamination and checking to prevent mistakes or harm. But the rituals can also be invisible to others, such as thinking a good thought to undo a bad one or praying for forgiveness.

Give your patient the What Is OCD? handout.

T: It seems like you know quite a bit about OCD already. I have a handout here that provides you with some details about how common it is, its course, and the typical treatments. Could you please read this before the next session? We can talk about your reactions.

Discuss OCD Symptoms

Before you ask your patients about their symptoms, history, and current situation, be sure to review material from the pretreatment assessment. The OCD Assessment Form will then lead you through the topics for your own initial assessment. You don't need to ask every question in order, but just use this as a general guide. Whenever your patient tells you about relevant life events or problems the form doesn't ask for, be sure to record the information at the end of the form. Try to complete this form during your first meeting with the patient. In doing so, you won't be able to dwell on each item, but just get a basic and preliminary understanding of your patients' OCD symptoms and the context. Your goal is to develop a formulation of the case to enable you and your patient to arrive at a mutual understanding of all the factors that contribute directly to the problem and which of these need to be addressed during therapy.

Treatment Goals

If you have concerns about comorbidity, lack of motivation, or other factors that might prevent you from implementing CT immediately, you can indicate the need to assess this further or treat it prior to CT. In some cases, you may decide to refer your patient for medication or other intervention (e.g., panic control methods) before beginning the cognitive therapy for OCD.

If your review of your patient's OCD and related symptoms and history indicates it is appropriate to proceed with CT, briefly discuss the goals of cognitive therapy:

T: The goal of this cognitive treatment is to reduce the frequency of your
    obsessions and compulsions. In addition, we also want to reduce the severity
    of the anxiety and guilt associated with them. To reach those goals, we'll
    need to examine the way you think. Once we detect thoughts or beliefs that
    are unhelpful or false, you and I will work to change them so that ultimately,
    your thinking is more helpful and accurate. Changing your negative thinking
    will reduce your distress and enable you to realize that your compulsions and
    avoidance behaviors are no longer necessary. Do you have any questions
    so far?

If you have already identified themes pertinent to CT, you can mention those here as well:

T: From our discussion of your symptoms, it seems that we might want to focus
    our treatment on beliefs about _____ [e.g., responsibility,
    overestimation of danger, etc.].

At this point, you can also discuss secondary treatment goals if your patient has comorbid conditions tied to the OCD. Typical examples are major depression or dysthymia, which might have developed secondary to the OCD symptoms.

T: You mentioned that you got depressed shortly after you started having OCD symptoms about harming others. Our main focus in treatment will be on your OCD, but since your depression might actually be a result of the OCD, the strategies we will use to identify faulty thinking and unhelpful beliefs will apply to both OCD and depression. So, I think it's quite likely that your depression symptoms will benefit from the cognitive therapy, and in fact, the research literature suggests this as well.

Other goals might include anxiety disorders (e.g., social phobia, panic disorder, generalized anxiety disorder) that are partly related to the OCD, as suggested below:

T: You've told me that in addition to your OCD symptoms, you'd also like to work on your panic attacks and social anxiety. Because your OCD is so much more severe than your panic problem, I suggest that we deal with that first. Your other anxiety problems might improve as well, if the beliefs that underlie those disorders are similar to the beliefs that underlie the OCD. In any case, if you still have significant problems in those other areas after the OCD treatment, we can address those later. How does this sound?

Assign Homework

For homework, ask your patient to read the handout entitled What Is OCD?

Summary and Feedback

In this first session, briefly summarize the major points covered during the session. This should be a positive summary to avoid activating distressing thoughts. Ask your patient to add any comments about what he/she learned during the session. Finally, ask your patient for feedback.

T: Do you have any concerns about our session today? Did anything bother you? It is very important for me to know if you have any negative reactions.

If your patient expresses any concerns, respond thoughtfully and without defensiveness, to help your patient feel more comfortable or to plan for desired changes that are feasible within the CT therapy for the next session.

During and after each session, you should complete the Cognitive Therapy Session Report to remind yourself what was discussed during the session. These forms will eventually be used at the end of treatment to help you develop a relapse prevention plan (see chapter 14) based on the CT methods that worked best for your patient.

SESSION 2

Handouts

Personal Session Form

Intrusions Reported by Ordinary People

Rituals and Neutralization Strategies

Cognitive Triangle

Cognitive Model of OCD

Graph of Progress in Therapy

Treatment Contract

Cognitive Model of OCD—Blank Form

Therapist Forms

Cognitive Therapy Session Report

Agenda

- Check on patient's OCD symptoms and mood since last session and provide the Personal Session Form.

- Briefly review content of previous session.

- Set the agenda jointly with the patient (why people develop OCD, what maintains it, and what treatment will look like).

- Review homework (reading of handout).

- Provide rationale for cognitive therapy using handouts for Intrusions Reported by Ordinary People and Rituals and Neutralization Strategies.

- Discuss the Cognitive Triangle.

- Develop the Cognitive Model of OCD.

- Describe the treatment process, using the Graph of Progress in Therapy.

- Discuss and sign the Treatment Contract.

- Assign homework to complete Cognitive Model of OCD—Blank Form.

- Ask for summary and feedback about the session.

Begin the Session

Start this session by handing your patient the Personal Session Form and checking on OCD symptoms and mood in the previous week. To provide a bridge between sessions, ask if your patient remembers the focus of the previous session. If not, remind him or her that you defined what OCD was, gathered information about OCD symptoms, and discussed treatment goals. Briefly state what the patient's most important symptoms and related goals were. Ask about your patient's reaction to the handout assigned for homework.

Next, set the agenda:

T: Today we'll talk about why people develop OCD, and what maintains it, and what the treatment process will look like. Would you like to add anything?

Rationale for Cognitive Therapy

Your main task for today is to provide a rationale for why cognitive therapy is appropriate for your patient's OCD symptoms.

Discuss Intrusions As Normal Events

Begin by educating your patient about intrusions. Note that intrusive unwanted thoughts or images may appear to come out of the blue or can be triggered by objects and situations or by internal events such as thoughts or impulses. Provide your patients with the Intrusions Reported by Ordinary People handout.

T: This list shows you the types of intrusions experienced by almost everyone. These are not thoughts from OCD patients, but from ordinary people. Eighty to 95 percent of people in the community have these sorts of thoughts. Several studies from Europe, Canada, and Australia have demonstrated this very clearly by polling many ordinary people to see what intrusive thoughts or images or impulses popped into their minds. Here's a list of the kinds of thoughts they had.

This is a good opportunity for self-disclosure. If you feel comfortable sharing personal material, tell your patients what kinds of intrusive thoughts you've experienced. Continue with a discussion of the meaning people assign to intrusive thoughts:

T: It's not the fact that people have these kinds of thoughts or images or the specific things that people think about that distinguishes people who develop OCD from people who don't. Rather, it's the meaning that people attach to these thoughts. The average person generally ignores these intrusions or dismisses them fairly easily.

On the other hand, people who develop OCD feel that they should not have these kinds of thoughts and try to stop them. They also believe that stopping these thoughts is possible and a good thing to do. But soon they find out that they can't actually control their thoughts or images because this is not really possible. So it is no surprise that people with OCD who are trying to do the impossible experience a lot of distress and spend a lot of effort trying to remove these intrusive thoughts. This just adds more fuel to the fire—the thoughts actually occur more frequently, they last longer, and cause more upset.

Emphasize the normality of intrusive thoughts and the effects of interpretation:

T: It's important to realize that it's not at all abnormal or pathological that you experience intrusive ideas, images, or impulses. Nearly everyone does, though they usually don't talk about their intrusions to others. What's important is how you interpret these thoughts or images. The goal of this cognitive therapy is not to eliminate intrusive thoughts entirely. That would be impossible. Instead, our goal is for you to react quite differently to these kinds of thoughts. If we are able to decrease your distress when you do have them, you will experience them far less often and with less intensity.

Now discuss the role of beliefs and efforts to control thoughts in maintaining intrusions:

T: People with OCD appear to develop certain kinds of beliefs that are actually a distorted way to think about the world and about themselves. Some people believe that the presence of some types of thoughts is terrible and that they are weird or even bad people. For example, someone might believe that thinking about a disaster happening or having a sexual thought in the presence of children [substitute examples pertinent to your patient] is awful. They believe that they could and should control those thoughts by not thinking them. But thoughts are simply what our minds generate naturally. Random thoughts probably serve a very important purpose. They help us be aware of problems and potential harm, so we can decide if we need to do something about it. However, no one can actually control his or her thoughts and research indicates that trying to control thoughts by suppressing them actually makes them return more frequently and with more strength. This happens because we become so vigilant to make sure they don't come to mind that we are even more attuned to them than if we'd just left them alone in the first place. Thus, trying to control obsessive thoughts just makes them worse.

If your patient asks why intrusive thoughts occur, provide the following explanation (adapted from Freeston et al., 1997):

T: We're not sure, but spontaneous thoughts and images are needed by humans to be creative and to solve problems. So intrusive thoughts are probably adaptive and crucial to our existence. But since our thought generation system in the brain is imperfect, sometimes we spontaneously generate unpleasant thoughts that we'd rather not think about. Most people simply do not pay attention to these intrusive thoughts.

Describe Rituals and Coping Strategies

Next give your patient the handout entitled Rituals and Neutralization Strategies to review. Point out the wide variety of things people do to reduce their discomfort after intrusions or obsessions. Ask your patient to identify the ones on the list that fit his or her own experience. Decide on the terminology your patient likes best to describe what he/she does to try to terminate the obsession and reduce discomfort ("neutralization," "rituals," "compulsions," "undoing," etc.) and use this language throughout treatment. Ask the patient if these coping strategies really work.

T: You're right, rituals and avoidance behavior might make you feel better in the short run, but long-term they don't work very well, because anxiety goes down only briefly and comes back again. But there is a problem with rituals and avoidance: they actually increase the strength of your OCD. Because they reduce the unpleasant feelings, people are even more likely to use them next time the obsessions occur. In addition, people with OCD do not learn that the discomfort will decrease on its own if they don't engage in rituals or avoidance behavior. Rituals also prevent a person from learning to use other more effective coping methods to relieve discomfort.

Cognitive Triangle

Begin the description of the cognitive therapy model and methods by providing the Cognitive Triangle.

T: Thoughts are statements that you automatically say to yourself, whether you want to or not. Thoughts aren't in your control. Emotions are what you feel. Behaviors are what you do. Thoughts, feelings, and behavior are very much linked to one another, and each strongly influences the other. Thus, change in one of these three areas will also lead to change in another. So the basis for cognitive therapy is the idea that changing what we think in a situation will change how we feel and also how we behave.

Illustrate the connection between ordinary triggering events and the resulting thoughts, emotions, and behavior, making it clear that many events can be interpreted in more than one way:

T: For example, imagine that you are in a shopping mall and you suddenly see several people running toward a door. You might think: "Oh no! There must be a terrorist attack! There's probably a bomb in the mall!" What would you feel? And what would you do? [Allow time to respond.] Now, imagine that instead you think, "Someone must be giving away free stuff in the parking lot!" What would you feel and do now? [Allow time to respond.]

Discuss with your patient that his or her actions in the above case would depend on his or her interpretation of the situation. Next, discuss how this example relates to your patient's OCD:

T: Let's think how it works for you when you get an intrusive thought. Can you give me an example? How did you interpret this intrusion? How did this make you feel? What did you do?

Use the Cognitive Triangle handout to illustrate the back-and-forth effects of interpretations of intrusions, emotions, and behavior (including neutralization and rituals). Note that treatment will focus mainly on the thoughts and how the patient interprets these (the meaning the patient assigns to them). This, in turn, will influence emotional responses and behaviors.

Develop the Cognitive Model

Next, develop the model for OCD from a cognitive perspective, using your patient's own obsessive thoughts and compulsions. You will try to identify the following contributing and maintaining factors in the OCD symptoms:

- Typical triggering circumstances for OCD symptoms

- The maladaptive obsessive thoughts, images, or impulses

- Interpretations of these obsessive intrusions

- Rituals and avoidance strategies

- Underlying beliefs that contribute to symptoms

- Probable core beliefs (your patient's views of him- or herself, the world [including other people], and the future)

- Personal experiences that have contributed to the OCD symptoms and beliefs

- Current or recent stressors and mood that might be contributing to the problem

You can provide the Cognitive Model of OCD handout as a guide to help your patients create their own model, but it may be more powerful to derive the model from their own experiences. The dialogue suggested below is interactive as you ask questions and guide your patient to use the responses to develop a model that represents his or her OCD experience. Begin by selecting the most disturbing obsession.

T: Let's figure out how the OCD process works for you. Usually, the process begins with some sort of trigger or cue for your intrusive thoughts [images, impulses]. You seem to be most bothered by the idea that you could harm your child, so let's start with that intrusive thought. What are some common triggers for this idea?

Help patients describe the thought, image, or impulse briefly as they recall it.

T: So, then what thought [image, impulse] went through your mind immediately? Did you have any immediate thought or reaction to the obsession? ... So it seems that you interpreted that intrusion as having a particular meaning. You assumed ...

Use or modify the patient's own words to clarify the interpretation and confirm that you have understood it correctly.

Ask about what influences interpretations:

T: Your interpretation could be influenced by several things. For example, your mood or stressful events might affect how you viewed this intrusion. What mood or emotions do you think make you more susceptible to interpreting thoughts negatively? What about stressors, like work, home, social events, etc.? Do any of these play a role? Sometimes people interpret intrusions differently when they have heard or read something recently in the news or heard about it from someone they know. Various sources of information can affect how you think about an intrusive experience. Does this apply to you? Early life experiences can also affect people's interpretations. For example, experiences in your family or with others or perhaps some medical history or family history of OCD or other mental illness. Are any of these relevant for you?

Identify the type of emotion and the rituals:

T: OK, now let's fill in this part about negative emotions and this one about coping strategies. When you get an intrusion and interpret it in this way, how do you feel? If your interpretation provokes a lot of anxiety or guilt, you will probably try to avoid situations that provoke intrusions, and when that doesn't work, you do rituals or some kind of neutralization. Of course, these strategies only work temporarily as we've already discussed. In your case, what do your intrusions and interpretations lead you to avoid? Okay, now let's write in the rituals or neutralization strategies here. Notice that these efforts to neutralize or suppress thoughts also provoke more intrusions and negative interpretations. This is because they actually reinforce the notion that the thoughts or images are bad and should be stopped or prevented. Since it is really impossible to prevent them, you are sort of caught in a vicious cycle, an exercise in frustration.

Point out the probable effect of a neutral instead of negative interpretation:

T: Notice that if you reacted to the intrusion with a benign interpretation like, "Oh, I wonder why that just popped into my head? It probably came from the movie I just saw," your emotional reaction would have been more neutral, maybe only a bit of surprise, and you wouldn't have felt the need to avoid and do any rituals. Of course, this is what we are aiming for in the treatment.

Draw the link between change in beliefs and change in behaviors:

T: It is also important to realize that changing beliefs can change behaviors. Maybe you already have some examples of this from your own experience in the past. Can you think of any? ... So, if we can change your interpretations and beliefs about the triggers of your OCD, chances are this will also change your emotional reactions and your rituals. Does this make sense to you?

Discuss the possible role of family history of depression or anxiety, which may indicate a biological predisposition. Then discuss how negative mood states like anxiety and depression may worsen OCD symptoms.

Review the model as it is drawn and be sure that your patient agrees with it. It may be useful now or later in the therapy to ask your patient to explain the model, especially as other variations on obsessive thoughts and rituals are being discussed.

If there are points of disagreement in the initial discussion of the model, you may respond to these by asking more questions or, if you have concerns, suggesting that the patient's idea can be tested as treatment progresses. It is important that the patient begins to understand the linkages among symptoms, and especially the role of interpretations and beliefs in generating emotional discomfort, avoidance, and rituals or neutralizations. These avoidance efforts may also generate other negative interpretations and beliefs (e.g., "If I can't get rid of this thought, it means I must want to think it and I'm a bad person"). The model is unlikely to be complete at this point, since it is difficult to know this early in treatment all of the patient's interpretations and beliefs. As treatment progresses, your patient can make changes and additions to the model to fit the information that emerges. Make a copy of the cognitive model developed during the first session for your patient to put in his/her notebook.

Describe the Treatment Process

A discussion of the treatment process should take place fairly early in treatment, to ensure that your patients are familiar with and agree to their role in therapy. Note that therapy will be different from any unsystematic attempts your patients may have tried on their own to overcome their fears. It is also different from traditional talk therapy. Whenever possible, you should try to relieve any fault or self-blame for OCD or for failing to correct these symptoms.

T: The way we work to correct some of the mistaken OCD thinking is to discuss the way people find themselves thinking about the obsessive fears. This requires you to learn to be a good observer of your own thinking process. We'll systematically examine how you think about obsessive cues and what you believe when you are thinking these things. We can then examine together whether your interpretations and beliefs make sense to you. This is very hard to do by ourselves, because our thinking is so automatic that it's hard to even notice our thoughts and beliefs. Therefore, having the help of an objective person familiar with OCD is usually necessary.

T: The major focus of our treatment sessions will be identification of intrusive thoughts [images, impulses] and how you interpret these thoughts. You'll learn to examine these interpretations carefully using various cognitive therapy techniques, and we can also work on strongly held beliefs about yourself and the world that might be contributing to the OCD problem. This treatment is really a skill-building program. You'll develop skills to identify your interpretations of intrusive obsessions and determine whether your assumptions are reasonable. You'll also learn very specific methods to test the usefulness and validity of your thoughts and beliefs. We'll keep records of your interpretations and use logical discussion strategies and experiments to help you evaluate the OCD-related thinking.

T: Together, you and I will decide what methods work best for you and emphasize these as we go along. This process might temporarily cause you some distress, but these feelings are usually quite manageable, and we'll work at a pace that is comfortable for you. Our treatment will be done in a structured way, so each session will follow a usual format of checking on how you are feeling, setting an agenda, discussing homework, working on skills, and reviewing what we have done and how you feel about it. Most of the time, treatment takes about twenty sessions, but you and I will decide together how many sessions you need. Early sessions occur weekly and our last few sessions will be spaced farther apart. Each session will be about fifty minutes long, and we'll agree on homework assignments during each session.

If patients have questions about biological aspects of OCD and whether CT can be effective when OCD has biological underpinnings, explain:

T: Yes, OCD certainly has a biological basis. We know that genetics plays some role and that certain parts of the brain are associated with excessive activity when OCD is present. Also, many patients benefit from certain types of medications. It is especially interesting that some researchers have clearly shown that successful treatment using medications and psychological treatments actually alter brain activity that is associated with OCD. That is, the brain functioning actually becomes more normal, more like the brains of people without OCD, when these treatments are successful. So it is clear that medication is only one way to normalize brain functioning and that psychological therapy can also do this quite well.

You will also need to address the patient's and possibly family members' expectations during treatment:

T: It's important to be realistic about what we can accomplish during treatment and how long the therapy for OCD should last. The goal is to substantially reduce, but probably not eliminate, obsessive thinking. That's because intrusive thoughts and images of all kinds are normal, even if they are uncomfortable for a little while. That means that you can't really get rid of intrusive thoughts that we now think of as obsessive thoughts for you. In treatment we'll try to make them much less disturbing so you don't have to avoid them or carry out your rituals to feel okay. That's the way most people respond. They have intrusive thoughts or ideas occasionally and think, "Oh, where did that come from?" or, "I wonder why this is bothering me now." The idea stays with them a short while and then gradually goes away if they don't try hard to get rid of it. Eventually, your obsessive thoughts will also become less frequent because they won't bother you much and won't produce an intense urge to get rid of them. Instead, you just live with them for a bit until they go away.

T: However, it's important for you to know that there will be ups and downs in helping you get to the point where the thoughts and images just don't bother you much. So expect that sometimes you'll feel very good about your progress and sometimes you might feel stuck. Just stick with the process, even if it seems to be going slowly at some points. This is the way change in obsessions and compulsions often looks for people in treatment. [Show the patient the Graph of Progress in Therapy handout and suggest that the two of you keep a record of the patient's progress.]

Once you are sure your patient understands the treatment plan and the rationale for this approach, ask for a formal agreement to attend therapy sessions and complete assignments. Both you and your patient should read the Treatment Contract and sign it.

Assign Homework

Ask your patients to complete one or two blank forms of the Cognitive Model of OCD for typical obsessive intrusions that occur during the coming week. Ask them to observe their thinking with regard to triggers for the obsessive thought, image, or impulse, immediate interpretations, emotional reaction, and subsequent neutralizing strategies and the effect of these on emotions. Also ask your patients to see whether any past or recent experiences or information and any long-standing beliefs seem to contribute to interpretations on these occasions. Encourage your patients to bring in the models they develop to the next session for discussion.

Summary and Feedback

Ask your patient to summarize the session. Allow sufficient time to verify your patient's basic understanding of the CT model and treatment plan. You can then add comments to expand on any aspects your patient has left out and ask if there are any questions. Finally, ask your patient for feedback about the session.

SESSION 3

Handouts

Personal Session Form

Types of OCD Beliefs

List of Cognitive Errors

Thought Record and Guide—Five Column

Therapist Forms

Cognitive Therapy Session Report

Agenda

- Check on patient's OCD symptoms and mood since last session.

- Briefly review content of previous session (Cognitive Triangle, Cognitive Model of OCD, treatment process).

- Set the agenda jointly with the patient.

- Review homework (completed blank forms of the Cognitive Model of OCD).

- Discuss Types of OCD Beliefs in relation to the cognitive model and treatment.

- Discuss List of Cognitive Errors.

- Explain the five-column Thought Record and Guide.

- Assign homework.

- Ask for summary and feedback about the session.

Start this session by handing your patient the Personal Session Form and by checking on your patient's recent OCD symptoms, related problems, and mood. Then ask if your patient remembers the focus of the previous session. Ask about any questions or any additions your patient wants to make. Next, set the agenda:

T: Today we'll talk about certain types of beliefs that typically occur in OCD and about cognitive errors people make and how these apply to you.

Review Homework

Ask if your patient completed and personalized the Cognitive Model of OCD for obsessive intrusions that occurred in the past week. Discuss the most important points.

Help your patient complete any unfinished sections of the model. If your patient reports any problem completing the homework, you should take this very seriously and try to resolve the problem before continuing with any other assessment or treatment. See suggestions in chapter 2, where we discuss managing problems in therapy. Also consider the following discussion:

T: Tell me why you weren't able to do the homework. What got in the way?

P: I just didn't have time this week. It was so hectic.

T: Do you think that this will be a regular problem, that your life is so hectic that you don't really have time to do the work in therapy?

P: Well it's hard for me to find the time with the kids always needing my attention. Sometimes I'm just so tired, especially at night.

T: [conveying sympathy but firmness] I can understand the difficulty. Let's see if we can figure this out. First, do you think that now is just not the right time to be working on the OCD problem?

P: Oh no, I have to work on this because my rituals are part of why I am so tired.

T: You think that the OCD symptoms are part of the problem?

P: Definitely. Just doing one load of laundry chews up at least a couple of hours each day.

T: Let's brainstorm a bit. If you look back at this past week, can you think of any way you might have found time to do this assignment?

This type of dialogue conveys the message that homework is critical to the success of the therapy and that patients are expected to work seriously on their OCD problem.

Types of OCD Beliefs

After reviewing the model, identify the specific cognitive domains that apply to your patient, choosing the domains that seem especially pertinent from the Types of OCD Beliefs handout:

T: People with OCD also seem to have several types of beliefs that are problematic. Our job is to figure out which of these apply especially to you, because this is what we need to pay close attention to in therapy. So as I speak about these, let's see what fits your experience and we can discuss these in more detail throughout the treatment. Let me show you this list of Types of OCD Beliefs while I mention them. These fall into various categories.

As you and your patient review the handout, ask which ones seem to apply most and ask for examples. Talk about how these belief domains are not completely distinct and that a given thought can fall into more than one.

Cognitive Errors

Next, introduce your patient to cognitive errors.

T: There are different ways of looking at thoughts and beliefs. As described above, cognitive domains are types of thoughts that might be unhelpful. Another way to evaluate interpretations is to identify thinking errors in the specific thoughts you have. Cognitive errors are mistakes in thinking, or in logic. Identifying your thinking errors might help you look at your thoughts more critically and ultimately develop more accurate and helpful ways of thinking.

Provide your patient with the List of Cognitive Errors and review them together. For each error, ask if your patients think they make this kind of error and ask for examples. For example, blaming yourself in advance for a feared outcome ("If _____ happens, it will be my fault") is an example of jumping to conclusions (specifically fortune-telling) and also illustrates beliefs about responsibility. In this case, the patient doesn't allow for the possibility that outcomes may be neutral or even positive or that responsibility may lie elsewhere. Magnification or catastrophizing ("That would be terrible") is a common cognitive error in which the patient exaggerates the probability of harm or its seriousness. This fits closely with the cognitive domain of overestimation of danger. Another error is emotional reasoning in which the patient has a strong emotional reaction (anxiety, depression) to an experience and then believes that because he/she feels upset, the situation must be dangerous or hopeless. An example would be "Because I am upset by the thought, it really could happen." This can also be considered a special form of jumping to conclusions and is related to interpretations about overimportance of thoughts. All-or-nothing thinking may be evident in thoughts like "If I have any recurrence of OCD symptoms, it means therapy doesn't work at all."

Introduce the Five-Column Thought Record

Explain that according to the cognitive model, OCD is maintained by the failure to evaluate and consider alternative interpretations and beliefs in light of contrary experience. This rationale helps patients alter their implicit account of their difficulties. For example, you can help patients with harming obsessions change their thinking from "I have crazy thoughts, which means that I am very dangerous" to "I have thoughts that seem crazy and that I interpret in a way that makes me anxious. In fact, my intrusive thoughts result from normal mental processes and are unimportant. I should just observe them."

Help your patient realize that people's thoughts influence how they feel and what they do. Then, ask your patient to give a personal example:

T: Think of a time this week when you felt a strong emotion. What was going through your mind?

Record the patient's example on a copy of the five-column Thought Record and Guide to begin to illustrate how to use this record. Review the instructions on this handout to be sure the patient understands how to use the thought record. An example of typical dialogue for training patients to complete the form is given below.

T: Okay, what was the unpleasant situation that occurred?

P: I was holding a little baby. She is my niece and only three months old.

T: Let's put "holding three-month-old niece" in the column entitled "Situation/Trigger." And what was the thought or impulse that was running through your mind just then?

P: Well, it was awful. I thought, "I am going to smash her head against the wall."

T: Okay, let's put that in the column entitled "Intrusions." And what was your immediate reaction to this intrusive thought?

P: I thought that because I had this thought of smashing her head, I'd act on it.

T: Okay, let me write this in the column for interpretations. How strongly do you believe in this interpretation on a scale from zero to one hundred percent? Zero means that you don't believe it at all, and a hundred means that you completely believe it.

P: Very strongly. Maybe ninety!

T: And what kind of feelings did you have?

P: I was very anxious.

T: How anxious, on a scale of zero to one hundred percent?

P: Eighty-five.

T: Okay, let me write "anxious, eighty-five percent" in the column on emotion. Did you have any urges to ritualize or avoid, and if so, how strong were they?

P: Well, my urge to avoid was one hundred percent. I gave the baby to the mother right away.

T: Okay, I am going to write this down in the column on compulsions/avoidance.

When you complete a thought record, be especially alert for statements that contain absolute phrasing of words, such as "always," "never," and "constantly." At this point, do not identify each of these statements as representing a domain or faulty thinking, but make a note of them for later work.

Assign Homework

For homework, ask your patient to self-monitor situations, intrusive thoughts, and emotions using the five-column Thought Record and Guide handout. Ask the patient to select very common situations or intrusions that seem especially disturbing and to complete at least four thought records during the week. These might be in different cognitive domains or they might be the same intrusions or interpretations on different occasions. Also ask your patient to identify the cognitive errors in the interpretations and the domains the interpretations belong to. From this point forward, at each session, give the patient enough forms to last until the next session (one or more per day).

Summary and Feedback

Ask your patient to summarize the session. You can add any comments to expand on any aspects your patient has left out. Inquire about any questions. Finally, ask the patient for feedback about the session.

SESSION 4

Handouts

Personal Session Form

Thought Record and Guide—Seven Column

Therapist Forms

Cognitive Therapy Session Report

Agenda

- Check on patient's OCD symptoms and mood since last session.

- Briefly review content of previous session.

- Set the agenda jointly with the patient (working on evaluating thoughts).

- Review thought-monitoring homework.

- Evaluate interpretations using Socratic questioning.

- Explain the seven-column Thought Record and Guide.

- Assign homework.

- Ask for summary and feedback about the session.

Start this session by handing out the Personal Session Form and by checking on your patient's recent OCD symptoms, related problems, and mood. Review what your patient learned in the previous session. Next, set the agenda:

T: Today we will work on one of the most important strategies in cognitive therapy. You'll learn how to take a step back from your thoughts and how to critically evaluate them. Now, let's take a look at your thought record from this past week because this will be a very good place to start.

Verify that the patient used the thought record correctly and select one or more thought incidents to discuss in the session. Comment positively on the patient's efforts to use the forms, or if he/she did not complete some forms, determine why and emphasize their importance. If your patient tried but had problems completing thought records, be empathic in asking what was difficult and suggesting ways to resolve the problem. Patients may feel embarrassed about their writing or spelling or about recording upsetting thoughts on paper. It's important that you don't inadvertently reinforce patients' existing views of themselves as "stupid" or "incompetent" or "bad." Let your patient know that filling out thought records will get easier with repeated practice and that spelling and being neat doesn't matter. What is important is that he or she learns to observe thinking.

Ask your patient to discuss his or her experience during one or more of the situations that provoked considerable discomfort. Review these in sufficient detail to gain a clear understanding of the sequence of triggers, thinking, feelings, and actions.

Work with your patient to restate the thoughts as bluntly as possible to capture the actual thinking at the moment. For example, "Having this thought means I'm a pervert" is more direct than the vaguer version, "If I think a sexual thought in relation to my daughter, it might mean that I'm a bad person." To avoid putting words in your patient's mouth that don't correctly represent what he or she is thinking, ask directly whether the reformulated simpler statement accurately reflects what was in the back of his or her mind. Reword it until your patient confirms that it is accurate. Both you and your patient should then record the statement verbatim on the thought record form.

Next, move to evaluation of the interpretation.

Evaluating Interpretations with Socratic Questioning

In the course of discussing the thought records, you should remind your patient that certain beliefs or automatic assumptions result in faulty interpretations of intrusive thoughts. For example, if someone believes that it is important (or even possible) to control their thoughts, they are more likely to be upset when an unwanted thought occurs. This is more likely to lead to an interpretation that loss of control is imminent. Someone who believes that thoughts can always be controlled will likely be very hard on themselves for failing to control their thoughts. The patient who is prone to believing that he or she is a bad person is likely to attribute special importance to thoughts about harming others.

You can then propose the following:

T: We'll now start to look more carefully at the faulty interpretations to see if there might be another way of viewing the thoughts you have recorded for homework. We'll be evaluating your belief that _____ . We can consider whether there are other assumptions that might be equally valid.

If your patient expresses concern that the thoughts are too entrenched to change, you can suggest that people's beliefs do change and ask for examples of this from the patient's own experience outside the realm of OCD thinking (for example, current attitudes about people that differ from initial impressions).

With regard to style, you should encourage your patient to collaborate in this process of investigation or detective work. Concrete strategies are often useful. For example, use paper to draw or illustrate any aspects of the cognitive evaluation whenever useful. Whenever your patient develops a new idea that seems helpful or finds one of the cognitive techniques useful, encourage him or her to make notes on the personal session forms or on any of the handouts. Do not argue with your patient and avoid using "yes, but . . ." statements or any other comments that might imply that your patient is incorrect or, worse yet, stupid. Initially, patients rarely believe that there is an alternative way to view a thought or situation related to an obsession. You need to be respectful and accepting of this and present treatment as an opportunity to explore other views and review the evidence for and against their own beliefs. Validation strategies are essential to encourage your patients to notice and think about their reactions to intrusions. It's best to adopt the view that patients have always done the best they can to follow instructions. It will be up to them to decide if a new idea is valid.

Explaining the Seven-Column Thought Record

Next take a seven-column thought record and fill in the first five columns (you can just transfer what the patient had completed for homework on the five-column thought record, or you can select a new OCD trigger situation). Then provide instructions on completing the last two columns.

T: These columns here are used for evaluating automatic thoughts/interpretations. So after you have completed the first five columns, you can use a strategy called Socratic questioning. This means you basically ask yourself some questions that may be useful in evaluating interpretations and formulating rational alternatives. Questions you might use can be found at the back of your form, such as "Is this thought helpful right now?" or "What is the evidence for and against the specific interpretation?" You will find that depending on the context, certain questions are more useful than others. Just select the ones that fit the interpretation you are trying to work on best. So for the interpretation "If I think of smashing her head, I'll act on it," which questions would you select?

P: "What would a friend say to me about this?"

T: Good. And what would a friend actually say? Can you try to reply to this?

P: A friend would point out that I have had these thoughts several thousand times and I never acted on them ever . . .

T: That's a good way of looking at this. So why don't we put in the column for rational responses: "This is just a thought. I have had this thought over a thousand times and I never acted on it. . . . This shows me that thoughts cannot cause actions." [Patient writes this thought in rational response column.] How strongly do you believe that rational response?

P: Well, I think it's true, so at least seventy percent.

T: Now let's take a look at the last column of the thought record. How credible is the original interpretation now?

P: Not as much, maybe thirty-five percent.

T: Okay, let's put that down. Which emotions does it cause now and how strong are these?

P: Some anxiety, maybe twenty percent.

A seven-column sample thought record appears at the end of this chapter.

Whenever you provide educational or corrective information, you must be careful to avoid giving reassurance, especially when your patient is clearly making a mistaken assumption. It's also important to avoid reinforcing a patient who appears to be trying to give you a "correct" answer to the questions listed above but is not really buying into it. In such cases, mention that he or she appeared doubtful and simply suggest, "Be as honest as you can about your reactions. It's your thoughts that count here." Discuss whatever it is that causes your patients to be doubtful. Usually they'll report that they thought of something that supports their original interpretation. If this is the case, address this "evidence" with Socratic questioning.

Assign Homework

For homework, ask your patient to practice evaluating interpretations a few times each day using the seven-column Thought Record and Guide handout.

Summary and Feedback

Ask your patient to summarize the session. You can add any comments to expand on anything your patient has left out and inquire if there are any questions. Also ask the patient for feedback about the session. Finally, ask your patient to complete another OBQ-Ext before he or she goes home, as you will need this score before your next treatment session.

SELECT THE NEXT COGNITIVE DOMAIN

After the fourth session, you need to decide which treatment module from the following chapters to start with. Your decision should be informed by the beliefs you have identified during treatment sessions and on your patient's thought records completed for homework, as well as the subscale scores of your patient's most recent OBQ-Ext. Usually it's best to address the belief domain in which your patient has the most severe problems first.

In general, we recommend completing the OBQ-Ext, OCRS, and BDI-II every month or every four to six sessions. The subscales of the OBQ-Ext that reflect domains addressed in therapy can help you determine whether sessions focusing on a particular module should be terminated or extended. The other two measures will give you an idea of whether your patient is improving on OCD and depression symptoms, which will indicate if you are on track with your approach.

Thought Record—Seven Column

Patient's Name: Date: Compulsions/Avoidance:

Situation/Trigger	Intrusion	Interpretation	Emotion	Maladaptive Coping Strategies	Rational Response	Outcome
Describe what led to the intrusive thought and unpleasant emotion.	Describe unwanted thought, image, or impulse.	a) Write interpretation. b) Rate belief in interpretation, 0 to 100 percent.	a) Specify emotions. b) Write strength of emotion, 0 to 100 percent.	a) Rate urge to neutralize or avoid, 0 to 100 percent. b) Specify rituals or avoidance.	a) Write rational response to interpretation. b) Rate belief in rational response, 0 to 100 percent.	a) Rerate interpretation, 0 to 100 percent. b) Specify and rate subsequent emotions, 0 to 100 percent.
Holding three-month-old niece	"I am going to smash her head against the wall."	a) "If I am thinking that I might smash her head, I'm going to do it." b) 90 percent	a) anxious b) 85 percent	a) urge: 100 percent b) Gave baby to mother right away.	a) "This is just a thought. I have had this thought over a thousand times and I never acted on it. This shows me that thoughts cannot cause actions." b) 70 percent	a) 35 percent b) anxious, 20 percent

This table is adapted from *Cognitive Therapy: Basics and Beyond*, by J. Beck (page 132), 1995, New York: Guilford Press. Copyright 1995 by J. Beck. Adapted with permission.

Chapter 5

Overimportance of Thoughts

This is one of the most important chapters in this book because many, if not most, patients with OCD overestimate the importance of their thoughts. Those who have harming, sexual, and religious obsessions, or magical thinking will benefit from the techniques contained in this chapter. These patients tend to confuse thoughts with actions, often termed *thought-action fusion,* believing that merely having a negative or frightening thought can lead directly to unintended actions or outcomes.

You will need to determine whether your patient has a significant problem with overestimating the importance of intrusive thoughts. Base this on your own assessment during the first few sessions, on information from the patient's thought records, and on your patient's scores on the overimportance-of-thoughts subscale of the Obsessive Beliefs Questionnaire. If your patient clearly has such symptoms, apply the strategies suggested below. We have typically spent at least four sessions teaching patients how to apply these techniques.

HANDOUTS

Personal Session Forms

Thought Record and Guide—Seven Column

Intrusions Reported by Ordinary People

Cognitive Model of OCD—Completed and Blank Forms

States of Mind Diagram

List of Cognitive Errors

Behavioral Experiment Form

Downward Arrow Form

THERAPIST FORMS

Cognitive Therapy Session Report

AGENDA

As always, begin each session with a brief check on your patient's mood and ask about the frequency and intensity of intrusive thoughts since the last meeting. Also ask about any reactions to previous sessions. Set the agenda with your patient, and review the homework assigned for the previous session. The following cognitive techniques are included in this chapter to challenge your patient's interpretations and beliefs about the overimportance of their intrusive thoughts, images, or impulses:

- Review of the CT model
- Wise mind = rational + emotional thinking
- Psychoeducation
- Metaphors and stories
- Patient as scientist or detective
- Courtroom technique
- Downward arrow
- Socratic questioning
- Behavioral experiments
- Consulting an expert
- Double-standard technique
- Continuum technique
- Advantages and disadvantages

After teaching and practicing one or more of the above methods, assign your patient homework as recommended at the end of this chapter. At the end of every session, ask for a summary of what your patient learned and for feedback about any problems during the session or positive aspects of the discussion and exercises.

REVIEW HOMEWORK

Review the seven-column thought record forms (see chapter 4), attending to the patient's rational responses and ratings of the strength of belief before and after these responses. When rational responses are not reducing negative emotions, ask about both the strength of the emotional/gut level belief and also about the strength of the intellectual or rational belief. Sometimes patients know what the rational answer is or should be, but emotionally they are on a different level. Select two to three thoughts from the thought records to review in detail. Your goal here is to help your patient evaluate the relevance and importance of the evidence for and against OCD beliefs and identify more adaptive, alternative beliefs. Begin by commenting positively on your patient's efforts and successful use of the strategies assigned. Correct any simple mistakes, such as recording something other than an intrusive thought, incorrectly putting a statement of emotion in the box for cognitive interpretations, forgetting to rate mood or strength of belief, etc.

Depending on the specific assignment given at the end of the previous session, you may want to ask one or more of the following questions:

T: Did you find any of the evaluation questions on the back of the thought record useful? Which ones? Did you notice yourself making any cognitive errors when you looked at the interpretations you wrote down? Which ones? How did you deal with that? Did you try to correct the errors? How well did that work?

When you spot mistakes in applying rational alternatives, use Socratic questioning to help your patient discover the problem or consider another solution.

T: I wonder if there is another way of looking at that? What would your friend Jodie say about the rational response you used here?

This dialogue should always be honest in tone, not merely asking leading questions to which you know the answer and are waiting for your patient to figure it out. The attitude needed is one of curiosity and genuine interest in learning and considering the patient's views, as well as other possible viewpoints or explanations. Your stance enables your patient to step back and gain some perspective, learning to modify the automatic negative interpretations that follow obsessive intrusions.

Inquire about the outcome of any other homework given and review any forms assigned during the previous session. If your patient followed instructions, but the results do not match expectations, probe further to understand the procedures your patient used and why these might have resulted in the pattern observed. Discuss possible explanations and reassign the tasks if needed.

Whenever your patient fails to complete a homework assignment, be sure to find out why. If the explanation sounds like a legitimate excuse, there is no need to pursue the issue further unless a pattern of failed homework assignments develops. If the explanation implies a misunderstanding of the assignment, reexplain the homework and the rationale for requesting it. However, if the excuse given suggests your patient lacks motivation, do not proceed further without a thorough discussion of the importance of patients' efforts to complete all homework they have agreed to do. Failure to complete homework constitutes a therapy-interfering behavior and must be addressed (see chapters 2 and 4) before proceeding to teach cognitive techniques.

COGNITIVE THERAPY TECHNIQUES

The techniques presented below are intended as options from which you can make choices, based on judgments about the nature of your patient's symptoms, accompanying interpretations and beliefs, and personality style, and the likelihood that your patient will benefit from a particular method. This judgment requires some experience. If you are a beginning therapist, try each method once or twice and then concentrate mainly on the techniques that seem to work best with your patient.

Remember that your task is not to have patients directly evaluate their intrusions ("I might stab my daughter with that knife"). Instead, help your patient evaluate the interpretation that follows the obsession ("I'm a bad mother for having such a thought" or "I will lose control and do it"). Don't try to convince your patient that she will not stab her daughter. Instead, help her to examine whether only bad mothers have these thoughts or whether intrusive thoughts mean that loss of control is imminent.

The main interpretations related to overimportance of thoughts are:

- Just having the thought (or image or urge) means it is important: "I shouldn't be thinking about this" or "Oh, I need to be concerned about that."

- Thoughts can cause behaviors or actions (thought-action fusion): "Thinking about this embarrassing thing means it will happen," "Having violent thoughts means I'll lose control and become violent," "Having thoughts about molesting a child means I will do it," or "If I think about a plane crashing, it will actually happen."

- Thinking something is as bad as doing it (moral thought-action fusion): "Having this urge is just as bad as doing it," "Having aggressive images means I secretly want to hurt someone," "Having a blasphemous thought is as sinful as committing a sacrilegious act," or "If I don't fix this thought about others having an accident, I'm a lazy and bad person."

Review the CT Model

Reviewing the cognitive model is beneficial in early sessions of therapy and will also be helpful periodically throughout therapy to make sure your patients retain a clear understanding of how their beliefs play an important role in their OCD symptoms. This is particularly true for patients who have problems with overimportance of thoughts (or images or impulses). Review the most important aspects of the model by referring to the cognitive model of OCD that you developed with your patient during assessment and education sessions. If the original model does not refer specifically to obsessions that represent overimportance of thoughts, create another version of the cognitive model based on these obsessive ideas. Review again the Intrusions Reported by Ordinary People handout, focusing on the ordinary intrusions that are especially similar to your patient's obsessions. Ask your patient to comment on the likely validity of the other people's intrusions that are similar to his or her own.

T: Do you think the person who wrote this belief should be concerned that it will come true? Why or why not?

Now, discuss what beliefs of your patient's might have led to interpretations about the importance of thoughts and his or her distress about this?

T: Why do you think you are especially bothered by this type of belief? Was this an important issue in your family when you were growing up? Did you have any special experiences that make you think these thoughts are really important?

Use this information to encourage your patient to talk about the overimportance of thoughts and to write in pertinent examples of beliefs in the Cognitive Model of OCD—Blank Form handout.

Wise Mind = Rational + Emotional Thinking

It may be helpful to remind patients of the difference between rational thinking and emotional thinking when addressing the overimportance of thoughts. Borrowing from Linehan's (1993) work, we have found it useful for some patients to draw two large, slightly overlapping circles (see States of Mind Diagram handout). The left circle represents emotional thinking when thinking is controlled mainly by feelings such as anxiety, guilt, or sadness. The right represents rational thoughts, based on empirical facts and logic. You can point out that patients often seem to hold both types of thoughts in mind at the same time when obsessive ideas occur. That is, they are very fearful while at the same time realizing that their fears aren't reasonable, but nonetheless the fearful state seems to dictate much of their mental airtime and their behavior. In the diagram, the patient can write examples of rational and emotional thoughts next to each circle. The aim of CT is to strengthen the rational mind circle so eventually it overlaps more fully with the emotional mind circle, creating what Linehan calls "wise mind." In the wise mind, both types of thinking are more balanced, so that the person is aware of his or her concern but readily able to apply factual information and logic to dispel unreasonable fears. Some patients find it helpful to return to these circles to determine what type of thinking they are using to evaluate the dangerousness of their obsessions. An example of how this might work follows:

States of Mind Diagram	
Emotional Thoughts: "Oh my God, what if I can't stop myself from using these scissors to stab my son? This is terrible! I'm such an awful person for even thinking this!"	**Rational thoughts:** "I've had this thought before and have never done anything like that. I don't have any history of doing impulsive things like this. No one else who knows me is worried about my attacking anyone."
Wise thoughts: "These are common intrusions for most people, although they don't usually tell others about these thoughts. I am just having a strong emotional reaction that's a habit by now, but it would be jumping to conclusions to believe that just thinking something means that I'm going to act on it or that I really want this to happen. What I think is not who I am. If that were true for everyone, lots of my friends and family would be bad people too, and I don't believe that. In this case, I can't let my emotions overwhelm what I know to be true, that I'm basically a kind person."	

Psychoeducation

You can normalize interpretations about the overimportance of sexual obsessions by educating patients about how sexual thoughts, fantasies, and arousal can arise from many stimuli, including those unrelated to preferred sexual orientation and behavior. For example, if your patient has homosexual intrusions, educate him or her that this is very common. If your patients have experimented with same-sex partners in the past, or have looked at same-sex pornography, also educate them that this occurs very frequently (for a more detailed description on addressing same-sex thoughts and fantasies, see chapter 8). Encourage your patients to read sex education books. *The Mind and Heart in Human Sexual Behavior* by Alan Bell (1997) is a great general text; *Male Sexual Awareness* by Barry and Emily McCarthy (1998) is especially helpful for homosexual fantasies and concerns regarding masturbation; and *My Secret Garden* by Nancy Friday (1998) is helpful for women's sexual fantasies.

For patients with religious obsessions in which overimportance of thoughts is a prominent feature ("Thinking a blasphemous thought is as bad as blaspheming God"), consider helping them review the teachings from their own religion that they believe support their obsessive concerns. If the teachings they recall were learned as a child, ask them to consider whether they might have interpreted the information as black-and-white thinking (a cognitive error) because they were too young to understand the real teachings. Examining their childhood-based religious beliefs in relationship to current teachings within their church/religion designed for adults may help them notice important differences. This may also require consultation with an expert from their religion and should be used only when the therapist strongly suspects that their thinking is more childlike than typical of an adult within the religious faith. Thus, patients from strongly fundamentalist religions may require other strategies. In general, it's important that the therapist affirms the patient's faith. If patients have difficulty letting go of neutralization strategies, it is therefore often useful to ask, "Given what you know about God, would he want you to?"

For patients who fear their obsessions indicate that they are "crazy," or mentally ill, you may ask them to define the illness more clearly. Often their ideas are based on newspaper stories in which individuals killed family members or went on a rampage and killed others. Your patient may fear that he/she shares important characteristics with these people and have a feared diagnosis such as pedophilia or paranoid schizophrenia. In some cases it may be helpful to actually review the criteria in the *DSM-IV* for the feared disorder to clarify the meaning of diagnostic terms. You should help your patient identify the differences between clinical symptoms, age of onset, and familial patterns of these disorders and OCD. This will obviously be most useful when the diagnosis is clearly mistaken. After it has been established that the belief ("I am a pedophile") is not supported by any evidence, you and your patient should try to formulate a more accurate belief ("I am not a pedophile. I am just someone who is terribly afraid of being a pedophile and hurting children").

Patients will often ask why they developed a particular subtype of OCD (a loving mother might have thoughts about stabbing her children; a very religious person might have blasphemous thoughts). In general, people develop OCD in those areas where it bothers them the most. You can explain that this is because OCD patients have an ambivalent sense of self. For example, they fear that a core belief like "I am bad" may be true, whereas at other times they can recognize that they are actually pretty decent individuals. Because of this ambivalence, they are fighting the intrusive thoughts that they consider to be supportive of the negative core beliefs much more than the average person would, which according to the research on thought suppression, only leads to an increase of intrusions.

Metaphors and Stories

You can use metaphors and stories to convey information in a compelling way. The following story, adapted from Michael Otto (2000), provides a model for understanding the nature and effect of the thoughts we have.

> Last night, I made a really good spaghetti sauce. It tasted so great served over pasta, and best of all, I didn't finish it. I have some leftover in my refrigerator now. The flavors have been melding over night. All I have to do is go home, heat it up, and I'll have a great dinner. I can see it, I can smell it, I can almost taste it—the melding of tomato

sauce, garlic, and basil, and I have fresh parmesan cheese to put on top.... There's only one issue. I made up this story. I don't have pasta with homemade spaghetti sauce in the refrigerator. But this reality did not stop me, and perhaps you, from getting a little hungry, and perhaps even salivating a little. This teaches us something about thoughts. They don't have to be accurate to have an effect on us. During therapy, it's important that we keep this principle in mind, that our thoughts can have a strong effect even though they may be false.

Use this to introduce a discussion of how often patients may have been accepting their intrusive thoughts and resulting interpretations as correct and meaningful, when they could be testing their accuracy. They might be disturbed by their intrusions even though they are not true.

You can also use metaphor to make a salient point. Ask your patient to think of their intrusions as static. Perhaps they can tune them out without missing anything crucial (D. Chambless, personal communication, 1998).

Patient As Scientist or Detective

This is a general strategy to encourage your patients to examine other vantage points and to evaluate the evidence for and against their beliefs about the importance of their thoughts.

T: If you were the chief detective, how would you proceed to examine the evidence for or against your belief?

Encourage your patient to generate alternative explanations for the interpretations and then collect information that supports or refutes these alternative interpretations.

T: How many times have you had this type of harming thought? ... Okay, you've had it many many times. Now, how often have you actually acted on it?

Although these questions can help patients recognize that their fears have not materialized, they may attribute this to their rituals. In this case, you will need to help them identify more basic intermediate or core beliefs about themselves that may be driving their interpretation (see the downward arrow method). Once you and your patient have identified intermediate beliefs (for example, "If I didn't stop myself, I really would do it because I can't be trusted"), consider the evidence that supports or contradicts this view (also see section on behavioral experiments). If your patient reports core beliefs (e.g., "I'm an immoral person"), go to chapter 13 to select methods that will help him or her challenge these basic negative concepts and consider alternative core beliefs.

Courtroom Technique

The courtroom technique follows logically from thinking about evidence like a detective.

T: You've said you believe that having the thought that you might deliberately drop your baby down the stairs means you are a dangerous person and unfit to be a parent. Let's use the courtroom technique to examine this possibility. In this method, we both participate as if we are in a courtroom, and we can take various roles, such as the lawyer defending the belief and the judge or member of the jury evaluating the evidence. Of course, in a courtroom, only factual evidence is allowed. First, I'd like you to take the role of the prosecuting attorney. Pretend I'm on trial, and you try to show to the jury that I am guilty of being a dangerous person who is unfit to parent. Pretend you are talking to a judge.

P: Well, you admitted that you have thought about throwing your baby down the stairs, and you actually walked over to the stairs to test it. You even imagined what would happen to the baby if you did throw it down, and you've had many of these thoughts over the past several months. Before that, you had thoughts about hurting little children. You are a very dangerous person and must be put in jail to keep you away from children.

T: Anything else?

P: Oh yeah, when you were fifteen, you got mad and broke your little brother's toys. That made him cry, and you felt smug about it until your dad found out and you got punished. Even he said you were a bad boy who couldn't be trusted.

T: Is that it? Okay, it's my turn. Now, I'll be the defense attorney, you be the person on trial, and I'll cross-examine you. "Mr. J., please clarify for the court how often you have actually thrown your baby down the stairs."

P: Well, never actually, but . . .

T: Never. I see. And how often have you thrown your baby onto the floor?

P: I haven't but . . .

T: And what about throwing your baby on a table, on the couch, on a chair? How often have you thrown or even dropped your baby anywhere at all?

P: Well, I did toss him up in the air a little.

T: And what happened then?

P: He laughed.

As you continue to play defense attorney, you can show that the evidence does not support the charges brought against the defendant. At this point you can ask your patient whether the judge would agree with this assessment or pursue further questioning. You can then suggest reversing roles, so your patient can be the defense attorney doing a cross-examination while you respond as if you were the patient. This will help consolidate the patient's conceptualization of the problem as a psychological fear rather than a probable action. The courtroom technique is also illustrated in chapter 7 on overestimation of danger and in chapter 9 on responsibility.

Downward Arrow

The downward arrow technique is useful in identifying both catastrophic fears ("I'll go to jail") and also core beliefs ("I'm a bad [immoral, dangerous] person"). As part of this technique you keep asking a series of similar questions over and over again until you uncover these fears and deeper level beliefs (see the Downward Arrow Form handout). The example below illustrates how this technique can be used in the context of overimportance of thoughts.

P: I'm afraid I might molest my daughter (age three), you know, by touching her wrong or something. It's horrible.

T: So, while you are bathing her, you have the thought that you will touch her in the wrong way, in a sexual way. Let's see if we can understand more about this fear. If you were bathing her and thought about touching her genital area, what would that mean?

P: That I had done a bad thing, that I might be molesting her.

T: And if you got the idea that you might be molesting her, what would that mean to you?

P: That's a terrible thing for a parent to touch their child sexually. It's immoral.

T: And why is it immoral to have thoughts about touching your child sexually?

P: It would mean I was a pedophile.

T: And what would be so bad about that?

P: I'd be unfit as a parent. I'd probably lose my child, maybe even go to jail.

T: What's the worst thing that would happen?

P: Losing my child is the worst.

T: And what would be so bad about that?

P: I'd be totally devastated.

T: What would it mean about you?

P: I'm an immoral person, really bad, bad.

T: So when you have the idea that you might touch your daughter on her genitals in a sexual way, this leads you to think you are an unfit parent who might lose your child, an immoral bad person. Is that right?

P: Yes . . .

T: Okay, this is important. Let's see if we can find some ways of determining whether you are an unfit parent or an immoral person or whether there is another viewpoint about your thought about touching your daughter sexually.

In the case of harming, sexual, and religious obsessions, a downward arrow might lead to uncovering fears of catastrophic outcomes such as actually causing bodily injury or death, sexually assaulting someone, or going to hell. Core beliefs that emerge might include being out of control, defective, dangerous, immoral, unlovable, or bad. The validity of these types of beliefs can be examined using various strategies as described in this and subsequent chapters, especially chapter 13 on core beliefs. Of course, as the downward arrow yields information pertinent to the case formulation, you can revise the patient's cognitive model accordingly.

Socratic Questioning

Socratic questioning is a series of questions designed to help patients examine the reasoning behind their obsessive beliefs. It's especially useful to help correct the faulty beliefs that the mere presence of a thought gives it special significance or that thinking about something increases the probability that it actually happens (thought-action fusion). Ask your patient for an example during discussion in the session or from thought records completed for homework. Highlight the following common tautology: "It must be important because I think about it, and I think about it because it is important" (Freeston et al., 1996, p. 437). Using your patient's own examples, ask the following:

T: Are all of the thoughts and images you just had in the past few minutes important? If not, how do you decide which ones are important? What role does your emotional reaction to the thought play? What role should it play?

You can also refer to the List of Cognitive Errors handout to review the description of emotional reasoning and use Socratic questioning to determine how this applies to assigning importance to thoughts.

T: Let's take a look at the importance of this particular thought. You were just telling me that the airplane you just heard overhead might crash because you just thought about it. So now let's identify several other recent thoughts you've had while sitting here. What were you thinking about before you had that thought?

P: [sheepishly] I was thinking about that figurine on your shelf and how it was not very pretty.

T: [laughing] I totally agree. So you thought, "That's an ugly figurine." What else?

P: I thought about whether I needed to get food at the grocery store on the way home.

T: What else?

P: I wondered if you drove a safe car for the snow that's coming down now. I thought about a car crash.

T: Okay. Those are good examples of a random assortment of thoughts. If you like, I can also tell you some of my random thoughts. [This strategy may be especially useful if the patient has difficulty recalling his or her own thoughts.] Now, how does someone who doesn't have OCD determine whether a thought is meaningful or true?

P: Well, if it's upsetting. That would be important.

T: If a thought is upsetting that means it is true? So does that mean that all thoughts that produce unpleasant emotions, like fear or anxiety or guilt, are meaningful? When you thought about your coworker yesterday, you felt frustrated. Does that mean the thought was important or you needed to do something?

P: In this case no, but it might. It depends on what happened.

T: I agree. When people feel bad, they think more about an incident, but they decide whether to do something based on the context of the situation. Now, you also had a thought about my car. Suppose either one of us had a thought that my car would break down [Note: select the less disturbing vision of a breakdown rather than an accident, because the patient obsesses about accidents in relation to airplanes]. If we got worried about this, felt bad, would my car break down?

P: Well, not really unless it's got a problem.

T: So without evidence that there's a problem, we wouldn't think we needed to pay attention. For example, if one of us read about someone getting cancer, would we get it?

P: Well, maybe, but not because of reading about it. Lots of people are getting cancer these days.

T: So, what you are saying is that just thinking about it doesn't necessarily make it happen. Something else has to occur to make it likely. Is that right?

P: Yeah.

T: How does this apply to the thought that you can crash airplanes just by thinking about airplane crashes?

At this point, your patient has begun to consider the possibility that thinking does not necessarily directly affect outcomes, although he or she might not yet be willing to concede that this would be true of really upsetting thoughts. You will need more thought examples in future sessions for your patient to become more convinced of this. Notice that in using Socratic questioning, the therapist also asked about not only the patient's thoughts but also other people's thoughts, including the therapist's. This taking of other perspectives can be very helpful and is discussed further below.

Thought-action fusion often has a moral or religious overtone (e.g., harming others, blasphemous thoughts). In this case, normalize the occurrence by referring to the Intrusions Reported by Ordinary People handout, and then question your patient's belief that "I think about it because I secretly want it or it is my true [bad] nature."

T: How would you know that you were really dangerous? What would you do if you were dangerous? What kind of behaviors would you engage in? Are people who have these thoughts [images or urges] likely to act on them? What evidence would you use to determine if someone with these kinds of thoughts would act on them?

Behavioral Experiments

You can also use behavioral experiments to evaluate the importance of thoughts or images. You'll need to be somewhat creative in devising behavioral experiments that address your patient's faulty interpretations. The experiment should be manageable, not too anxiety-provoking for your patient. Each experiment must include a prediction or hypothesis that is being examined (the likelihood of a feared consequence occurring) and a record of the actual outcome. Follow this with a discussion about the validity of the prediction. As your patients become more familiar with this method, they can eventually take over the responsibility of setting up their own behavioral experiments as homework, using the Behavioral Experiment Form.

As part of the process, patients rate their belief in their predictions, and they rate their discomfort levels during the experiments. After the experiment is completed, they should write down the results. Did their predictions come true? What actually happened during the experiment? The goal is that, over time, they will observe a decrease in their fears and beliefs and a greater belief in alternative explanations and interpretations.

The amount of time and number of days of each experiment should be set to match your patients' expectations associated with the belief being tested. For example, if planes will crash, the outcome can be tested within hours. If storms or health problems may occur, this could take days or weeks. Ask your patients to predict the outcome and then test it by thinking the harming thought about something relatively tolerable. You can also propose experiments with similar types of thought-action-fusion occurrences that are less intense than your patients' actual obsessions. Ask whether your patients believe these would lead to outcomes like the ones they are afraid of in relation to the obsession. Some examples from Freeston et al. (1996) follow:

- Buy a lottery ticket on Monday and think about winning for five minutes (or more) per day.

- Make a minor household appliance like a hairdryer or toaster break down within the next week by thinking about it for five or more minutes per day.

- Cause a public figure to break a limb by picturing this image daily.

- Cause therapist to have a heart attack in the session by thinking about it.

The last one is especially useful for patients whose fears are focused on causing harm to people they care about. Some patients will refuse to try to kill a goldfish by thinking about it, but are willing to try to cause a person to break a finger by thinking. Let your patients determine what they are willing to try. At the end of the experiment, ask patients to report the outcome and their explanation for that outcome. If your patient doesn't believe that the feared consequence will occur for these kinds of benign situations, emphasize the inconsistencies in thinking, using Socratic questioning.

T: You aren't worried about causing this kind of harm, but you do think you can cause other kinds of harm. How would that work exactly? Why wouldn't you be able to at least cause this minor accident?

Socratic questioning and behavioral experiments should make it obvious that just because your patient has certain thoughts or images does not mean they are important, and that your patient thinks about many things that are not particularly important. Ask what implication this observation might have on interpreting whether the particular intrusive thought under consideration is important. Also ask your patient to generate an alternative interpretation, even if he or she does not yet believe it. One patient whose intrusive thoughts concerned a vague harm to her family concluded, "This thought just means that I care about my family—nothing more."

Consulting an Expert

Patients who fear punishment by God may believe that having a bad thought means they want it to happen or thinking something sacrilegious is as bad as doing it. These ideas are usually acquired through early religious training. In this case, you can ask your patients whether they agree with this early teaching now that they are an adult and know more about religious teachings.

One of us recently treated a Catholic patient who experienced recurrent blasphemous thoughts while praying. She had to repeat her prayers over and over again because she was concerned that God would punish her if she was unable to complete her prayer without intrusions. The patient was asked, "Given what you have learned about God, what would he know about you? What kind of a person would he think you are, all in all? Would he be aware of your struggle with OCD? Could he forgive you for your recurrent blasphemous thoughts?"

You may also wish to suggest that your patients consult with an expert from their religion to discuss the obsessive ideas. In this case, we strongly advise that you speak to the consultant beforehand. The priest, minister, rabbi, or other religious leader will then know to focus the discussion on the interpretation rather than on the obsession. That is, obsessive images of Christ's penis or thoughts about thumbing one's nose at God would not be the focus, but instead, the expert can directly address interpretations like "it is unacceptable to think these thoughts," "if I ignore these thoughts, that is antithetical to my religion," or "these thoughts mean I'm a bad person." Often it's helpful for you to be present at the interview with the consultant to help focus the discussion on the validity of your patient's interpretations.

Double-Standard Technique

To determine whether your patients are using different standards for themselves than for others, ask whether they would hold the same attitude about someone else they know well (another mother, a coworker) who had the same thought.

Help your patients notice contradictory thinking about themselves and others. If your patient explains the difference based on personal negative traits that others don't have, explore this further with Socratic questioning and the downward arrow technique. Your goal here is to determine whether presuming differences from others reflects core beliefs that can eventually be tested. In some cases, it may be helpful to role-play and trade roles. You can take the role of the patient, presenting the arguments why your thoughts are worse than the other person's while your patient plays the therapist or a friend who does not have OCD. This strategy is similar to the courtroom technique but without the legal tone.

Continuum Technique

Described by J. Beck (1995), this method can be used to evaluate the belief that thinking about something is as bad as doing it and is especially useful for patients who have sexual, religious, or harming obsessions. Consider, for example, a patient who believes he is dangerous because he has thoughts of pushing someone down the stairs. Discuss with your patient whether there are really only two categories (i.e., dangerous or not dangerous; moral or immoral) or whether there are different levels of being dangerous. Draw a horizontal line. Label one end 0 percent (not at all dangerous) and the other end 100 percent (extremely dangerous). Then ask your patient to rate how dangerous he is for thinking the intrusive thought. Encourage your patient to make the initial rating first on an emotional or gut level and then from an intellectual perspective. If the emotional and rational ratings are different, point out these differences. Below is an example of what a scale for "I am dangerous" might look like:

0%	50%	*patient's initial rating*	100%
not at all dangerous	moderately		extremely dangerous

In the example above, most patients initially rate themselves as highly dangerous, around 90 on the scale. After this, you and your patient together can generate several examples of other dangerous people. For example, you can ask your patient how dangerous or immoral a serial killer is who tortures his victims before he kills them. After each example, ask your patient to rerate his or her own position on the scale. The goal of this exercise is to provide patients with perspective about where they belong on a scale of dangerousness or badness.

Similarly, the mother who considers herself to be a "bad mother" because she has thoughts about sexually molesting children could be encouraged to use the scale in relation to examples of mothers who actually do bad things:

- a mother who molests and beats her son

- a mother who signs her children into prostitution

- a mother who fondles her son and asks him to fondle her

- a mother who tells her child to have sex with his uncle

- a mother who allows her child to be used for pornographic photographs

- a mother who deliberately observes her child masturbating

Advantages and Disadvantages

You can also help your patients examine the pros and cons of their interpretations and beliefs. Begin by inquiring, "What are the advantages of believing in this thought? What are the disadvantages?" and then listing under each heading all of the pros and cons generated. You may have to help your patients list a few examples in each category to obtain a fuller picture of the value of holding the beliefs. Once the advantages and disadvantages are established, help your patients evaluate the validity of the advantages and develop an adaptive response to the thought. This is intended to help your patients see that they are engaging in a fruitless pursuit of hoped-for advantages that almost never happen and are suffering several serious disadvantages. The example below illustrates this method.

T: Let's try a technique in which we examine the advantages and disadvantages of your interpretations related to the obsessions. When you see knives and scissors, you get thoughts about harming others and then you think that it's better to avoid the knives so you can't stab anyone. Let's write that thought down [stating it again while writing]: "It is better for me to stay away from knives, so I cannot stab anyone."

P: That's pretty much what I think anytime I see something sharp.

T: For the moment, we'll just stick to knives because your thought is especially strong there. Now, I'm guessing that your plan to avoid knives leads to your feeling less anxious, so one potential advantage of this thought could be "It keeps others safe." Let's put that under the advantage heading. Do you see any disadvantage to having this thought about avoiding being around knives?

P: Sure, it's a pain to avoid the knives because I have to go to all sorts of trouble to cook without cutting, or else I have to make sure my daughter isn't in the house when I cut up the vegetables and other stuff.

T: Agreed. It's very inconvenient for you. Any other disadvantages?

P: I feel stupid doing it when nobody else I know does this.

T: Okay, I'll write those down. I'd like to add another one. I think the thought might actually help maintain your OCD, because it prevents you from finding out what would happen if you did handle knives.

P: Yeah, I suppose that's possible, like maybe I'm not really so dangerous as I think, but I'm too afraid to find out.

T: Exactly. Not only does your avoidance of knives interfere with making dinner, but it also causes you to feel different from other people, affecting your relationships. I'm also guessing it reduces your confidence and makes you feel dangerous. What do you think?

P: Oh yes, I do feel different—bad.

T: So, let's put those down on the list.

Continue with the examination of the advantages and disadvantages, and then use Socratic questioning to determine the validity of the advantages your patient has listed. After this, help your patient go on to develop an alternative viewpoint:

T: Let's take a look at what this means for you. What I'm hearing you say is that even you think that staying away from knifes doesn't really help keep others safe—they were safe in the first place. Can you say more about what this means about you as a person. Are you dangerous?

P: No, probably not really, but I worry about it.

T: I understand that concern. But in fact what is the more accurate belief? What about the belief: "I am not a dangerous person, and I have never acted on any of those aggressive thoughts. It is just my OCD that causes me to avoid anxiety-provoking situations." Is this closer to the truth about you?

ASSIGN HOMEWORK

The following homework assignments may be useful based on techniques from this chapter. In assigning these techniques, be sure to specify verbally and in writing (with a copy for yourself) what you expect your patient to bring to the next session.

- Ask your patients to complete the seven-column Thought Record and Guide to provide several examples of relevant intrusions about the importance of thoughts during the week. A range of examples will enable your patients to apply the techniques taught in this module to their common thoughts.

- Ask your patients to refine their personal cognitive model of OCD based on findings from thought records.

- Assign the Downward Arrow Form if you think it will help your patients better understand the thoughts and beliefs that underlie certain types of obsessions about the importance of thoughts.

- If more education about sexual urges and fantasies is needed to allay feelings of being different or weird for having sexual thoughts, assign relevant reading.

- Assign behavioral experiments to test whether particular thoughts come true using the Behavioral Experiment Form.

- Ask your patients to call or make an appointment with an expert consultant (such as a religious figure) after initial discussion about what information would be useful in resolving the patients' overestimation of thoughts.

- Ask for a list of the advantages and disadvantages of particular interpretations.

SUMMARY AND FEEDBACK

Ask your patients to summarize the major points covered during each session, and if several ideas were covered, assist in filling in any gaps or correcting any confusion. Also ask for comments and questions about what they learned during the session. Finally, ask for feedback about your own behavior and how the session went from their perspective, especially if anything was problematic. If your patients express concerns, respond in an understanding manner and develop a plan for how to address this.

Chapter 6

Control of Thoughts

In chapter 5, you applied a variety of treatment strategies to help your patient more accurately estimate the true importance of his or her intrusive thoughts, images, and impulses. As we indicated at the outset of that chapter, patients who overestimate the importance of obsessive thoughts are also very likely to try to control these thoughts. This will be especially true of those with harming, sexual, and religious or magical thinking. To control these thoughts, many patients use maladaptive coping strategies that, paradoxically, actually help maintain the very thoughts and fears they are trying to stop. These patients will benefit from the cognitive methods recommended here to help them reduce their problematic efforts to control their obsessive thoughts.

HANDOUTS

Personal Session Forms

Thought Record and Guide—Seven Column (introduced in chapter 4)

Thought-Suppression Graph

THERAPIST FORMS

Cognitive Therapy Session Report

Cognitive Model (developed during session in chapter 4)

AGENDA

Begin by briefly asking about your patient's mood and OCD symptoms, especially intrusive thoughts, during the past week. Also ask about any reactions to the previous few sessions, which probably focused on overimportance of thoughts. Together, set the session's agenda and review the homework assigned from the previous session. On the agenda, you will want to put one or more of the following techniques:

- Thought-suppression experiment

- Metaphors and stories

- Advantages and disadvantages

- Socratic questioning

After teaching and practicing these methods during the session, decide with your patient what homework might be especially useful. This is likely to include completing thought records and the Thought-Suppression Graph. At the end of each session, ask for a summary of what your patient learned and for any feedback about any problems or positive aspects of the session.

REVIEW HOMEWORK

For your first session in this module, most likely you will be reviewing homework assigned from the previous module on overimportance of thoughts from chapter 5. In reviewing the seven-column thought records, focus on your patient's rational responses and ratings of the strength of beliefs before and after using rational responses. Reinforce or correct your patient's efforts as appropriate. You can use Socratic questioning to help your patient identify problems and logical errors, making sure to keep an attitude of genuine curiosity and interest.

As always, record homework information on your Cognitive Therapy Session Report. Help your patient draw conclusions from the homework to reinforce cognitive change and the benefits of using these methods. Probe further regarding any problems, but be careful to avoid comments that might embarrass or sensitize your patient about making mistakes.

COGNITIVE THERAPY TECHNIQUES

Remember that at no point will you and your patients directly evaluate the intrusions/ obsessions, but instead you will focus only on the interpretation that follows them. Thus, you would not evaluate a patient's images of her child being naked but would focus on her idea that "I must be completely out of control for even having such an image" or her associated belief that "only child molesters have these kind of images." In this module, you will work specifically on your patient's efforts to suppress the images to understand the opposite effect this has on emotions and on obsessions.

Thought-Suppression Experiment

Begin by providing some education. State that based on your observation of your patient and other patients with OCD, you believe that your patient's efforts to suppress intrusions in fact lead to just the opposite. That is, efforts to stop thoughts actually increase their frequency and assigned importance, and probably also increase the discomfort associated with the thoughts. To illustrate that trying to control intrusive thoughts via suppression is counterproductive, first ask your patient to picture a pink elephant or a camel or some other exotic animal. Then, ask your patient to try very hard *not* to think about that animal for the next five minutes:

T: Now, I want you to suppress this image. Keep this white bear out of your mind at all costs. Work hard to avoid thinking about white bears or forming any image of these bears. If the idea or image pops into your mind, raise your finger like this while we are talking so I will know.

Talk about something else for five minutes, noting the raised finger whenever it occurs. Then ask your patient about the experience. Comment on the fact that scanning your mind internally to make sure a thought or image is not present actually causes a person to pay more attention to the idea and think about it more (see Wegner, 1989). Next, review last week's thought records with your patient to select one of the obsessive thoughts that your patient usually tries to suppress. Ask him or her to experiment with suppressing the thought for the next two days and not suppressing it on the remaining days of the week before the next session. Decide how to keep a frequency count of the thought and agree on how to graph it on the Thought-Suppression Graph handout. An example of a completed graph is given on the next page.

In your next session, review the form and ask your patient what happened when he or she tried to stop the thought compared to what happened when allowing the thought to remain. Your goal is to help your patient register the negative effects of thought suppression, including that it does not work, it requires exceptional effort, and it provokes emotional discomfort. Use this to lead into a discussion of how your patient might respond differently to intrusive thoughts. You and your patient may need to brainstorm a bit to agree on useful methods for consolidating this cognitive learning experience.

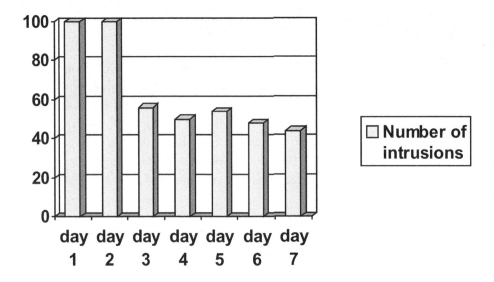

Figure 2: Thought-Suppression Graph

Ideal strategies are to leave the thoughts and images alone (no mental response) and to keep doing the tasks you are already engaged in, regardless of the thoughts (no behavior change). Your patients might remind themselves that suppressing only made it worse during the experiment, so it is better to just wait out the discomfort until it habituates. If this proves very difficult, consider using some distraction strategies, such as absorbing tasks, until discomfort declines to a manageable level.

Beware of patient suggestions that are simply alternative versions of suppression, such as changing the thought or "coping" with it in special ways that appear likely to have similar effects of strengthening the obsession. These too can be tested against the alternatives of merely allowing the intrusion to remain in mind as long as it naturally occurs.

Metaphors and Stories

There are several metaphors you can use to illustrate how your patients might respond to an intrusive thought. These include

- Allowing a train (the obsession) to enter the station and leave on its own timetable (J. Buchin, personal communication, 1998)

- An image of Wiley Coyote on the train tracks, stepping aside to let the train pass, rather than standing in the middle of the tracks and being flattened by the train; his hair gets mussed and he sways from the rushing air a little, but he isn't hurt (M. Freeston, personal communication, 1997)

- Imagining the intrusive thought as a leaf floating in the wind or on the water, swirling around and around, ultimately landing on the ground, still, unmoving

Advantages and Disadvantages

You can also discuss the advantages and disadvantages of holding the belief that some thoughts or images need to be controlled. Help your patients examine the pros and cons of the belief by inquiring: "What are the advantages of believing in this thought or making this decision? What are the disadvantages?" List all of the pros and cons on paper and provide assistance to add to the list for both categories to obtain a fuller picture of the value of holding this belief. Consider the following example:

T: Why don't we take a look at the advantages and disadvantages of your efforts to suppress your thoughts about saying blasphemous words such as "hell" or "damn" in church.

P: Well, one advantage is that it makes me feel like I am doing the right thing, you know, following God's teachings.

T: Okay, that's one advantage—you *think* you are behaving in a manner consistent with your religious beliefs. Do you also feel less upset emotionally when you try to suppress the words?

P: Only for a short while, actually.

T: So that's both an advantage in the short run but also a disadvantage in the long run. Let's put that down in both columns. What other advantages are there for suppressing?

P: Well, maybe it works sort of. I don't think bad words for a little bit.

T: Again, sounds like this is both an advantage and a disadvantage. Let's put that in your list. Any other advantages?

P: I can't think of any.

T: Now, what about disadvantages?

P: It doesn't really work, I guess. You know every time I go to church, I have to keep doing this. Sometimes I have to leave the room, I'm so afraid I'll say it out loud.

T: Okay, that's an important disadvantage. Suppressing doesn't seem to work very well. Does it take much energy?

P: Oh yeah, lots. Sometimes I'm just exhausted when I get home after church, just fighting to keep it under control.

T: So that's another disadvantage—it's very tiring to try to control your thoughts. Okay, let's review the list.

Here's the list that the above conversation would generate:

Thought Suppression	
Advantages	**Disadvantages**
1. I think I'm doing the right thing from a religious standpoint—God would approve. 2. I'm briefly less upset. 3. It works for a short while.	1. I'm still upset about the thoughts in the long run. 2. It doesn't work for very long. 3. Sometimes it doesn't work at all and I have to leave the sanctuary. 4. It takes a lot of emotional energy; makes me tired.

You could then continue the conversation:

T: Let's take a look now at the advantages you listed, especially this first one. The other two have distinct disadvantages, which you are already aware of. So, would God approve of your thought suppression? Do you think God thinks that all people who have intrusive thoughts about these kinds of words should be very upset and work really hard and get really tired trying to control them?

P: I guess I can see your point. I hadn't really thought of it like that.

At this point you can engage your patient in a thoughtful discussion of what he or she was taught from a religious perspective, using Socratic questioning methods as noted below. You can also consider involving an expert, in this case a minister or priest, if your patient needs clarification of religious teachings and how they might apply to this sort of problem.

Socratic Questioning

The downward arrow methods described in detail in chapters 3 and 5 may also be very helpful in identifying maladaptive beliefs about the value and importance of controlling intrusive thoughts and images. These beliefs can then be evaluated using Socratic questioning to elucidate cognitive errors and mistaken assumptions:

T: Why don't we think a little about this right now? What do you know about how God would likely view a person who has a problem with obsessive thoughts? Suppose you had obsessive thoughts that you had made a mistake at work and began to check over and over. What would God think about this?

P: Oh, he would know that that was an OCD problem, and it wasn't the person's fault, although the person should try to get help to fix it.

T: That make sense to me. If God is all-knowing, he would know this.

P: Yes, people have problems; that's just human. God wouldn't punish someone for that.

T: I agree. Let's see if your situation is any different. Do other people besides yourself have a problem worrying about their thoughts, especially blasphemous thoughts? And do you think this is OCD?

P: Yes, I know they do because you showed me that book (Ciarrocci, 1995) which was all about it. I've also seen it described in the OCF newsletter. Yes, I'm sure this is OCD. Lots of experts seem to think this, and it makes sense to me.

T: So, if your thoughts about blasphemous words are because of OCD, would God know this?

P: Yes, of course, he knows I have OCD.

T: What does that mean about how God would react if you didn't try to control your thoughts in order to get over your fears? If you just let your thoughts stay in your head without trying to get rid of them?

P: Maybe ... I suppose God would think I should get help. But what if I let my thoughts alone and I blurted this out in church?

T: Well, of course, that is your obsession, right? That you will lose control and blurt out obscenities and swear words in church and similar places. In the past few sessions, you and I have talked about how you have attributed a lot of importance to this idea, and have been thinking that it is an important thought. But, in fact, this is just a hypothesis you have and the evidence suggests that you are someone who is worried about saying your thoughts, but not someone who swears and blasphemes a lot in public.

P: Yeah, I am still worried about losing control, though.

T: Of course, and we didn't think we could undo this with just a few sessions, so of course you still worry about this. Right now, let's look at your idea that your thought-suppression efforts are really doing the right thing from a religious perspective, that God would approve of your actions and therefore this really is an advantage for continuing to do this.

P: Okay.

T: You said God would think you should get help for OCD. But here you said "God would approve" of trying to suppress your thoughts. What do you think now?

P: I guess it doesn't really make sense. If he wanted me to get help, he probably wouldn't want me to keep doing stuff that doesn't work very well.

T: So, are you saying that maybe from a religious perspective, thought suppression isn't really a good idea?

P: I guess not, but it is very hard to see it that way when the thoughts happen in church.

T: How strongly do you believe you should try as hard as you can to suppress your thoughts?

P: Not really. No, I don't think that. Maybe only 30.

T: So God might not actually approve of this method, or at least continuing to do it isn't very consistent with what he would want you to do?

P: Yes, I'm not sure he would disapprove, but he would want me to work on this problem.

T: Let's decide on an experiment [thought-suppression test] to try out an alternative.

This dialogue illustrates a typical and slightly meandering Socratic dialogue to first elicit from the patient her own beliefs about God and her religious teachings that may not match her automatic conclusion. The therapist focuses on other less threatening OCD symptoms to first establish the patient's belief about God's response and then apply it to her own situation. The patient's reluctance to accept even her own belief about God is evident as she expresses her obsessive fear. The therapist redirects her back to the task at hand after normalizing her concern. This ultimately results in some significant change that will need reinforcing in future sessions using related CT methods.

After applying the several strategies outlined here and in chapter 5, help your patients reexamine their case formulation from the original cognitive model developed during the assessment (chapter 4) to see if any changes are needed.

ASSIGN HOMEWORK

The following homework assignments are likely to be useful after sessions in this module:

• Assign the advantages and disadvantages technique for homework if it seemed useful during the session.

• Ask your patient to graph the frequency of a target thought each day over seven days using the Thought-Suppression Graph handout.

In the next session, you should inquire about the outcome of this experiment during suppression and nonsuppression days and review the graph. The expected pattern should be one of high frequency on thought-suppression days and relatively low frequency on days of not suppressing. If the pattern differs from this, determine whether your patient has followed the instructions correctly, especially in allowing the thought to come without interference, or using neutralization or coping strategies. Reassign the experiment if needed. If the assignment goes as expected, compliment your patient on the work and draw the obvious conclusion that thought suppression produces a paradoxical increase in obsessions rather than a reduction.

SUMMARY AND FEEDBACK

Ask for a summary of each session's content and for feedback about your own behavior as a therapist, responding appropriately if any concerns are raised.

Chapter 7

Overestimation of Danger

Overestimations of the probability or severity of danger or harm are very common in OCD and in individuals with anxiety disorders in general. Most of your patients with contamination fears or compulsions to prevent negative events (fire, burglary, accidents, illness) will benefit from this module. Note that unlike the focus of cognitive therapy for overimportance of thoughts or control of thoughts, cognitive techniques for working on overestimation of danger, directly evaluate the content of the obsessions themselves. However, take care to avoid implying that your patients should not have such thoughts, but instead focus on their estimates of the likelihood and severity of harm. We suggest various treatment strategies to help with this below. Allow two to four sessions for this module.

HANDOUTS

Personal Session Forms

Thought Record and Guide—Seven Column (introduced in chapter 4)

Downward Arrow Form

Behavioral Experiment Form

List of Cognitive Errors

THERAPIST FORMS

Cognitive Therapy Session Report

Bring a calculator.

AGENDA

Start each session by inquiring about your patient's mood and OCD symptoms. Also ask about any reactions to the previous session. Jointly, set the agenda and review the homework assigned during the last session. On the agenda, you'll want to put one or more of the following techniques to evaluate overestimations of probability or severity of harm:

- Socratic questioning
- Downward arrow technique to identify catastrophic fears
- Calculating the probability of harm
- Conducting a survey
- Behavioral experiments
- Consulting an expert
- Identifying cognitive errors
- Metaphors, stories, and analogies
- Betting money
- Role-play

After learning and applying these methods during the session, decide with your patient which homework exercises might be especially useful. At the end of each session, ask for a summary of the session highlights and for feedback about any problems or positive aspects of the session.

REVIEW HOMEWORK

For your first session in this module, most likely you'll be reviewing homework assigned from the last assessment session (see chapter 4) or a previous module. These homework assignments may include thought records and other cognitive strategies. In reviewing the seven-column thought records, focus on your patients' rational responses and ratings of the strength of beliefs before and after coming up with rational responses. Help your patients draw conclusions from the homework to promote cognitive change. Praise your patients whenever they do their homework well. Identify problems and provide corrective feedback as necessary. You can use Socratic questioning to help your patient identify problems and logical errors, maintaining an attitude of genuine curiosity and interest. As always, record information about the completed homework on your Cognitive Therapy Session Report, including the percentage of assigned homework that was completed, new insights, and any difficulties.

COGNITIVE THERAPY TECHNIQUES

The techniques described below are intended as a list of options from which you can choose. Pick the strategies that you think will have the highest likelihood of success first. If you are unsure, try different strategies and stick with the ones that seem to work best for your patient.

Downward Arrow

Particularly for overestimations of the severity of harm, use the downward arrow technique to identify immediate fears of catastrophic danger, as well as basic beliefs. Several fears may underlie patients' overestimation of the consequences of danger. Here's an example:

T: So, you saw a blue plastic bag on the highway last night. What does that mean?

P: That there was something in the bag someone was desperately trying to throw out, and they did not want to throw it in their own trash.

T: If someone wanted to throw something away but not in their own trash, what does that mean?

P: That there was something really toxic in the bag.

T: So, if there was toxic waste in the bag you saw last night, why is that important?

P: If I drove over the bag, my car is now contaminated with toxic waste.

T: So if your car was contaminated with toxic waste, what would that mean?

P: That I would bring the toxic waste home to my family.

T: And if you were to bring the waste home to your family, what's the worst part about that?

P: That my kids are going to die because I was not careful enough.

T: And if your kids were going to die because you were not careful enough, what would that mean?

P: That I am a bad father.

T: Does it mean anything else about you?

P: No, just that I am a bad father, a bad person really.

This patient's replies suggest that he overestimates danger and also has a core belief that he is a bad person. After identifying the beliefs, you can help your patient evaluate them using the other methods described in this chapter.

Note that the patient jumps to a conclusion about a catastrophic outcome and experiences considerable anxiety because of this assumption, even if he thinks the outcome is unlikely. Socratic questioning (see chapter 5) or comments expressing wonder may be helpful to evaluate maladaptive beliefs identified with the downward arrow technique.

Calculating the Probability of Harm

To modify inflated harm estimates, van Oppen and Arntz (1994) suggest contrasting the patient's original estimation of probability with the multiplied estimations of the sequence of specific events that would have to go badly to result in the dreaded outcome.

Start by identifying a recent obsession that is related to overestimation of harm and use the following steps:

- Record your patient's original estimate of the likelihood of harm.

- Together with your patient, specify all the different events or steps that would have to occur to result in the ultimate feared outcome.

- Ask your patient to estimate the probability of each of these individual events occurring.

- Using a calculator, ask your patient to compute the final cumulative chance by multiplying together all of the chances of each separate event.

- Compare this to your patient's original estimate.

Here is how this strategy can be applied for a patient with checking symptoms in an example modified from Söchting et al. (1996):

T: You've told me that you keep checking your door over and over again before you leave the house because you're afraid someone might break in. How likely do you think it is that a burglar will break into your home if you don't lock the door?

P: It's high. Maybe seventy percent.

T: Now let's take a look at all the different events that would have to come together for this to occur. How likely is it that you'd leave your house without locking the door?

P: Twenty-five percent.

T: Okay, you think that there is a one in four chance of not locking the door when you leave the house. And how many times, approximately, did you leave the house in the past year?

P: About once a day, so probably 365 times.

T: And how often did you actually find out that you'd left the door unlocked when you came back home?

P: Once I left the door unlocked, but I really just went around the corner to say hi to a neighbor.

T: So one time out of 365 days you left the door open. This is much less than one percent probability. Let me see [using the calculator] ..., to be exact it is .27 percent for leaving the door open any given day. This is much lower than your original estimate of one in four for leaving the door open.

P: Yes, I hadn't really thought of it that way. That's true.

T: So your biggest fear is that the burglar will come into your house when the door is unlocked. This means that we should multiply the probability of leaving the door unlocked by the probability that a burglar tries your door on that specific day, rather than any other door in the neighborhood. Can you give me an estimate of how many break-ins per year you have in your town? [If your patient is unsure, you could get the exact number from the local police department.]

P: It's pretty safe, I'd say about fifty at the most.

T: And how many houses do you have in your town?

P: I'm not sure. We have about 250,000 people, so probably at least 50,000 houses.

T: So now we need to divide the frequency of burglaries in your town by the number of houses. This is one chance in one thousand. Next, we need to multiply the probability that you left the door open by the probability of a break-in. Multiplying these two percentages gives us a yearly likelihood of a break-in at one chance in about 365,000.

P: Wow! I guess if you look at it this way, it's pretty rare.

T: Yes, let's see ..., if we assume that you will live to age seventy-five, it would take almost 5,000 lifetimes for a break-in to occur because you didn't check your door. Now, how does this compare to your original estimate of a seventy percent likelihood that someone will break in?

P: I guess I really overestimated the risk of leaving the door open!

A good follow-up strategy is to ask your patient whether this likelihood warrants the time and effort spent checking, as well as the anxiety about not locking the door. (Examples for assessing the advantages and disadvantages of beliefs or behaviors can be found in chapter 5 and chapter 9.)

Another method to address overestimates of danger includes establishing with the patient what has actually happened in the past and what the consequences were.

T: So how often have you been concerned that you contracted HIV?

P: Lately, all the time; at least two hundred times. That's why I've had so many tests.

T: And how often was your prediction that you contracted the virus actually true?

P: Never. All the tests were negative.

T: So given that you predicted two hundred times that you'd get HIV, and two hundred times you were wrong, what do you think you should remember next time you predict you'll get HIV from something?

P: That all my HIV predictions have been false so far. I thought that I might get HIV so many times, but it has never been true. I guess I need to change the way I think about this. But I get so anxious. I guess that's emotional reasoning, right?

T: Yes, that's what it is, and probably you also have a strong tendency to feel especially vulnerable [guessing at core belief]. We can take a look at this possibility as well. Let's note that on our forms to discuss in future sessions.

Conducting a Survey

The survey method can be used to determine the probability of feared events by asking other people, perhaps ten friends, neighbors, or coworkers, how often such events have occurred in their lives. For example, a patient who excessively checks that his or her car doors are locked might fear that forgetting to lock the car will result in car theft. First, ask your patient to predict how many out of ten people will have forgotten to lock their car at times. Instruct your patient to ask people about the consequences of forgetting to lock the car. Sometimes patients are very concerned about other people's attitudes toward individuals who make such a mistake. For example, your patients might worry that others would consider them stupid. As a result of the survey, your patient will likely learn that many people have forgotten to lock their cars at some point and that the cars were never stolen. Your patient will also hear that other people's attitudes are not nearly as harsh as your patient originally predicted. Make sure you emphasize the difference between your patient's original predictions and the actual outcome of the survey. Discuss with your patient possible reasons for misestimating others' experience and attitudes.

Behavioral Experiments

Another strategy for modifying overestimates of the probability of danger or adverse outcomes is to encourage your patient to do experiments to test predictions. The Behavioral Experiment Form can be used to test hypotheses. Below we describe the general steps:

1. Identify one or more typical situations that trigger your patient's overestimation of danger. The experiment will focus on the probability of negative outcomes and/or the severity (awfulness) of the outcome.

2. Formulate a hypothesis or prediction about feared consequence(s), trying to capture your patient's idiosyncratic fears as closely as possible. The downward arrow technique may be helpful for this. For example, a patient might predict that if she doesn't recheck an envelope before mailing a bill payment, her car payment won't be made and the car will be repossessed.

3. Ask your patient to rate how likely it is that the feared consequence will occur.

4. Ask your patient to rate his or her discomfort (anxiety, guilt, disgust) level.

5. Next, use Socratic questioning to ask your patient to think of ways to evaluate his or her original predictions and encourage your patient to specify and test alternative hypotheses. For example, someone who worries about making a mistake in an e-mail at work can deliberately make one or more of the errors she fears and observe whether she gets fired (negative outcome) or, alternatively, that no one seems to notice.

6. Next ask your patient to conduct the experiment and record the results on the Behavioral Experiment Form.

7. After the experiment, ask your patient to rerate the discomfort and discuss whether this rating has decreased significantly from the beginning of the experiment.

8. Examine whether the actual consequences matched the predicted ones. For example, you might ask the following questions: "Now, remind me of your predictions. What were you afraid would happen? Did your feared consequences come true? What did you learn in the experiment? What do you want to remember from it? Is there any evidence that supports your predictions? What alternative hypotheses would explain your findings?"

Consulting an Expert

A strategy to test whether the consequences of a feared outcome will be as severe as expected is to encourage your patient to obtain information from an expert. For example, the patient might discuss with their primary care physician the probability of contracting a deadly disease by touching a doorknob, or a person who is excessively concerned about chemicals in cleaning products might speak to a chemist. As in any situation in which an expert is consulted, you should discuss the option carefully with the patient to ensure that the strategy for obtaining information is likely to yield accurate knowledge rather than worst-case scenarios. It may be wise to check with the experts first to be sure that they are aware of the importance of not emphasizing what could happen but what typically occurs. In many cases, you will want to be present to ensure that the questions your patients ask are appropriate.

Identifying Cognitive Errors

Some patients discount objective or expert information because they focus exclusively on how anxious a situation makes them, rather than on the low probability of a feared event. In this case, it is useful to ask the patient whether this type of thinking represents a cognitive error, such as emotional reasoning or fortune-telling. If the patient agrees, you can inquire about an alternative viewpoint that is more accurate or more likely. Thought records also help prompt the patient to identify and challenge cognitive errors.

Metaphors, Stories, and Analogies

Metaphors and analogies are good teaching tools to illustrate similarities between concepts. For example, to point out your patients' overestimates of danger, you might want to ask, "Does rain always mean that a hurricane is coming?" or "Does a headache always indicate that a person is having a stroke?"

After introducing the metaphor, ask, "Does the fact that a disaster *could* occur make it likely? Are you presuming that because the catastrophic idea occurs to you, this somehow makes it more likely to happen?" You can then follow apparent discrepancies with questions about a more logical/accurate viewpoint: "If not, how do you decide that a particular outcome is actually likely and warrants special attention? What sort of logical thinking do you use about rain and hurricanes or headaches and strokes?"

One client gained some perspective by considering whether her thinking was more like imagining an asteroid hitting the earth or actually seeing the asteroid in a telescope headed toward the earth. This helped reduce her confusion about what thoughts she should pay attention to and which ones she could ignore.

Betting Money

For feared events in the future, ask your patients whether they would be willing to bet a large sum of money on the feared outcome and, if so, how much (M. Freeston, personal communication, 2002). Alternatively, you can ask whether you, the therapist, should bet a large amount of your savings on the predicted catastrophic outcome. In our experience, patients are rarely willing to bet any money on their feared predictions and indeed were much more inclined to bet money on more rational risk estimates. Thus, the financial considerations help promote rational thinking.

Role-Play

Role-plays can help your patient take another perspective on the situation and generate alternate hypotheses besides catastrophic ones. The hypotheses can then be tested through Socratic questioning or some of the methods suggested above. You can play the role of the patient, presenting his or her arguments about the likelihood of danger while the patient plays the role of therapist or friend who does not have OCD. For example, you might present your patients with their own arguments about why they should not be sitting in the chair in the doctor's office because after all, they could get AIDS. The goal is to have your patients evaluate the rationality of the arguments from a different perspective and examine realistically the logical basis for their estimation of the consequences of danger and resulting outcomes. As in the betting money example, patients are often surprisingly rational when it comes to giving advice to others.

ASSIGN HOMEWORK

The following homework assignments can be useful for patients completing this module:

- Record and evaluate beliefs pertaining to danger overestimates on thought records.

- Use the downward arrow technique to identify catastrophic beliefs.

- Calculate probability estimates.

- Use the survey method when appropriate.

- Conduct experiments using the Behavioral Experiment Form to test specific beliefs.

- Consult experts if appropriate.

- Identify cognitive errors.

SUMMARY AND FEEDBACK

As described in previous chapters, ask your patient for a summary of the major points covered during the sessions and for feedback about your own behavior.

Chapter 8

Desire for Certainty

OCD has been called the "doubting disease" because intolerance of uncertainty and difficulty making decisions are frequently observed in this disorder. Doubt and uncertainty are often linked to other OCD belief domains. For example, patients might feel uncertain whether they completed a task perfectly or whether they made a perfect decision. Patients might overestimate danger because they are uncertain if everything is absolutely safe. Similarly, patients might feel very uncertain if they cannot control their thoughts or if they don't fully understand the meaning of their intrusive thoughts.

Uncertainty is related to a wide range of clinical symptoms in patients, such as uncertainty about whether or not they are homosexual, uncertainty about whether they have made a mistake or said something inappropriate, uncertainty about whether they might have done something inappropriate (such as molested a baby), uncertainty about existential issues (such as who is to say what's morally right and wrong in this world?). In this chapter, we cover several techniques to address these symptoms.

HANDOUTS

Personal Session Forms

Thought Record and Guide—Seven Column

Downward Arrow Form

Behavioral Experiment Form

THERAPIST FORMS

Cognitive Therapy Session Report

AGENDA

Begin the session by inquiring about your patient's mood and OCD symptoms. Inquire about any reactions to the previous session. Agree on the agenda with your patient and review the homework from the previous session. We recommend the following techniques to evaluate the need for certainty with your patients:

- Downward arrow
- Identifying cognitive errors
- Socratic questioning
- Advantages and disadvantages
- Conducting a survey
- Continuum technique
- Behavioral experiments
- Fill in the blanks

REVIEW HOMEWORK

As always, your session should include an early discussion of the previously assigned homework (see chapter 5 for details on how to do this). Suggestions for various homework assignments are described at the end of this chapter.

COGNITIVE THERAPY TECHNIQUES

Below we provide detailed descriptions for techniques from which you can choose for patients who present with uncertainty. Choose the strategies that will have the highest likelihood for changing a maladaptive belief. If you are unsure, try different strategies and keep using those that seem to work best for your particular patient. Remember not to directly evaluate the intrusions/obsessions or images ("I am not sure, but think I might have seen a baby that was left on a supermarket shelf"), but rather enter into a discussion about different levels of certainty with the patient ("How certain do you have to be that nothing bad has happened?"). That is, do not discuss whether she has or has not seen a baby, but focus on the underlying issue—"Whenever I am not sure, something bad is likely to happen" or "I am bad if I don't keep on the lookout for babies in danger."

Downward Arrow

Use the downward arrow technique to identify beliefs that underlie the desire for certainty. As indicated on the Downward Arrow Form, keep asking similar questions over and over again to move from superficial to deeper level beliefs. Below is the result of downward arrow questioning of a patient who fears she has not understood everything her teacher was talking about in class (adapted from Freeston et al., 1996). Her typical compulsion was to call up her teacher and classmates frequently after lectures to inquire about material she didn't comprehend fully. Her downward arrow might look as follows:

What if I didn't understand everything the teacher was talking about today?

⇩

I won't know anything that is being asked on the test.

⇩

I'll fail the next test.

⇩

I won't pass my program.

⇩

Everybody will think I'm stupid.

⇩

I am a failure.

The example above illustrates how intolerance of uncertainty can be related to perfectionism ("If I don't understand *one* thing, I won't know *anything*") and over-estimation of danger ("I'll fail the next test"). It also provides opportunities for inter-ventions at different levels. Early on in treatment, we'd recommend work on the more superficial thoughts, such as "I won't know what's being asked on the test" and "I will fail the next test." Later on in treatment, you can work on the deeper level beliefs, such as "I am a failure."

Identifying Cognitive Errors

Let's assume that the student from the example above is still in the early stages of treatment. In this case, you can start by helping her evaluate her cognitive errors.

T: Do you think your wanting to be certain about everything your teacher talked about might reflect any cognitive errors?

P: Yes, I guess so. I think it might be black-and-white thinking.

T: How so?

P: Well, it's like either I understand everything perfectly, or I understand nothing. There's nothing in-between.

T: That's true. Can you think of another way of looking at how you learn in class? What would be an alternative way of thinking?

P: I could say, well maybe there are a few things I missed and a few things I'm still not sure about, but overall, I learned a lot and I know enough. I'll get by.

Another form of cognitive error evident in the above downward arrow sequence is fortune-telling or catastrophizing, because the patient predicts a number of negative outcomes without having any evidence to support them. Emotional reasoning ("I feel anxious and uncertain, therefore I am not knowledgeable") might also be contained in the sequence above. Labeling is another example of a cognitive error evident in the patient's core belief ("I am a failure"). As always, when erroneous thinking has been identified, the thoughts should be modified with Socratic questioning or other strategies suggested below.

Socratic Questioning

Socratic questioning will be helpful in exploring your patients' views about needing to be certain about everything, as well as alternative perspectives. For example, you might want to question the patient above about what her classmates would say about how much a person needs to know and understand in order to do well in school. Or you might ask her about her own experience:

T: Let's take a look at your belief that you won't know anything on the test and will fail. Have you ever failed a test?

P: No, actually, I never have.

Here you can either point out the discrepancy between the expectation and the patient's actual history or focus instead on the logical thinking about what is required to fail a test. The following is an example of the latter strategy. You can always return to the historical information later:

T: So actually, you don't have any real experience with failing a test, but maybe you have gained an understanding from observing other people's experience. What does it take to fail a test? How do people fail?

P: Well, they don't study, or they aren't very smart, so they don't understand the concepts, or they party a lot and are in bad shape when they take the test.

T: That sounds right to me. That's my observation as well. Let's see how these apply to you. Are you worried about failing because you haven't studied?

P: No, I always study, but maybe not enough. How can I know if it's enough?

T: What about the other two criteria you mentioned? Are you not smart enough to understand the concepts, or do you party too much the night before exams?

P: No, neither of those. I know I understand the stuff, at least most of it, because other classmates have often asked me for help, and I can explain well enough so they get it. I don't really go to parties or drink or even stay up very late.

T: Okay. So you don't meet any of the three criteria for failure. I don't really understand. Is there some other way to fail tests? Maybe your mind could just go blank? I'm trying to figure this out.

P: No, I'm not really worried about that. I think I'm just catastrophizing. It's not really making sense, is it?

Advantages and Disadvantages

You can also encourage your patient to identify the pros and cons of striving for certainty, in this case of "being certain I understand everything covered in class." We usually ask our patients to list the pros and cons. Here's an example:

Trying to Be Certain I Understand Everything Covered in Class	
Advantages	Disadvantages
1. I feel less anxious.	1. My classmates think I'm trying to be the teacher's pet.
2. I might do better on the test.	2. My worry makes me even more anxious before tests.
	3. I'm constantly preoccupied with needing to know everything.
	4. My classmates are frustrated because I ask too many questions in class and after school.
	5. I'm getting really nerdy. My head is always stuck in the book. I make lots of lists of stuff I need to remember, so I'm not having much fun.

Once the advantages and disadvantages are established, begin by evaluating the validity of the advantages:

T: How many times have you been certain that you really knew everything that was covered in class?

P: I never am!

T: Do you know for sure that you do better on tests because you always try to be certain about everything that's taught in class?

P: No, I am usually pretty preoccupied in tests with the question if I really know everything. I'm sure this doesn't help me.

Next, you can weigh the disadvantages of wanting to be certain about everything taught against the benefits of doing this:

T: Now let's compare the advantages you list here with the disadvantages. How do they compare?

P: Hmmm. Well the disadvantages are substantial and are the reason why I came to treatment in the first place.

T: And the advantages? How important are they? How often do they really happen?

P: Well, I guess they aren't important because they don't ever happen. But they seem so important at the time.

Your next step would be to identify an alternative belief that moderates the need for certainty.

This advantages and disadvantages strategy can be useful for other problems related to the desire for certainty, such as if your patient needs an excessive amount of information before making a decision. OCD patients often require excessive certainty about topics that are inherently ambiguous, such as sexual orientation ("How do I know for sure that I'm not gay?") and/or existential issues ("Who can say what's right and wrong?"). Together, you can examine the advantages and disadvantages of rigidly trying to gain certainty versus "just letting the question sit there."

Conducting a Survey

The survey method is a helpful strategy for evaluating the desire for certainty. Using the previous example, you and your patient could agree on how many people she would need to ask to determine whether certainty about every aspect of a lecture in school should be an important goal. For example, your patient could ask her classmates after a lecture what percentage of the material covered in the lecture they actually remember and how important it is to them to feel certain about every little detail. Patients are often surprised to hear that others retain only a very small percentage of what they learn in class. In this context, you might want to educate your patient about how low retention rates for lectures (5 percent) or reading (10 percent) tend to be. Surveys of this nature also tend to teach your patients that those students who try to get the big picture have higher retention rates than those who worry too much about details.

Alternatively, you could design this survey as a behavioral experiment. Prior to conducting the experiment, you would ask your patient to predict the outcome of the survey. After she completes the survey, you would encourage your patient to compare her predictions with her actual results. If discrepancies were found, you would then discuss whether your patient's beliefs should change. For example, a new and more adaptive belief to work toward could be: "It's not necessary for me to be certain about everything. Other people forget a lot, too, and they live just fine."

Continuum Technique

Patients who believe they need to be certain about everything often have many manifestations of this belief, such as reading very slowly, rereading things, trying to recall all aspects of a conversation, lecture, or movie, or seeking reassurance from others to verify their recall. These rituals are usually very time-consuming and can interfere with their educational and occupational requirements. We have modified the strategies below from Söchting et al. (1996) to address an excessive need for certainty.

Let's assume your patient holds the belief "I have to be certain about everything" and therefore tries to remember license plates, bumper stickers, messages on junk mail, and so on. To help your patient understand that different types of material require different levels of attention, certainty, and understanding, you can apply the continuum technique. Ask your patient to draw a scale from 0 (not important to be certain) to 100 (very important to be certain). Inquire what would be important facts to be very certain about. Examples include the patient's own name, address, spouse's name, or the salary figure on a job application. Then identify some facts that are less important and therefore would not require such a high degree of certainty—for example, a colleague's birthday, or the name of a favorite florist, a title of a novel, or the name of an actor in a movie. If needed, you can use survey techniques to help your patient avoid lumping everything toward the "very important to be certain" end of the continuum. Finally, inquire how the patient would rate the most recent forgotten item that provoked OCD-related discomfort.

The continuum technique might also be useful for patients who want to feel absolutely certain of their sexual orientation. They typically have a strong desire to fit neatly into the "straight" category. However, even heterosexual people often experience homosexual fantasies, often without any desire to make the fantasies reality. Some patients might have experimented with same-sex partners in the past or have looked at same-sex pornography. The degree of stress and self-doubt about sexual orientation may depend on upbringing and cultural context.

Using the continuum technique, you can discuss that sexuality is not confined to just three categories of homosexual, bisexual, and heterosexual. While there might be a few people who are exclusively heterosexual in their preference, most people fall somewhere other than entirely straight. Encourage your patient to draw a continuum ranging from 100 percent heterosexual to 100 percent homosexual, and rate his or her various experiences (such as frequent physical contact with partners, fantasies, or feelings of love). The sex education books mentioned in chapter 5 may also be helpful in this context, as may a discussion about thought suppression (see chapter 6). The main discussion point should be that rigid categorizing of people to achieve certainty is problematic. Instead, acceptance and exploration of ambiguity can actually be enjoyable.

As always, interventions should not stop here. Ultimately, you and your patient need to explore the most dreaded consequence of not being certain about facts, sexual orientation, or other elements about which your patient worries.

Behavioral Experiments

As mentioned above, behavioral experiments can help your patient evaluate the importance of certainty about facts and whether failing to remember them will indeed lead to the most dreaded consequences. A detailed discussion of how to conduct a behavioral experiment can be found in chapter 7. Other examples that specifically address the need for certainty are given below.

To test the prediction that "If I don't remember all the details of the assigned reading, my classmates will think I'm stupid," start by asking your patient how she'd know that others would think she was stupid (for example, they won't talk to her, will mock her, and so on). Help your patient to complete the Behavioral Experiment Form. She can then test the hypothesis by publicly admitting that she forgot a fact. For example, she could tell her friends something like "I just can't remember when the Berlin Wall was erected," and then note her friends' reactions. It's important to determine whether your patient's feared prediction comes true, that is, whether the classmates stopped talking to her or started mocking her. If the prediction does not come true, the next step is to discuss how important it really is to be certain about these kinds of facts.

Behavioral experiments may also be useful for patients with checking rituals. For example, a person might use checking rituals to be certain he hasn't accidentally hit someone while driving. In such cases, the need for certainty is usually connected to overestimation of danger. As an experiment, you could ask your patient to drive on a bumpy road without looking in the rearview mirror. When the thought about having hit someone occurs, assess his beliefs and feared consequences using the downward arrow method:

I might have hit somebody.

⇩

The person is dead.

⇩

I am a hit-and-run driver.

⇩

The police will find my car and arrest me.

⇩

I will be alone and in jail for the rest of my life.

Ask patients to rate their degree of uncertainty immediately after and again one day after behavioral experiments. Usually, over time, anxiety and uncertainty both decline.

A similar experiment may be useful for patients who have checking rituals intended to prevent fires, floods, and so on. For example, the patient who is uncertain whether he or she turned off the coffee maker and therefore fears a fire might decide not to check the coffee maker before going to work.

For these behavioral experiments, follow the format described in chapter 7, adding a rating for uncertainty (0 percent equals certain to 100 percent equals uncertain) under the discomfort rating. Encourage your patient to rate uncertainty on both an emotional/gut level and an intellectual level. And ask your patient to rate the degree of uncertainty both right after leaving the house and right before coming home. Debriefing after the experiment is completed should include the reinterpretation of intrusions and assumptions with more rational explanations.

Fill in the Blanks

Over the years, we have treated several people who were bombarded with obsessions about harm occurring to people. Patients with this type of concern fear they might have observed an awful situation (child who fell into a trash can or is trapped in a freezer) but are not certain this occurred. Patients respond to their intrusive images and ideas by trying to recall exactly what they've seen, asking for reassurance, and going back and checking. Although the circumstances of the fear change over time, the obsessions generally follow the same pattern. Freeston et al. (1996) recommended that patients with this type of problem should be encouraged to think of variations of this type of intrusion as one obsession for which they can fill in the blanks. For example, "I think I might have seen [something pink in a manhole]. This could perhaps be a [little child who might have fallen in]." Or "I think I might have seen [something white behind a tree]. This could perhaps be an [old lady who has fallen down]."

Conceptualizing these intrusions as only one obsession that varies slightly depending on the circumstances helps patients to feel less bewildered and more in control. Additional interventions can focus on the patient's overestimation of danger and responsibility (see chapters 7 and 9).

ASSIGN HOMEWORK

Decide with your patient which homework exercises might be most beneficial. We recommend the following homework assignments:

- Record beliefs related to an excessive desire for certainty on thought records.

- Use the Downward Arrow Form to identify catastrophic and core beliefs related to situations when an excessive desire for certainty seems to be prominent.

- Evaluate cognitive errors related to the need for certainty.

- Make a list of the advantages and disadvantages of wanting to be certain about details.

- Conduct a survey to determine how many facts others remember or how much certainty they require.

- Use the continuum technique to determine how much certainty is required for different situations.

- Conduct behavioral experiments to test catastrophic beliefs related to uncertainty.

- Use the fill-in-the-blank technique to record intrusive thoughts to determine whether they are all of a similar nature.

SUMMARY AND FEEDBACK

Toward the end of each session, ask for a summary of the session highlights and for feedback about any problems or positive aspects of the session.

Chapter 9

Responsibility

An inflated sense of responsibility is very common among patients with OCD and likely to surface as a problematic belief for most patients, accompanied by strong feelings of guilt. You should use this module if your patient reports strong guilt reactions in the emotional component of their cognitive model of OCD (chapter 4) or, in their thought records, and shows a high score on the responsibility subscale of the OBQ-Ext. Most of the time, responsibility concerns are also tied to fears of causing harm and failing to protect others. Thus, the techniques in chapter 7 on overestimating harm will also be relevant for most patients who overestimate their responsibility. Many of the strategies included in this chapter will already be familiar to you from working on other types of beliefs; they are illustrated here specifically in relation to responsibility beliefs, along with new methods like the pie chart technique which are used mainly for excessive responsibility.

HANDOUTS

Personal Session Forms

Thought Record and Guide—Seven Column

Downward Arrow Form

List of Cognitive Errors

THERAPIST FORMS

Cognitive Therapy Session Report

Cognitive Model (developed in chapter 4)

AGENDA

After the usual brief mood and symptom check, identify items for the agenda. While you and your patient are working to evaluate over-responsibility and consequences of responsibility, the following techniques will be most useful:

- Socratic questioning

- Downward arrow

- Pie chart

- Courtroom technique

- Double-standard technique

- Continuum technique

- Advantages and disadvantages

REVIEW HOMEWORK

As always, your session should include an early discussion of the previously assigned homework (see chapter 5 for details on how to do this). Suggestions for various homework assignments are described at the end of this chapter.

COGNITIVE THERAPY TECHNIQUES

For some patients, feared consequences associated with obsessions are perceived as unacceptably high. Patients who have learned to reduce their overestimate of the likelihood of danger (see chapter 7) may still perceive the risk to be high if they consider the consequences unacceptable. Van Oppen and Arntz (1994) proposed a formula for computing risk:

$$Risk = Probability \times Consequence$$

So, even if your patients consider the probability of harm low, they will still find the risk unacceptably high if the consequences seem too awful. Therefore, you need to focus on what makes the consequences so unacceptable. Often overestimation of personal responsibility is the culprit.

Common reasons for patients' excessive concern about responsibility pertain to (1) having the thought at all (such as about stabbing someone or having blasphemous thoughts) and (2) taking or not taking an action (misplacing a paper at work, not picking up a stone in the road, failing to verify that no one was run over, and so on). In these cases, two aspects of responsibility should be addressed: the amount of responsibility and the expected consequences. The most common interpretations and beliefs associated with excessive responsibility are convictions about personal guilt, worthlessness, and likely disapproval and rejection by others or God. These typically take the following form:

- "It's my fault (I'm to blame)."

- "I should go to hell."

- "God will punish me."

- "Others will reject me."

Cognitive strategies for reducing these intermediate beliefs about responsibility are described below. Deeper level beliefs ("I am worthless"; "I am bad") that commonly underlie these interpretations can be addressed with strategies recommended in chapter 13.

Socratic Questioning

You will want to use Socratic questioning often to elucidate the specific elements of your patient's interpretations. Below is a brief example of Socratic questioning pertinent to responsibility for contamination from germs after a behavioral experiment.

T: Before you went into the bathroom, were you thinking anything about what you were going to touch?

P: Well, I guess I had the idea that this time I was really going to get it. I mean, somebody would have been in there who really had a problem and I was going to get sick.

T: Uh huh, so you had the thought that you would get sick this time. Anything else?

P: Yeah, I thought it'd be my fault. You know, because I've decided to do this treatment. I'd have brought it on myself when I could have avoided it.

T: So, your idea was that you'd be responsible if something happened to you and that the risk seemed maybe higher than before. [Two types of erroneous beliefs are evident here: risk and responsibility.]

P: Yes, sometimes I get afraid that there could be a problem and I wouldn't know about it and couldn't avoid it. Sort of a whim of fate that I'd be the one in the wrong place at the wrong time. It'd be just my luck.

T: [Trying to clarify patient's thinking] Are you afraid that it will just be bad luck that you get sick from what you touch here, or that there is really a high risk and you are being foolish to take the risk?

P: I think I alternate. It's a bit easier if I think about luck, but I have a lot of doubts that I'm not doing the right thing, that I'll make a bad decision. I think this applies to other situations, too.

T: Let's stick to this one for the moment. You seem to be saying that if you think that a bad outcome, like sickness, could be just because of luck, that it is easier for you than thinking that you were responsible for a bad choice.

P: Yes, that's right.

T: Do you think you are making a bad choice right now by touching the bathroom doorknob?

P: No, but that's partly because you're here. I'd have a harder time deciding to do this if I were alone, because it'd all be on me. I'd be responsible if it turned out to be a dumb thing to do.

T: So let's focus on responsibility. You are trying to avoid being responsible for causing yourself to get sick. Is that it?

P: Yes.

As in this example, Socratic dialogue is designed to help you elucidate your patient's thinking, so the main beliefs become clear, in this case a prediction that "I will make a bad decision" (perhaps accompanied by a generalized version of this belief that "I am a bad decision maker"), followed by the belief that "it would be my fault [if I got sick]." You may need to examine beliefs in two or three different contexts that provoke discomfort to be certain that you and your patients have identified their main beliefs and corollaries.

Downward Arrow

You can pursue the discussion of responsibility further by determining your patient's worst-case scenario to see what the most basic fears are. The downward arrow technique (see Downward Arrow Form) is especially useful for identifying catastrophic ideas and underlying fears or core beliefs. For one woman whose little daughter wanted a friend to come over to play, the therapist asked the usual variation of downward arrow questions in response to her evident discomfort ("What are you concerned about? ... What would that mean? ... What's so bad about that? ... What's the worst part about that?"). The following sequence of concerns emerged:

I'm afraid to let my daughter's friend come over to play.

⇩

She might touch the woodwork in our old house.

⇩

She'd eat the paint and get lead poisoning.

⇩

Her parents would blame me for letting her come near the paint.

⇩

I'd be an irresponsible parent.

⇩

Other people would never let their kids play with my daughter.

⇩

My daughter will be rejected and I'll be responsible for ruining her life.

⇩

I won't be able to live with myself.

The example includes overestimation of harm as well as responsibility beliefs. To focus on the latter, you would highlight these beliefs.

T: What I am hearing you say is that you are especially concerned about responsibility for ruining your daughter's life. You've also mentioned this issue of responsibility on your last thought record when you wrote the belief that if you take food to the potluck, it might be contaminated and people would get sick and blame you. It sounds to me like you tend to assume responsibility for things more than others might. Would you agree with that?

When your patient confirms this, you can then proceed to examine the evidence for the validity of this belief. Use the following strategies.

Pie Chart

A good way to examine responsibility is by using the pie chart technique which we have adapted from Söchting et al. (1996). This technique has several parts:

- Estimate the patient's responsibility for a feared outcome.
- Make a list of all possible factors that could account for the outcome.

- Assign percent responsibility to all factors that are not personal and include these in a pie chart.

- Assign the percent of patient's responsibility last.

- Compare the initial percent responsibility to the final one.

For example, a mother feared that the food she fed her child and her child's visiting friends would cause a bacterial infection, which would be her fault. You would begin by asking the patient, "If the children got such an infection, how much of the responsibility would be yours? What percentage?" Then, you would help her generate a list of all other factors that could possibly play a role. For example, contributing factors to food poisoning might be the producer of the food (40 percent responsible), the packaging and the transport of the food (each 10 percent), the shopkeeper who sold the food (10 percent), the functioning of the refrigerator it was stored in (10 percent), bacteria on the child's hands at the time of eating (10 percent), and so forth. Next, you would draw a circle and divide and label all of the pieces of the pie according to the percent contribution that your patient believes should be assigned. You would save your patient's own contribution for last. Usually, only a small portion of the circle is left for the patient's own personal responsibility or control over the event. Finally, comment on how this personal responsibility compares to your patient's original estimate, allowing your patient time to process the information.

Note that the pie chart technique may not be useful for patients whose concerns about harm to others are very diffuse. For example, one of our patients engaged in various magical rituals to prevent family members from coming to harm. Because her

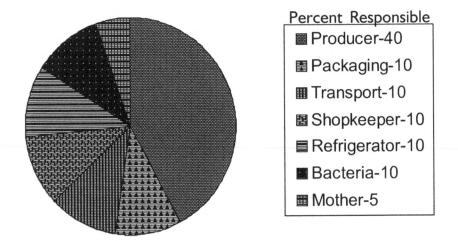

Percent Responsible
- Producer-40
- Packaging-10
- Transport-10
- Shopkeeper-10
- Refrigerator-10
- Bacteria-10
- Mother-5

Figure 3: Example of Pie Chart Technique

obsessions never focused on any specific sources of danger, it was impossible to partial out who might be responsible and this technique could not be applied.

Courtroom Technique

An additional way to evaluate interpretations of responsibility is the courtroom technique, in which your patient acts as an attorney to argue the case. This is similar to the method of role-playing mentioned earlier for use with overestimates of danger. Note that anxious patients often use emotional reasoning as evidence of danger: "If I feel anxious, there must be danger" (Arntz, Rauner, & van den Hout, 1995). It is usually easiest to begin by asking your patient to act as the prosecuting attorney, while you play the judge; later on you can reverse roles and ask your patient to be the judge or a jury member while you present the patient's arguments.

In the courtroom technique, ask your patient to argue for his or her guilt using only empirical evidence that would be allowed in a court of law. This means that emotional reasoning (the subjective feeling of guilt) would be disallowed as evidence ("I feel guilty, therefore I am responsible for the crime") unless your patient can generate factual proof. Remind your patient that it is essential to present only the facts.

As the judge, you can disallow inadmissible evidence such as hearsay or arguments based on emotional logic.

T: Okay, now present the evidence for the prosecution in our little mini court of law. Why don't you start by arguing why you were responsible for the woman who got sick after the potluck. Pretend that I am the judge, or if you prefer, I can be in the jury. Try to convince me.

P: Well, she got sick about an hour after the potluck and that must have been food poisoning.

T: Keep going, why are you responsible? Remember this is a trial, and you are the lawyer. Your job is to argue the evidence. I'm listening.

P: Okay, your honor [putting on a serious face]. My client here baked a brand new dish she'd never made before, and it might have had something in it.

T: Excuse me. In my court, "might have" is insufficient. You must state the facts.

P: Yes, well, there was a woman who got ill after the potluck, an hour later, and that means food poisoning.

T: Are you certain she had food poisoning? Do you have a doctor's statement that it was food poisoning?

P: Well, no, but she threw up.

T: I see, no doctor's statement, but she threw up. Interesting. Go on.

P: Well, then I ... I mean my client, looked at the leftover casserole she'd made and it had little dark spots in it. They could have been mold or something.

T: Or something. . . . Can you be more specific? When was this and what proof do you have of mold?

P: It was the next day, actually two days later, when I . . . my client heard about the sick woman.

T: Let me understand this now. There was a potluck dinner with a variety of dishes, including your client's casserole, yes? One woman and only one woman threw up about an hour later. Two days later, your client's leftover dish had dark spots in it. Do you have independent verification that the spots were mold? Can you be sure they were not dark spices?

P: Well maybe, but they looked like it to my client.

T: So, you have no independent evidence, things "seem" but cannot be verified. Only one woman was ill rather than most of those who ate the food. She threw up, but there is no information about the source of her illness. Do you have any other more concrete evidence?

At this point, you and your patient can discuss the alternative explanations that the judge hinted at. A good next step is for you to play the attorney arguing in favor of your patient's view, while your patient acts as a member of the jury to judge whether the evidence is "beyond a reasonable doubt." This forces your patient to observe his or her own arguments from an outsider's vantage point. You will probably need to employ this technique more than once for different but similar obsessive concerns before your patient can begin to use the method alone to evaluate irrational interpretations.

Double-Standard Technique

This technique is useful for challenging the perceived social consequences (disapproval, rejection) and religious consequences (God's disapproval, going to hell) of having been responsible. Many patients hold one standard of responsibility for themselves but another more relaxed one for other people.

In using the double-standard technique, be as concrete as possible in selecting other people for comparison to ensure that your patient has real people in mind. You can ask your patient questions like the following:

- "Would you think a friend of yours was responsible in the same situation? For example, what if it were Mary in this situation?"

- "Would you condemn her in the same way?"

- "Do you think other people you know would consider Mary responsible? Would they condemn her?"

- "Suppose they did blame and condemn Mary, would you agree with them?"

If patients agree that they hold different standards for themselves than for others, you can explore this further with Socratic questioning to determine if there are any maladaptive core beliefs that need to be addressed (see chapter 13).

Continuum Technique

Closely related to the double-standard technique is the continuum technique, which is designed to reduce black-and-white thinking. This can help patients learn to distinguish between being a good citizen (someone who helps when somebody is indeed hurt) from being everybody's guardian angel (someone who tries to prevent all types of improbable harm for everyone) (Freeston et al., 1996). To accomplish this, draw a horizontal line on paper and anchor the endpoints from 0 percent (completely irresponsible) to 100 percent (completely responsible).

0%	50%	100%
completely irresponsible	moderately	completely responsible

Ask your patient to provide examples of behaviors that would qualify for each of the extremes and for the middle point of the scale. Examples might be 0 equals never keeping promises or never admitting egregious mistakes and 100 equals always keeping appointments and promises. It should become clear fairly quickly that both extremes of the scale can be problematic because they represent absolute thinking (refer to the List of Cognitive Errors handout). Many situations require judgment to deal with competing responsibilities and obligations. Use this scale to determine what degree of responsibility your patient considers reasonable in some situations and to identify where your patient's actual responses would lie. Examine whether your patient's earlier evaluation of these behaviors with regard to responsibility matches his or her rating of them on this new scale.

Advantages and Disadvantages

In using this strategy, you and your patient would discuss the advantages and disadvantages (or costs and benefits, pros and cons) of continuing to accept responsibility in the absence of good evidence or of maintaining a double standard. As always, all advantages and disadvantages should be listed and evaluated to determine their relative weight or importance. Ask your patient what course of action makes sense after evaluating the pros and cons. An example of this list is given below:

Over-Responsibility	
Advantages	Disadvantages
1. It's the moral thing to do. 2. It prevents other people from getting hurt and being angry with me.	1. It makes me very upset, sometimes without good reason. 2. It maintains my OCD. 3. I avoid social situations where I'm afraid I might cause a problem. 4. More difficulty deciding what to cook for others.

In this example, you should review the disadvantages with your patient in enough detail to emphasize the problems caused by accepting responsibility too readily without good evidence. In addition, it is important to help your patient examine closely the advantages because these are important to maintaining beliefs. You can use Socratic questioning for this purpose. For example, ask whether your patient thinks it is truly the moral thing to accept responsibility when there is little evidence that a person is really responsible for a problem. What evidence does your patient have that accepting responsibility prevents others from getting hurt? Similarly, pose a hypothetical situation in which your client made a mistake but didn't realize this until someone revealed it; your patient then apologized as soon as it was clear that he or she was wrong. Would your patient get angry with others who did this? Would others get angry because your patient didn't accept responsibility in advance? Now, draw the general principle from this discussion in the form of a statement: "It is okay to wait until you actually make a mistake before accepting responsibility for it."

ASSIGN HOMEWORK

The following homework assignments can be useful for patients completing this module:

- Record perceived responsibility beliefs on thought records and identify alternative beliefs.

- Use the Downward Arrow Form to identify catastrophic and core beliefs related to situations when guilt and responsibility seem to be prominent.

- Use the pie chart technique for situations in which clients seem to be presuming responsibility that should be shared with many others.

- Write down the evidence for their own responsibility and imagine a judge reviewing whether this evidence was admissible in court.

- Think carefully about whether they would hold the same viewpoint if it were a friend of theirs in the same situation (double standard).

- Make a list of the advantages and disadvantages of accepting more responsibility than others would.

SUMMARY AND FEEDBACK

Ask your patient for a summary of the major points covered during the sessions and for feedback about your own behavior.

Chapter 10

Perfectionism

Many patients with OCD exhibit perfectionistic tendencies, defined as the belief that there is a perfect solution to every problem, that it is possible and desirable to do something perfectly (without mistakes), and that even minor errors will have serious consequences. Perfectionistic traits are also typical of people with a number of other types of mental health problems (such as eating disorders). Thus, this type of thinking is not exclusive to OCD, but here we present specific strategies for modifying it in relation to obsessions and compulsions.

As Freeston et al. (1996) point out, therapists need to be flexible when working with patients with perfectionistic attitudes. They describe a patient who believed she was not as compliant as she could have been and who therefore felt that she did not deserve to get better. This example points to an inherent contradiction in insisting on perfect homework assignments while at the same time claiming that perfectionism is a counterproductive strategy. That is, you should be clear that your patient's goal should be to learn to cope better with his or her intrusive thoughts, avoidance, and compulsive rituals, rather than to try to master these assignments perfectly. At times you may wish to use the therapy itself as a laboratory for behavioral experiments in which your patient makes deliberate small errors in following instructions to see whether this leads to a failure to benefit from treatment.

HANDOUTS

Personal Session Forms

Thought Record and Guide—Seven Column

Downward Arrow Form

List of Cognitive Errors

Behavioral Experiment Form

THERAPIST FORMS

Cognitive Therapy Session Report

AGENDA

After a brief mood and symptom check, set the agenda. You will likely include one or more of the following methods to evaluate perfectionistic attitudes:

- Cognitive errors and downward arrow
- Socratic questioning
- Taking another's perspective
- Behavioral experiments
- Advantages and disadvantages
- Identifying cognitive errors
- Continuum technique
- Metaphors and stories
- Psychoeducation

REVIEW HOMEWORK

Plan to assign homework at the end of each session in this module and to review the homework early in each session.

COGNITIVE THERAPY TECHNIQUES

A wide range of cognitive strategies are useful for working on perfectionistic beliefs. Because perfectionism also occurs in the context of the desire for certainty (chapter 8), the need for control (chapter 6), and excessive responsibility (chapter 9), you should refer to these modules for further treatment strategies as needed.

Cognitive Errors and Downward Arrow

All-or-nothing thinking is a common cognitive error present in patients with perfectionistic thinking. Such thinking often takes the form of "If it is not absolutely perfect, it is bad." This leads your patient to be excessively concerned about even minor errors tolerable to most people. In some cases, patients' perfectionism is compartmentalized in particular areas of their lives, but in many cases it is pervasive, affecting nearly everything they do. Perfectionism may also serve as a coping strategy for a patient's fear of failure; failure would therefore figure prominently in the feared outcomes during the downward arrow procedure. A somewhat different feared outcome was evident for a woman who worried about her boss's reaction to mistakes:

What if I make a mistake at work?

⇩

I can't do my job right.

⇩

I am inadequate.

Another example from a woman with a somewhat rigid and authoritarian husband was

What if I make a mistake at home?

⇩

My husband will notice.

⇩

He'll be upset with me.

⇩

He'll stop loving me.

⇩

If he doesn't love me, no one will.

⇩

I'm unlovable.

These examples contain intermediate beliefs, such as "If I make a mistake at work, it means I can't do my job right" and "If I make a mistake at home, my husband will stop loving me." These beliefs can be examined using some of the strategies given below. In both examples, the final beliefs of being inadequate and unlovable are core beliefs. You and your patient can work on changing these using techniques from chapter 13.

Socratic Questioning

In most cases when you uncover perfectionistic beliefs about overly high standards or severe concerns about making minor mistakes, Socratic questioning will enable you to explore your patient's views and evaluate the usefulness and validity of various alternative viewpoints. Below is an example.

T: So, at your accounting job you've been getting behind because you have to keep checking and rechecking to make sure there is no error in your calculations. Do other people check as much as you do?

P: No, not at all. I've seen them check, but only once and then they don't seem to have any problem just passing in the forms. I get incredibly anxious and have to go back till I'm sure it is perfect.

T: Your colleagues don't seem to be worried, so they do normal checking, just once. Why do you think it worries you so?

P: I've always had to do stuff perfectly. In school, my teachers used to complain because I was late with stuff, and the papers were erased a lot because I was trying to fix it, just so. You know, it's ironic, my schoolwork often looked pretty bad, a lot worse than if I had just done it once and left it alone.

T: So you are already clear that the perfectionism didn't work well for you when you were younger, and it doesn't work for you now either.

P: Yeah, that's certainly true, but it makes me incredibly anxious not to make sure. It drives me nuts.

T: Where do you think this really high standard came from? Why does your work have to be perfect?

P: I'm not really sure, but my dad always used to say that if you couldn't do it right, it was better not to do it at all. He was a perfectionist too, and I was always a little afraid of him. He didn't give much encouragement. I remember once he said I did a good job when I won a prize at graduation, but that's the only time I remember.

T: So your dad was very hard to please and it sounds like you tried hard to get his approval. Do you think his standards were reasonable when you look back on it now?

P: I haven't really thought about it much. Maybe they were a bit rigid.

T: Are they the same standards your current boss has for you and your coworkers?

P: No, my boss expects good work, but he's pretty reasonable. Of course, he's frustrated with me, but that's because I'm always late, not because he complains about my work. But you know, I'm always very careful to get the figures right, and I'm not so sure how he'd react if I did make a mistake.

T: Sounds like you think maybe your high standards and checking are keeping you from getting into trouble. How has he reacted when other coworkers made a mistake? Was he very angry?

P: Hmm, I'm not sure I've ever seen him angry. I don't really know of a situation where somebody made a mistake.

T: Do you think no one has ever made a mistake at your office?

P: Oh, that can't be true. Somebody had to. It happens.

T: So someone has certainly made a mistake while you were employed there; it's been six years, right? But you don't recall your boss being really angry. What does that tell you?

P: I suppose that he doesn't get upset easily when somebody makes a mistake.

T: How likely do you think it is that he'd get upset with you if you made a mistake?

P: Not really likely, I guess. But it seems like such a big deal to me.

From this point, further Socratic questioning could address the patient's personal beliefs and standards compared to the actual reality of the job situation, also noting the difference in values of the boss and the patient's father. Other options after this dialogue would be to use another technique, such as taking another perspective or designing a behavioral experiment, to test the idea that the boss would tolerate a small mistake.

Taking Another's Perspective

You can help your patients challenge perfectionism by encouraging them to take a different perspective, preferably that of someone they know and like, such as (1) a child, (2) an adult family member, (3) a close friend, or (4) another adult they respect and like.

If your patient has a child, ask how he or she would instruct the son or daughter (choose a same-sex child if you have the option). If your patient does not have a child, select a well-liked niece or nephew, a friend's child, or the child your patient hopes to have someday. Consider asking the following: "What rule or standards do you want your own child to have for him- or herself in this situation?"

If there is a discrepancy in standards set for self and child, ask for the rationale: "Why? Explain to me why you wouldn't want him or her to try to follow the rule you just told me about."

Then emphasize the new rule: "How does this apply to you? What does this mean for your own behavior in this situation?" Note that this last question would likely lead to a homework assignment for your patient to try out new behavior.

You can also ask about the point of view of other well-liked adults and about your patient's own views of how other adults should behave in this situation. This latter strategy is akin to the double-standard technique used in chapters 5 and 9.

If your patients use faulty thinking to hold themselves to a higher standard, you will probably want to use Socratic questioning to help them identify the flawed logic and replace it with more rational thinking.

Behavioral Experiments

You can use behavioral experiments to challenge perfectionistic attitudes by asking your patient deliberately to make small mistakes or moderate rigid habits. Use the Behavioral Experiment Form to compare the predicted negative consequence to the actual outcome.

T: You've been getting very behind in your work because you have to keep checking and rewriting to make sure that your memos and notes are perfect. You have also figured out that your standards for this are excessive and that it doesn't actually make sense for you to do this. I think it might be helpful to you to conduct an experiment to test your beliefs. Would you be willing to try this?

P: I guess I'm going to have to do something different, but it sure seems scary.

T: It makes sense to start small and work your way up, so you can manage your feelings. How about we start with writing a note to your coworker in which you deliberately misspell something or use small letters instead of capitals . . . something like that?

P: I could do that. I'm forever fixing the dumb mistake of forgetting the "s" on the end of a plural word. I could try leaving that alone.

T: Great idea. Let's start there, so when you forget the "s," you'll just leave it and see what happens. This means you would not reread it very carefully, just once only, but leave this mistake. Right?

P: That'll be hard, but okay.

Advantages and Disadvantages

Another strategy is to ask your patients to make a list of all the advantages and all the disadvantages of holding themselves to perfectionistic standards. In doing so, explore alternatives to rigid standards, so your patient has a point of comparison to help determine the disadvantages. For example, you might ask the following questions of a patient who is concerned about perfectly aligning the items on his desk:

- "What are the benefits of doing this?"

- "What are the costs?"

- "What alternatives are there to doing it this way?"

Help your patient understand that what he or she is doing is not necessarily wrong, just costly. If your patient believes that holding on to perfectionistic standards helps him or her work harder and better, likely disadvantages are that anxiety over performance is high and that the work is not very enjoyable.

Perfectionism may also interfere with accomplishing tasks in a timely manner. You can point out that time spent on doing compulsions could be used more advantageously. For example, if your patient decreased her compulsive stove checking by 8 minutes per day, this would result in a decrease of 56 minutes per week and 48.5 hours per year—time that your patient could spend doing more enjoyable activities.

Identifying Cognitive Errors

After establishing that a change in perfectionistic behavior may be advantageous, you and your patient should also discuss whether a change is safe. Often patients expect disastrous consequences to result from giving up their perfectionistic behavior. If this is the case, ask your patient whether he or she is engaging in any cognitive errors. Common errors related to perfectionistic standards include:

- All-or-nothing thinking

- Overgeneralization

- Jumping to conclusions

- Magnification

Continuum Technique

For patients with all-or-nothing thinking, it may be helpful to define a continuum of standards with at least three points:

1. Best (perfect, flawless, or right)

2. Average (usual, typical, intermediate, okay)

3. Worst (defective, flawed, or wrong)

You can illustrate this and write standards under each heading for the perfectionistic problem under consideration:

Best	Average	Worst

The example below illustrates this approach for a woman with cleaning compulsions related to perfectionistic standards (M. Freeston, personal communication, 2002). The therapist and patient established three categories:

1. Best equaled cleaning the house as if *House and Garden* magazine were sending a photographer.

2. Average equaled cleaning the house before the arrival of a noncritical personal friend.

3. Worst equaled not cleaning at all.

The therapist asked whether the average standard would be tolerable and preferable to either extreme. Eventually, the patient filled in the continuum with more graded responses, showing that different levels of cleanliness might be appropriate for different situations. This gradually replaced her rigid rule of trying to achieve the "best" possible state of cleanliness at all times.

Metaphors and Stories

As noted in previous chapters, metaphors and stories are useful methods for conveying information. The following story adapted from Michael Otto (2000) can be used to illustrate perfectionistic standards and self-statements that patients hold toward themselves:

> Little Jane [Little Joe if your patient is a man] wanted to learn to play softball and was very excited about it. She went onto the field one day to practice with her team. She wasn't very skillful yet because she hadn't played much, but she had learned the rules and was delighted to be out in the field with her new mitt. The batter hit a high fly ball in her direction, so she looked up and started to back up holding her mitt up high. She missed the ball. Immediately, the coach (let's call him Coach A) stormed onto the field and yelled at her, "I'll tell you something. If you screw up like that again, you'll be sitting on the bench for the next several innings!" Jane stayed through the inning but began to worry that a ball would come her way again. She came home that day, and her parents noticed that the mitt ended up under her bed gathering dust, and she seemed to lose interest in baseball.

Now imagine what might have happened if a different coach (let's call him Coach B) had instead walked out onto the field and said to her, "Okay, Jane, that was a good try. Next time, just back up a little farther because the ball often seems to be coming closer than it really is. Also if you hold your hands right here with the mitt, you'll be able to catch it better. Now go on and try that next time."

This story helps illustrate the effects of holding overly rigid standards. Most patients are readily able to apply the moral of this tale to the effects of their own rules and self-statements.

For patients whose perfectionism centers on remembering or knowing information, consider using the following metaphor (R. Frost, personal communication, 2000). Compare people who want to know or keep everything perfectly to a librarian or a museum curator. Librarians and curators usually just know where to look for information. Explore with your patient the consequences of having to store all kinds of details in their heads or keep everything just so. Compare this to just knowing where to look up information to find what is needed.

Psychoeducation

Your patient might also benefit from reading the "Dare to Be Average" chapter in the book *Feeling Good* by Dr. David Burns (1980). This chapter describes some additional techniques for exploring perfectionism.

ASSIGN HOMEWORK

Assign tasks to evaluate perfectionistic ideals based on the methods described above.

- Complete thought records to identify cognitive errors and generate rational alternatives to perfectionistic thinking.

- Practice the taking another's perspective technique.

- Design and complete a behavioral experiment to test a perfectionistic hypothesis and its alternative using the Behavioral Experiment Form.

- List the advantages and disadvantages of doing certain behaviors perfectly, and consider alternatives.

- Apply the continuum technique to move planned behaviors away from the perfectionistic end toward the middle range of performance.

SUMMARY AND FEEDBACK

Ask your patient to summarize the session content and give you feedback about how the session went.

Chapter 11

Consequences of Anxiety

While beliefs about the consequences of anxiety and discomfort may not be critical for the development of OCD (Freeston et al., 1996), they can play an important role in maintaining OCD symptoms. To avoid unpleasant feelings, patients may engage in rituals and avoidance behavior that prevent their learning that things would have turned out just fine if they hadn't neutralized. Thus, beliefs about the need to avoid anxiety can interfere with successful treatment. Typical beliefs include "Anxiety is harmful and needs to be controlled," "Anxiety stops me from functioning," and "Anxiety will overwhelm me so I can't cope." The patient may be concerned about the current or immediate results of being anxious or about anxiety occurring in the future.

HANDOUTS

Personal Session Forms

Thought Record and Guide—Seven Column

Downward Arrow Form

Behavioral Experiment Form

THERAPIST FORMS

Cognitive Therapy Session Report

AGENDA

After assessing your patient's mood and OCD symptoms, agree on the agenda. We've used the following techniques to evaluate consequences of anxiety with our patients:

- Downward arrow
- Socratic questioning
- Making extreme contrasts
- Retrospective review of the evidence
- Behavioral experiments
- Advantages and disadvantages

REVIEW HOMEWORK

Plan to assign homework at the end of each session in this module and to review the homework early in each session.

COGNITIVE THERAPY TECHNIQUES

Below we provide detailed descriptions of techniques you can choose when your patient is excessively afraid of experiencing discomfort and avoids it at all costs. We recommend you select the techniques that seem most likely to be useful for your patient.

Downward Arrow

We recently treated a patient who had intrusive thoughts about being unable to stop thinking about the air bubbles under her tongue. While using techniques from chapter 5 to address her problem with overimportance of thoughts, the downward arrow also revealed that she had a major problem with tolerating anxiety. Her example is given below:

What if I get intrusive thoughts about the air bubbles under my tongue?

⇩

If I have these thoughts in school, I might become very anxious.

⇩

If I get anxious, I won't be able to concentrate.

⇩

If I can't concentrate, I'll fail my classes.

⇩

If I fail, I won't be able to go to college.

⇩

If I don't go to college, I won't be able to get a good job.

⇩

I won't have any money, and nobody will respect me.

⇩

All of this will make me even more anxious and unhappy.

⇩

I won't be able to handle it and will have to kill myself.

The downward arrow sequence above is a typical example of fears that anxiety will prevent effective functioning. This patient is also concerned that she won't be able to cope with anxiety. You can use the Downward Arrow Form to help your patients identify deeper level beliefs and modify them with Socratic questioning.

Socratic Questioning

In the downward arrow technique described above, the patient believes that intrusive thoughts will provoke such terrible anxiety that she won't be able to function.

Next, the therapist intervenes using Socratic questioning about the role of anxiety and its effects:

T: So, you've told me that you think that the anxiety related to the thoughts about air bubbles will make it difficult for you to pass your tests. Have you actually ever been anxious during a test before?

P: Yes, I am terrified all the time.

T: And the last time you took a test when you were anxious, what grade did you get?

P: I got a B.

T: So what does this tell you about your original hypothesis that you'll fail when you are anxious?

P: Hmm. I guess I won't fail. I can do okay in terms of my grade, but it will be really unpleasant because of the anxiety.

If the patient in the example above had been disappointed that she was not able to function at maximum performance (she got a B when she was really hoping for an A), you'd need to address perfectionistic beliefs about needing to perform at maximum levels all the time (relevant interventions can be found in chapter 10).

The patient in the example above was able to address her fears relating to failure, but she still expressed a low tolerance for the anxiety symptoms themselves. Therefore, as a next step, her therapist separated anxiety into two parts: a physiological component and a cognitive component (there is a behavioral component of anxiety as well, which is not discussed here). This intervention is usually especially helpful for patients whose symptoms border on panic disorder.

T: So the last time you were anxious, what was it like? What kind of physical symptoms did you have?

P: Well, my heart was beating faster than usual, and I started sweating. Maybe I was breathing a little faster, too.

T: So how unpleasant was it to have faster heartbeat, to sweat, and to breathe faster?

P: Really unpleasant.

T: As unpleasant as taking this door right here and slamming it against my finger? [Note how therapist makes an extreme comparison; see below for a more detailed description of this technique].

P: Oh no, not that bad! Just somewhat unpleasant, I guess.

T: So, when we consider the big picture, anxiety symptoms are only somewhat unpleasant. I know you like to go to the gym. How do the symptoms you have right after doing your cardio workout compare to the OCD-related anxiety you were just describing?

P: Actually, the physical symptoms are very similar.

T: Are the symptoms unpleasant when you have them in the gym?

P: No, of course not. They're related to my workout, so they're not scary.

T: So you have all those symptoms in the gym several times per week, but they don't bother you. You might even get them when you walk fast or run up a flight of stairs. And the physical symptoms are the same as what you experience when you are anxious about your air bubbles, right?

P: I hadn't thought of that.

T: So it's not the physical symptoms themselves we need to be concerned about. We know you can tolerate them because they don't bother you when you have them in other contexts. It is the meaning that you attach to them.

P: Yeah, I guess you are right. So maybe next time I get concerned about being anxious, I just need to remind myself that anxiety is really just a bunch of physiological symptoms and I can handle them. I do it all the time. If I don't think that the symptoms are scary, they won't be!

Making Extreme Contrasts

Besides being unable to function or cope, other common beliefs that are identified with the downward arrow technique are beliefs that the anxiety will cause the person to lose control or "go crazy." In this case, you should ask your patient about a recent situation when he or she felt anxious and on the verge of going crazy. Then, ask for a comparison of his or her own behavior to that of someone who displays the negative extreme of the behavior your patient is concerned about.

T: What does "losing control" mean? If I told you that I saw a guy who totally lost control yesterday, how would you picture his behavior?

P: Well, I'd picture someone who pulls out his hair . . . and screams . . . and throws himself on the floor.

T: So did you ever do these things when you got anxious? Did you pull out your hair, scream, and throw yourself on the floor?

P: No! I've never done that!

Retrospective Review of the Evidence

In the above example, the therapist also compared this patient's definition to the patient's behavior in the past to see if they matched. In the section below, note how the therapist focuses especially on retrospective recall to modify the patient's belief.

T: And how many times in your life have you been afraid of losing control?

P: Oh gosh, several thousand times? Maybe more.

T: Okay, so several thousand times you've predicted that you might lose control, but it actually never happened. So next time you think you're going to lose control, how likely do you think this prediction will come true?

P: It's not likely at all. It won't happen.

Behavioral Experiments

For patients who overestimate the negative consequences of anxiety, you can also conduct behavioral experiments. For example, you can inquire about a patient's predictions about performance while anxious about an exam or other specific task. Your patient will probably predict failure. You can then agree on an experiment to test this prediction by observing actual performance. Complete the Behavioral Experiment Form (as described in detail in chapter 5, in the module on overimportance of thoughts). Tell your patient to just let thoughts and feelings related to anxiety come and go naturally and not to do anything about them. Indeed, for the behavioral experiment to be a true test, your patient cannot engage in any rituals or avoidance behavior. Afterward, ask your patient to compare the predicted performance to his or her actual performance.

Most likely, your patient's feared prediction will not come true. Accordingly, you and your patient will need to generate a new belief to explain what happened. You should also discuss whether your patient's anxiety decreases over time after realizing that predictions about danger and harm don't come true. An additional strategy is to encourage patients to actually try to lose control as an experiment. This usually demonstrates pretty effectively that it's not possible.

Advantages and Disadvantages

You can also help your patients examine the advantages and disadvantages of holding on to beliefs about consequences of anxiety (see chapter 5 for a detailed description of this technique). Your patients could list the pros and cons of neutralizing behavior. For example, your patient might state that the belief that "anxiety is dangerous and needs to be avoided" has protected him or her from anxiety and harm. The disadvantages are usually pretty obvious (spending a lot of time ritualizing, and so on). Of course, a potential short-term advantage of avoiding a feared situation or of ritualizing is an immediate decrease in anxiety. In this case, it's important to review the original cognitive model that shows that rituals and avoidance guarantee that maladaptive OCD-related beliefs cannot be disconfirmed. Also encourage your patients to explore whether trying to avoid anxiety (by rituals or avoidance behavior) has actually reduced their fears about anxiety. Review what has happened on previous occasions when they tried to avoid anxiety, and identify the advantages and disadvantages of following former OCD behavior.

ASSIGN HOMEWORK

The following homework assignments can be useful for patients completing this module:

- Use the Downward Arrow Form to identify beliefs related to your concerns about coping with anxiety or functioning impairments/loss of control due to anxiety.

- Evaluate the validity of thoughts and beliefs pertaining to anxiety with the help of thought records.

- Conduct behavioral experiments to test assumptions about what it means to get anxious.

- Make a list of the advantages and disadvantages of holding on to current beliefs or behaviors related to anxiety.

SUMMARY AND FEEDBACK

Ask your patient for a summary of the major points covered during the session and for feedback about your own behavior.

Chapter 12

Fear of Positive Experiences

Some OCD patients are afraid of or avoid positive experiences. Use this module if your patients report that they don't deserve positive experiences, that intrusive thoughts might ruin whatever they are doing, or that good experiences are always followed by bad ones. This module is also relevant if you notice that your patients never seem to engage in any experiences that could be pleasurable or associated with a sense of mastery. These issues are likely to emerge when you are developing your patient's cognitive model of OCD (see chapter 4) or reviewing thought records. The fear of positive experiences subscale of the OBQ-Ext can also provide an indication of the need to apply strategies from this module. Because fears of positive experiences are often tied to overimportance of thoughts and efforts to control thoughts, the techniques in chapters 5 and 6 might also be relevant.

HANDOUTS

Personal Session Forms

Thought Record and Guide—Seven Column

Downward Arrow Form

Behavioral Experiment Form

THERAPIST FORMS

Cognitive Therapy Session Report

AGENDA

As usual, you'll start each session with a brief mood and symptom check and inquiry about reactions to previous sessions. In deciding on agenda items for this module, the following strategies will likely be most useful:

- Downward arrow

- Socratic questioning

- Retrospective review of the evidence

- Behavioral experiments

- Conducting a survey

- Double-standard technique

- Role-play

- Advantages and disadvantages

REVIEW HOMEWORK

Plan to assign homework at the end of each session in this module and to review the homework early in each session.

COGNITIVE THERAPY TECHNIQUES

Patients sometimes report avoiding pleasurable experiences, because of moralistic attitudes about enjoyment, or because they fear such experiences will lead to negative intrusions. For example, Freeston et al. (1996) described a patient who avoided pleasurable experiences because unpleasant thoughts might intrude and impair the positive experience. Typical beliefs include the following:

- "I don't deserve to have fun because I have these terrible thoughts."

- "I won't be able to enjoy myself because I'll get these horrific images."

- "If I start to make progress, I won't be able to maintain my gains."

- "If my symptoms improve, I won't be able to handle everybody's expectations."

Here are some strategies you can use to address these concerns.

Downward Arrow

The downward arrow method helps patients identify their central fears. If it is helpful, suggest that your patient use the Downward Arrow Form as a guide to identifying the main fears. Fears of positive experiences are often related to fears of failing in some important way (in the role of parent, spouse, student, employee, or even patient), of being unable to maintain treatment gains, of disappointing others, and of not deserving good experiences ("I've never succeeded at anything important anyway"). Patients may also believe that if they get better, they'll be even more devastated when they ultimately relapse. Sometimes superstitious fears are related to the fear of symptom improvement ("Acknowledging that I'm getting better could precipitate a relapse"). The downward arrow strategy may uncover core beliefs about being inadequate, a failure, or unworthy of positive experiences (see chapter 13 for methods to work on core beliefs).

Socratic Questioning

Here's an example of how assumptions generated by the downward arrow technique can be addressed with Socratic questioning. Note that this is also an example of thought-action fusion, which can be addressed with techniques from chapter 5.

T: So you think that if you acknowledge that you're getting better and start getting excited about it, you'll cause a relapse.

P: Yes, that's right. I'll jinx it if I admit that something good is happening.

T: Let's take a look at the evidence that this is true. We've discussed that the large majority of people improve with appropriate treatment. How many of those people who get better, do you think, acknowledge that they do?

P: Most of them, I guess, because they are excited about their progress. So I'd assume that about eighty percent acknowledge that they are improving.

T: Do you think that eighty percent of all OCD patients who improve in treatment relapse because they say that they're improving?

P: No, I don't think so. I guess if this was the case you'd have warning signs all over your clinic not to talk about improvement. But I think it might be different for me.

T: Why would it be different for you than it is for others?

P: Because bad things always happen to me. Good stuff never happens. Whenever I get excited about something, it never works out. So now I have to be careful not to mess it up.

T: Okay. Let's look at the evidence for this. Was there ever anything good you were hoping for that *did* work out?

P: Maybe graduation from college?

T: Yes, definitely. This is an important accomplishment that did work out. So there is some evidence against the belief that good things never happen to you. Did you ever tell anyone about your good grades before you graduated?

P: Yeah, I mentioned them to my parents.

T: And did you ever mention that you were planning on graduating?

P: Yes, of course!

T: And did all this jinx the graduation?

P: No, it didn't.

T: Seems to me we found some compelling evidence *against* the belief that talking about good stuff jinxes it.

P: I guess so.

T: Now, let's look at the evidence *for* the belief that talking about good stuff will jinx it. Do you have evidence to back this up?

P: Yes! I tried to work on the OCD on my own before coming here. I even bought a self-help book. I improved a little, and then I was so excited, I told my boyfriend all about it. But then I really crashed.

T: Are there any other possible reasons why you might have relapsed besides that you mentioned your OCD work to your boyfriend?

P: Hmm, I don't know.

T: Did you consistently follow the advice in the book?

P: No, after a while I was getting bored reading so much, and I didn't understand everything that was described in the book, anyway. It's hard to do this stuff on your own, you know? So I kind of stopped doing the exercises.

T: What's more likely to account for your crash, that you stopped following the advice in your OCD book or that you mentioned your improvement to your boyfriend?

P: I guess that I stopped following the program.

T: So, it seems like we've been able to identify situations in which talking about something good didn't ruin the experience. And we also came up with an alternative explanation for why you might have relapsed after your previous efforts in dealing with your OCD. What does this tell us about your original thought that you shouldn't acknowledge your improvement in OCD treatment?

P: That acknowledging it has nothing to do with how well I do.

T: How much do you believe what you just said? Use the 0 to 100 scale.

P: Um, maybe fifty percent. I have to think about it more. It makes sense, but I'm not sure.

T: That's fine, it takes time to realize things that don't match your usual thinking.

Retrospective Review of the Evidence

In the dialogue above, the therapist uses a retrospective review of the evidence to modify a superstitious belief about jinxing something positive by acknowledging that things are going well. Patients can also be encouraged to review their actual experiences in other situations related to fear of positive experiences. Have they ever enjoyed situations or activities despite the presence of intrusive images? This may lead to the use of techniques from chapter 10 on perfectionism (such as identifying all-or-nothing thinking) to help your patient notice that a few bad thoughts need not mean that the experience is ruined completely.

Behavioral Experiments

Behavioral experiments might also be very useful to test predictions about superstitions ("If I allow myself to get excited about my progress, I'll relapse") or about your patients' predictions that they won't be able to enjoy themselves because of intrusions. For example, if patients are concerned about not being able to enjoy themselves, you can ask them to identify a pleasurable activity (going to a ball game) and use the Behavioral Experiment Form to record the task. Ask your patient to rate the expected level of enjoyment before the ball game, and then to go to the game regardless of any thoughts, and rerate the enjoyment after the game. As always when completing behavioral experiments, encourage your patient to explore the difference between the predicted and actual consequences. Also see chapters 5 and 7 for more discussion of behavioral experiments.

Conducting a Survey

Conducting a survey can be very useful when working with patients who think they don't deserve to feel good. Your patients could ask their friends or family members if they think that your patient or other people in your patient's situation (akin to taking another's perspective) deserve to enjoy themselves or to improve with respect to symptoms of guilt, shame, and anxiety. Often, just suggesting the survey makes it clear to patients that others around them would certainly consider them deserving of improvement and good feelings. This can lead easily into the double-standard method described below.

Double-Standard Technique

If your patients believe they don't deserve to get better, you can ask if they'd hold the same attitude toward someone else—for example, toward another person with similar OCD symptoms. If not, discuss why. Look for inconsistent thinking about themselves and others and explore this further using Socratic techniques. For example, your patients might explain a different view of what others deserve when they refer to special negative traits that they possess and others don't have ("Yes, but I've had an abortion and I need to be punished"). Explore this further with Socratic questioning to identify the gaps in your patient's logical thinking, especially by inquiring whether they know anyone else who has had an abortion and, if so, whether she too does not deserve to get better. If others do deserve to get better or enjoy themselves in some situations, you can ask why to help your patients clarify their values and the consistency of these values. Often, this discussion of presumed differences from others reflects deeper level beliefs, such as "I am bad." These can be modified with strategies outlined in chapter 13.

Role-Play

A similar strategy to address fears about improving in treatment might be a role-play. You can take the role of your patient while your patient plays the role of the therapist or a friend who does not have OCD. Usually, your patients will come up with good suggestions as to why you should improve and why you deserve to improve. Ultimately, you will need to discuss how your patients can apply this same advice to themselves.

Advantages and Disadvantages

Examining the costs and benefits of holding on to certain beliefs about positive experiences will often lead your patients to change their original perspective. For example, you might want to encourage your patient to examine the advantages and disadvantages of thinking "If I start to make progress, I won't be able to maintain my gains." Your patients might mention as an advantage that they are preparing themselves to avoid disappointment. Disadvantages might include not feeling motivated to try hard in treatment, feeling depressed or hopeless, and missing out on potential improvement. You can then examine the relative weights of advantages and disadvantages and evaluate the validity of the advantages.

ASSIGN HOMEWORK

The following homework assignments can be useful for patients completing this module:

- Use the Downward Arrow Form to identify beliefs related to fears of positive experiences.

- Record thoughts pertaining to fears of positive experiences and evaluate them using thought records.

- Review the evidence that supports or refutes beliefs pertaining to fears of positive experiences (retrospective review of the evidence).

- Conduct a survey among friends to determine if they would agree that your patient shouldn't improve in treatment.

- Have your patients think carefully about whether they would hold the same viewpoint if a friend of theirs was in the same situation.

- Make a list of the advantages and disadvantages of holding on to beliefs related to fear or avoidance of positive experiences.

SUMMARY AND FEEDBACK

After each session, ask your patient for a summary of the major points covered and for feedback.

Chapter 13

Modifying Core Beliefs

This chapter is designed for use any time core beliefs are identified while you are working on other belief types. This usually happens in the course of a downward arrow procedure or during Socratic questioning. You will need to decide whether to continue working on the intermediate beliefs or whether to focus attention on the core beliefs ("I'm bad," "I'm unlovable") using strategies suggested below. This decision often depends on the stage of therapy and the productivity of the cognitive strategies for intermediate beliefs. It is wise to avoid direct work on core beliefs until you have established a solid and trusting working relationship with your patient to enable them to tolerate very upsetting feelings and often crying in front of you. Although there is no standard rule, you might wish to wait until you have worked on one or two domains (for example, overimportance of thoughts or responsibility) before tackling core beliefs that support these interpretations. In our experience, therapists are more comfortable doing so after session 8 or 10. When your patient can readily identify and challenge their intermediate beliefs, and core beliefs are easily accessed, you can move to work on these as soon as they appear.

HANDOUTS

Personal Session Forms

Downward Arrow Form (previously completed forms that identified core beliefs)

Core Belief Filter

Core Beliefs Record

THERAPIST FORMS

Cognitive Therapy Session Report

Cognitive Model of OCD (from chapter 4 with core beliefs identified)

AGENDA

- Core belief filter
- Using the Core Beliefs Record
- Socratic questioning
- Continuum technique
- Making extreme contrasts
- Double-standard technique
- Courtroom technique
- Reframing the evidence
- Metaphors
- Historical testing of core beliefs
- Restructuring early memories

DEFINING CORE BELIEFS

Underlying the appraisals of situations and beliefs that support OCD symptoms are core beliefs, which are also called *schemas* or *basic assumptions*. Beginning in childhood, individuals develop fundamental beliefs or understandings about themselves, other people, and their personal worlds. Core beliefs are central ideas about the self. Most people, including people with OCD, have several positive core beliefs, including the following:

- "I am basically a good person."
- "I am likeable."
- "I am pretty competent at what I do."
- "I am a strong person."
- "I am thoughtful."

When elicited, these positive core beliefs are usually stated with some moderation, rather than in absolute terms like "I am all good" or "I am competent at everything." That is, they are not rigidly held beliefs, but the person considers them applicable in most situations.

In contrast, negative core beliefs are often absolute, global, and overgeneralized, and usually they can be stated in three or four words, such as "I am bad" or "I am vulnerable." Patients might also have negative core beliefs about others or the world, such as "The world is dangerous" and "people can't be trusted." Note that these beliefs about others have implications for your patient. For example, the belief that "other people are vulnerable" is interpreted to mean "I'd better be hypervigilant or I'll cause them harm." Thus, these beliefs about others are often linked to beliefs about the self, such as "I am dangerous." Negative core beliefs typically emerge during times of stress in response to strong emotional reactions or to behavioral mistakes.

Below is a table of typical negative core beliefs about the self and the world that occur often in relation to the types of beliefs common for people with OCD. Of course, many other core beliefs are possible in relation to OCD beliefs.

Cognitive Domains	Core Beliefs About Self	Core Beliefs About Others or the World
Overimportance of Thoughts	I'm bad/evil/dangerous. I'm defective/crazy. I'm unlovable. I'm not good enough.	No one could love me. People will reject me.
Control of Thoughts	I'm weak. I'm out of control.	People will reject me.
Overestimation of Danger	I'm vulnerable/helpless.	The world is a dangerous place. Other people are vulnerable.
Desire for Certainty	I'm defective/stupid.	
Responsibility	I'm bad/irresponsible.	People can't be trusted.
Perfectionism	I'm inferior. I'm inadequate/a failure. I'm incompetent.	People will reject me.
Consequences of Anxiety	I'm weak. I'm vulnerable.	
Fear of Positive Experiences	I'm unworthy. I'm unlovable/not good enough.	The fates are against me.

PREPARING TO CHALLENGE CORE BELIEFS

The strategies suggested in this chapter are intended to help patients alter their negative core beliefs, while also working toward alternative positive core beliefs and bolstering existing positive beliefs. Whenever your patient presents new information in therapy (for example, when your patient shares thoughts, emotions, and behaviors), you can hypothesize to yourself what core belief (negative or positive) might have been activated. It is up to you to decide when to focus on negative beliefs for examination and eventual change, as work on core beliefs is likely to initially increase your patient's anxiety. When you do suggest work on core beliefs, you might wish to warn patients of this possibility.

Most patients' core beliefs are evident based on previous use of the downward arrow strategy and from your work on their cognitive model, in which core beliefs are represented in a box on the left side. If you need to clarify why it is important to work on basic beliefs, remind your patient of the role of these beliefs as contributors to current intrusive thoughts and maladaptive interpretations by referring to their cognitive model.

To work on basic beliefs, you must first be aware of a more functional belief toward which your patient can be guided. Although new beliefs should be formed collaboratively, you should have several in mind that can be used as a goal so that strategies to alter the belief can be chosen wisely. For example, a patient with recurrent intrusions about cutting his or her baby's limbs off might hold a core belief "I am bad" or "I am dangerous." Consider guiding your patient toward an alternative and contradictory belief that "I am not actually dangerous, but I am someone who is very worried that I am dangerous." Another belief to aim for might be "Like other people, I get these types of violent images when I am under stress or have recently seen or read about violence. My thought just means I'm reacting normally." Thus, the revised core belief in the first case might be "I am sensitive" and in the second might be "I am normal."

COGNITIVE THERAPY TECHNIQUES

A variety of cognitive strategies are especially useful for helping your patients modify negative core beliefs. Many of these have already been introduced in previous chapters but are repeated here to illustrate their use with core beliefs. We have described them below in the order we most commonly use them. As always, select the methods that seem to best fit your patient's situation and your own skills.

Core Belief Filter

When a negative core belief is activated, most people immediately process information that is consistent with their core belief but ignore or distort information that is inconsistent with it. An information-processing model can help your patient understand how they can believe their core belief extremely strongly, even when it's obviously not true or substantially untrue. As J. Beck (1995) suggests, a person who holds a core belief very strongly does not process contradictory information. For example, a patient who believes "I am bad" (perhaps deriving from parental statements like "you are a bad person; that's the meanness in you coming out") does not process information that they are good, or not bad. Because this information does not fit their expected image, it is ignored or discounted. It does not register cognitively and thus has no impact on the person's self-view. In this way, a strongly held negative self-image becomes immune to change by contradictory evidence, such as positive comments by others or even positive behaviors that are inconsistent with the negative self-view.

To illustrate this analogy, provide your patient with the Core Belief Filter handout. This shows how information consistent with existing core beliefs is more readily accepted by someone than new information inconsistent with core beliefs. Information matching an alternative belief ("I am not bad"; "I am as good as others"; "I am good") bounces off because it does not fit your patients' long-held expectations of themselves.

You can liken this process to the childhood toy in which different geometric shapes are fitted into matching cutout spaces. Another useful analogy to illustrate this concept is a jigsaw puzzle in which your patient encounters pieces from several different puzzles, some more attractive than others. The goal is to fit together as many of the attractive pieces as possible to change the overall picture to a more satisfying and more accurate one.

Using the Core Beliefs Record

The Core Beliefs Record handout can be used to record an original negative belief, along with ratings of the current strength of belief (0 to 100 percent) based on your patient's gut feelings and rational thinking. As you can see in the example below, you and your patient should agree on a possible alternative belief, and the patient should rate the strength of this new belief on the same scale. The ratings should be repeated over the course of treatment. For some beliefs, it may be useful to have patients rerate daily how strongly they endorse both the dysfunctional and the alternative belief. These ratings provide steady information about progress during cognitive therapy and can help you decide when to change strategies. Typically, the alternative core belief will be less strongly held than the original one for quite some time until your patient has successfully applied a few of the techniques described in this chapter.

Core Beliefs Record

Patient's Name: ___CM_____   Date: ___4/8/05_____

Old core belief 1: I'm inadequate—I'll screw up badly._____

How much do you believe this right now in your gut? (0 to 100 percent) ___90___

How much do you believe this right now rationally? (0 to 100 percent) ___65___

Alternative belief 1: I'm adequate most of the time—I mess up occasionally.___

How much do you believe this right now in your gut? (0 to 100 percent) ___50___

How much do you believe this right now rationally? (0 to 100 percent) ___65___

Evidence that contradicts old core belief and supports new belief: At work, my boss has very rarely asked me to redo my work. When he has asked me to do something over again, he did not seem frustrated and has always told me he thought the instructions weren't very clear. In fact, he is pretty complimentary about my work and two of my coworkers are also complimentary._____

Evidence that supports old core belief with a reframe (yes . . . , but . . .): Sometimes I do screw up and make mistakes, but that just means I'm human, just like other people.___

Socratic Questioning

Socratic questioning is probably the most common method of helping patients challenge core beliefs. As always, you are helping your patient follow a logical line of argument to enable them to see the flaws in their thinking that have led to faulty conclusions. In general, use this type of questioning whenever it is clear to you that your patient has made a mistake in interpreting a situation as having dire consequences or meaning something about themselves or others when, in fact, this is very unlikely.

Take the case of a woman who feared she was a bad person because she had had an abortion when she was younger. She believed that God would punish her by taking away her child. To prevent this, she had to protect her daughter from contamination. The therapist followed a line of Socratic questions that included the following:

- "How do you know that God will punish you?"

- "Given what you know about God, could God forgive this kind of sin?"

- "Is this the kind of sin God could not forgive?"

- "If God knows everything, would God be able to understand this?"

This type of questioning is also illustrated below under the section Historical Testing of Core Beliefs.

Continuum Technique

Whenever core beliefs can be characterized as adjectives that are extreme and negative (weak, bad, dangerous), use the continuum technique to help your patient draw a scale from "very [bad]" to "not at all [bad]" and define the meaning of each of these endpoints. Work on additional scale points (25 percent, 50 percent, and 75 percent) to define what would qualify for these points and then ask your patient to place themselves along this scale. This strategy has been described in detail in chapters 5, 9, and 10.

Asking questions that emphasize the contrast between relevant patient behaviors and the core belief (examining recent evidence) can be especially helpful in this context. For example, ask, "So, when you went out of your way to help the little girl who fell down the stairs, would that be evidence that you are a bad person?" In a similar vein, you may be able to use your patients' own statements of attitude toward others to bolster the case for the alternative belief. For example, if your patient seems frustrated with someone else's unhelpful behavior toward others, you might inquire whether your patient's concern over this incident would most likely occur in a bad person or in someone who was not bad? This evidence of thoughtful concern can be used to support a self-image of a good rather than bad person.

Making Extreme Contrasts

Closely related to the continuum technique is making extreme contrasts (detailed in chapter 11). In this strategy, you compare your patient to someone real or imagined who is at the negative extreme of the core belief (someone with thoughts about harming others versus a convicted murderer). A similar approach to dealing with beliefs like "I am bad because I have violent thoughts" would be to ask your patient for a description of a really bad person he or she knows or has heard about. Next, ask your patient to compare him- or herself to this person.

Double-Standard Technique

The double-standard technique lends itself well for use with core beliefs whenever it seems evident that patients' views of themselves are not the same views they would hold about others in similar situations. Most likely you have tried this method out in chapters 5 and 9. In the case of core beliefs, your work will focus mainly on whether your patients would label and view others as they do themselves (bad, weak, unlovable, defective, inferior). Refer to chapters 5 and 9 for detailed examples.

Courtroom Technique

This method lends itself well to use with core beliefs whenever you find that the evidence your patients are using to justify their negative label has significant loopholes that would emerge if "tested in court." If you have not used this method earlier in therapy, follow the strategy in chapter 5 where the patient first plays the prosecuting attorney arguing the case for the negative core belief. Ask your patient to defend the belief using actual evidence that would be considered factual proof rather than subjective feelings and thoughts.

If you have already used this method, and your patient has used it well in the past, consider acting the role of the prosecuting attorney while your patient plays the judge. This enables you to state the negative core belief and the evidence for it in ways intended to emphasize the invalidity of the argument. Consider the following illustration:

T: Your honor, I submit to you that Mr. J. here is lazy and inadequate.

P: Okay. Let's hear your evidence.

T: My main evidence is that he himself thinks this is what his father thought. His father called him "lazy" and a good-for-nothing.

P: Is there evidence for this?

T: There are witnesses. The defendant's own sister heard the father say this.

P: What else did the father say? Did he believe this or was he just name-calling?

T: We have no statement from the father, your honor, he is dead. But I do have some additional evidence. Mr. J. admits that he called in sick to work on two occasions when he was not actually ill. This indicates weakness. The defendant has no backbone, he is inadequate.

P: Is this your only evidence?

T: No your honor, he himself states that he is inadequate. That is his own belief. It must be true.

P: [coming out of his role as judge] That sounds really ridiculous.

T: [staying in the role of lawyer] But your honor, it's the truth. He believes it very much.

P: That sounds even dumber. I get your point here. I need more evidence to support this.

T: Right. If you are going to walk around convinced that you are lazy and inadequate, it makes sense to me that you'd need more evidence than what you've given me so far. Do you have better evidence than this?

Reframing the Evidence

Consider reframing the evidence to be less overgeneralized and more specific to the situation (Beck 1995). Sometimes this can be facilitated with a "yes, but" method. For example, encourage your patient to state, "Yes, I have intrusive thoughts about harming others with a knife, but these are always just thoughts and images. In fact, in my behavior, I am actually someone who does not hurt others. If anything, I try to be very considerate." At this point, you might focus on the label of "considerate" to encourage the patient to evaluate whether this label is more accurate (has more supporting evidence) than the negative core belief.

To evaluate core beliefs about being a bad person because of intrusive thoughts, help your patient consider whether intention can be inferred based on thoughts or even based on behaviors. Ask your patient to think of examples of thoughts that bear no relation to a person's actual wishes or interests. For example, when a parent has a fleeting idea of how awful it would be to have a child die from disease or a car accident or some other disaster, does this mean that they want it to happen?

Metaphors

You might wish to identify relevant metaphors to help your patient adopt an alternative view. For example, a patient who has a negative view of herself based on parental attitudes can be reminded of the Cinderella story, in which a child is treated as if she is a bad girl when in fact she is not at fault. Various metaphors relevant to different types of OCD beliefs are described in previous chapters.

Historical Testing of Core Beliefs

This method is adapted form J. Beck (1995) and it works well for memories from childhood that patients have interpreted as evidence for their core belief. In this case, encourage patients to

1. Recall childhood memories that contributed to the core belief

2. Search for evidence that supports the new belief

3. Reframe each piece of negative evidence, using current adult knowledge

4. Summarize periods of childhood (for example, grade school, high school) with regard to the new belief

The following dialogue with an isolated and depressed young man with intrusive thoughts about harming others with knives or sharp objects illustrates core beliefs about being untrustworthy, rejected by others, and an unlovable person.

P: I don't see how anybody could even like me, actually. I try to keep away from people whenever there are knives around because I just can't trust myself to be safe. This is pretty hopeless because even if I did get to know someone, as soon as they find out I'm weird like this, they'll be out of here like a shot.

T: Okay. Let's unpack that one a little. You just said several things at once. Let's list them and decide which is most important to work on right now. You said, "No one could like me," "I can't trust myself," "I'm weird," and "I'll be rejected if people find out I have these thoughts." Does that cover it pretty well?

P: Yeah, so it's hopeless.

T: I understand that it looks like that, but do you remember what we said about how you see things in a particular way, based on your experience, and that we all do this? Remember the figure I drew [referring to the Core Belief Filter]? My job is to help you consider things that don't quite fit your usual interpretation. Okay if I keep going?

P: Yeah, I guess so.

T: Back to what you said. Which one is the most central part of the problem— not being trustworthy, being weird, or being rejected? [The therapist states the patient's ideas as simply and bluntly as possible to help him grasp the central concepts.]

P: Being rejected. That hurts a lot, but you know, these are all connected. How can people accept me if I don't accept myself, and how can I do that if I have these disgusting thoughts. I'm disgusted at myself.

T: Sounds like the rejection is about others and also about yourself. You don't accept yourself. Is that *just* because you have these thoughts about knives and hurting people?

P: No ... not completely. I know that other people have these. You know, that long list you showed me. I do believe that I'm not the only one, and I even think it might not be all that rare. That makes sense to me. But somehow, I'm not okay. I'm never okay just being me.

T: Where do you think that comes from? When we look back at your cognitive model, it seems like it might have something to do with your dad's expectations, but we haven't really talked much about this.

P: It must. Jeez, sometimes he was really unfeeling, even sort of mean. But mostly, just not sympathetic. Not to me or my sister. You know, it didn't matter what it was, but when I screwed up something, he would make out like I meant to.

T: Did you?

P: No, of course not. I was little. I didn't know how to do things.

T: So when he did this, what would happen?

P: He'd yell, call me names. You know, like "cheater" or "creep." The worst was actually "liar." He'd say, "Liar, liar, house on fire" in a really demeaning way. Like the kids' rhyme.

T: How old were you when you remember this most vividly?

P: Pretty young, maybe eight or ten.

T: So now you are at least ten years older, and you know more. Let's take a good look at whether he was right, now that you are older and can look back on it from an adult perspective. Was he correct that you were a liar or a cheat? As you define those terms now, were they applicable to you then?

P: No, not really at all. I sometimes lied a little, you know, to cover if I got home a little late or something like that, but I wasn't a liar. I did have a friend at school who made stuff up all the time. I didn't do that.

T: What kind of kid were you? How would you describe yourself then?

P: I was pretty quiet, I got along with my friends at school. I did okay in school. . . . I wasn't a behavior problem or anything like that.

T: What adjectives would have applied to you? Quiet? Friendly? Diligent? Nice?

P: Yeah, I guess. I haven't really thought about it . . . but that's probably right. Maybe passive too.

T: Okay, can you write those down on your session form? You think you were quiet, friendly, diligent, nice, passive [repeating these for emphasis]. Liked by teachers or other kids?

P: Yes, I think they liked me. My sister did, for sure.

T: Let's add that, liked by teachers and friends and sister. Now, how compatible is that with your dad's view?

P: Not very.

T: And how does this list of adjectives you just made fit with how you think about yourself lately?

P: Not so good a fit, I guess. I think I see what you're getting at.

T: Tell me what you think I'm getting at.

P: Maybe I've been walking around with my dad's view of me, not really me. Phew, that'd be freaky.

T: That's interesting. It seems new to you. What do you think is the next step?

P: I suppose I should really think about this more. You know, if I'm really so bad.

T: I agree, what would this mean about your being untrustworthy, weird, or rejected? We can take a close look at the evidence for this. Let's see if we can design a homework assignment that would help you move forward on this. It seems pretty central to working on the OCD when you really berate yourself.

P: Yeah, that makes sense.

ASSIGN HOMEWORK

A variety of homework assignments may be appropriate when working on core beliefs, as suggested below:

- Ask your patients to label the triangles and squares in the Core Belief Filter handout with the specific types of information they accept and reject. Along these lines, you might ask your patient to notice and describe actual instances of accepted negative information and rejected positive information during the week.

- Ask your patients to complete a Core Beliefs Record to identify information that supports or refutes a specific negative core belief and to indicate the more positive and accurate alternative belief.

- Suggest that your patients fill in several points on a continuum to provide specific examples to illustrate the range of behaviors representing a positive and negative self-view (such as "bad-good," "unworthy-worthy") under consideration.

- Recommend that whenever your patients notice a strong mood change signaling the presence of a negative core belief, they ask themselves whether the evidence for this belief would hold up in a court of law.

SUMMARY AND FEEDBACK

After each session, ask your patient for a summary of the major points covered and for feedback.

Chapter 14

Relapse Prevention

The focus of this final module is on reinforcing your patient's gains, reviewing the CT strategies to identify those that seemed most useful, and planning for how to minimize OCD problems in the future. A variety of strategies are included here for the final two sessions of therapy. These sessions should be spaced at least two weeks apart to encourage your patient to transition to increased reliance on self-treatment skills. Many of the strategies described below have been adapted for OCD from J. Beck (1995).

Before your patient stops treatment, you will want to repeat the assessment of OCD and mood symptoms using measures recommended in chapter 2 (Yale-Brown Obsessive Compulsive Scale, Obsessive Compulsive Symptoms Rating Scale, Obsessive Beliefs Questionnaire—Extended, Beck Depression Inventory-II) to determine how much progress your patient has made. Based on the results of this assessment, you will want to discuss plans for further work after therapy ends.

HANDOUTS

Personal Session Forms

Cognitive Model from chapter 4, with core belief descriptions

List of Cognitive Errors (review previous handout)

Types of OCD Beliefs (review previous handout)

Behavioral Experiment Form

Downward Arrow Form

Core Beliefs Record

Self-Coaching Session Form

List of Cognitive Therapy Techniques

Graph of Progress in Therapy

Problem Solving Worksheet

THERAPIST FORMS

Cognitive Therapy Session Report

AGENDA

Begin the first of these two sessions with a brief mood and symptom check, including asking your patient about the frequency and intensity of intrusive thoughts during the previous week. At this point, thoughts should be much reduced in frequency and intensity from pretreatment levels, although they may still be occurring periodically. Ask your patient about his or her interpretations when obsessive thoughts do occur. At this point, most interpretations should be neutral or only mildly anxiety provoking.

Ask about any reactions to previous sessions and about the previous session's homework assignment. Other agenda items for this and the final session include the following:

- Address concerns about termination.
- Review CT model, cognitive errors, and types of OCD beliefs.
- Review CT strategies that worked best.
- Credit progress to your patient.
- Plan to prevent relapse in the future.
- Introduce coping with stressors and using extra time.
- Introduce problem solving.
- Schedule self-treatment sessions.
- Discuss medication issues.
- Provide information about support groups.
- Get summary and feedback.

REVIEW HOMEWORK

In these final two sessions, as usual check on what your patient accomplished in the previous week. Just before the next to last session is a good time to review your own therapy session reports to determine which assignments seemed most useful. This can form the beginning of a list of treatment strategies to review what worked best during treatment and to develop a plan for preventing relapse in the future.

ADDRESS CONCERNS ABOUT TERMINATION

You will want to plan for the ending of treatment by reminding your patient that it makes sense to reduce treatment sessions from weekly to twice monthly for the last month of treatment. Do this at least one month before reducing the frequency of sessions. Identify your patient's thoughts about the reduced session frequency and eventual termination. Some patients may be afraid of relapse, concerned that they cannot handle problems on their own, and/or reluctant to end their supportive relationship with you as therapist. You can evaluate negative thoughts about stopping treatment by using Socratic questioning to identify your patient's specific concerns.

If appropriate, you can also review the potential advantages of treatment ending ("I will learn to rely more on myself," "I will have more time and money for other activities").

COGNITIVE THERAPY TECHNIQUES

It is especially important at this final stage of treatment to review your patient's progress, to identify the cognitive strategies that worked best, and to determine what problems remain that your patient will need to continue to work on. Strategies for this are provided below.

Review CT Model, Cognitive Errors, and Types of OCD Beliefs

It is very important at this point to review the cognitive model (refer to handouts from previous sessions) with your patient and ask your patient to articulate the principles of cognitive therapy on which he or she has been operating. At this time, it is often useful to review the List of Cognitive Errors and the Types of OCD Beliefs handouts as a reminder of your patient's specific types of thinking and beliefs and to determine the extent to which each of these has resolved or remains somewhat problematic. For example, has your patient gained control over perfectionistic standards and all-or-nothing thinking? What about overestimating danger and jumping to conclusions? Are excessive beliefs about responsibility largely resolved, or do these remain problematic?

Reviewing CT Methods That Worked

Most important is a review of all the cognitive techniques that your patient has learned in treatment in order to identify the most helpful ones. You and your patient will want to plan on how to apply these strategies over the coming months if some interpretations and beliefs are not yet fully reduced in strength. These are available in the List of Cognitive Therapy Techniques handout.

It may be helpful to review the general steps your patient has learned:

1. Identify intrusions (obsessive thoughts, images, or impulses).

2. Identify faulty interpretations of intrusions.

3. Evaluate these and generate alternative interpretations using various cognitive strategies.

4. Test alternative interpretations using behavioral experiments.

5. Record the actual results versus the predicted results.

Remind your patient that when behavioral experiments generate some discomfort, this is usually a sign that the technique is working. Your patient can expect that continuing to engage in these experiments will lead to changes in interpretations and beliefs and to a reduction in anxiety. Remind your patient that long-term gains are made through perseverance and commitment to continuing work, and that he or she is likely to experience some obsessive fears. That is, your patient will not be anxiety free, and this may be especially true now that treatment is ending.

Downward Arrow

If some of your patient's interpretations and/or beliefs have changed very little, a reassessment of the worst fears via the downward arrow technique may be necessary. It is possible that your patient may not have allowed him- or herself to get to the most basic fear. For a patient who has not made much headway, it may be necessary to identify novel strategies that have not yet been tried.

Crediting Progress to Your Patient

Throughout treatment you need to reinforce your patients for working hard and making progress. It is essential that your patients understand that they brought on the changes in OCD symptoms and mood, rather then crediting the improvement to you as the therapist. Clarifying how your patients accomplished the gains at the end of treatment will strengthen their self-efficacy beliefs and further consolidate gains. Talk about the specific actions and strategies that seemed to produce the most progress.

Preventing Relapse in the Future

Give your patients information about what the likely course of the OCD will be, depending on the extent of remaining OCD symptoms.

T: It is unlikely that you will walk out today free of your OCD. However, you have observed a significant decrease in the severity of your OCD symptoms. You now have the tools to continue to help yourself in these next several months. Research shows that people treated with cognitive therapy generally maintain their treatment gains, and some patients continue to show improvement in the months after treatment ends.

You should also address any unrealistic expectations your patient might have.

T: Don't expect that your progress over the next few months will be a straight course. Expect ups and downs, and try to avoid day-to-day comparisons.

This will help your patient not overreact if minor setbacks occur. If it seems useful, you can refer to the Graph of Progress in Therapy handout to illustrate that it is normal to have low points. You might also wish to suggest that setbacks usually get shorter and shorter and are less severe as time passes. It's important to take the big picture into account.

In addition, you and your patient should discuss the difference between a lapse and a relapse.

T: A lapse is a temporary period during which some of the OCD behaviors return. Just because you start to do a ritual does not mean that you will return to where you were before treatment. A temporary return of OCD symptoms may only be a sign that something stressful is going on in your life. We can set up periodic calls to check on your progress and troubleshoot if we need to. If you encounter problems you want to discuss or have questions, feel free to call me, but I think you are doing really well at this point.

Be careful not to imply that your patient is dependent on your help.

Coping with Stressors

Encourage your patient to identify potentially stressful situations that might exacerbate residual OCD symptoms. Examples might be difficult interpersonal situations or expectations, extra responsibilities, new media information about a harmful situation, or a serious loss. Ask your patient to describe what they anticipate their initial reactions might be to such circumstances in their lives. Identify the possible cognitive errors or mistaken interpretations in these reactions and inquire about alternative ways of thinking or interpreting situations. It may be helpful to ask your patient to anticipate potential problems and practice coping strategies through visualization.

Remind your patients of strategies that were helpful in the past and encourage them to use these to deal with setbacks. For example, suggest that your patients begin with self-monitoring of intrusions and interpretations when these occur. Are the interpretations faulty? If so, what techniques were useful in the past to evaluate them? Ask your patients to consider how they could conduct specific behavioral experiments with testable predictions in response to stressors. Plan a specific sequence in which your patients continue to evaluate themselves cognitively and behaviorally until the faulty interpretations are replaced with more adaptive ones.

Write down the CT techniques that worked best during therapy, so your patient can take home a list of strategies for use in the future.

Problem Solving

Sometimes patients describe problems in their lives that exacerbate their OCD symptoms. If these types of problems might provoke relapse, you and your patient can concentrate on them during the final sessions. First, teach your patient the basic problem-solving method and then help your patient to actively apply the method to specific problems. Follow these basic steps:

- Specify or define the problem.

- Determine what special meanings this problem has and the automatic thoughts or beliefs provoked.

- Give a rational response to beliefs.

- List all possible solutions to the problem, even silly ones, without evaluating them yet.

- Identify the solution that seems most likely to be effective.

- Implement the solution.

- Evaluate the outcome.

- If necessary, select another solution and implement it.

(Adapted from *Cognitive Therapy: Basics and Beyond*, by J. Beck, 1995, New York: Guilford Press. Copyright 1995 by J. Beck. Adapted with permission.)

One of our patients had contamination fears and was fearful of criticism from relatives at an upcoming family gathering. Whenever the criticism was about her OCD symptoms, it provoked depressed feelings and contributed to her negative beliefs ("I am defective/bad/crazy"), further increasing her OCD symptoms. She was encouraged to follow the above steps to identify and then implement potential solutions to manage her mood. This involved some creative brainstorming in which she decided to picture her critical mother as the Wicked Witch of the West, dressed in black and riding a broom. This helped defuse her mood and tune out the criticism, thereby avoiding a negative cycle.

Using Extra Time

For patients who formerly had very time-consuming OCD symptoms, plan what they can do with the extra time available. To identify potential problems, you can ask, "How is your life different now from how it used to be? How are you spending most of your time?"

If it is evident that your patient has not found healthy behaviors to replace OCD symptoms, you should prompt your patient to restart activities he or she used to do prior to the onset of OCD. Alternatively, you can discuss new activities your patient could engage in (joining a gym, finding a job, doing volunteer work, taking a class, and so on). It is essential that your patient use the new time in productive, satisfying, and engaging ways to help consolidate new behavioral patterns that are incompatible with OCD.

Scheduling Self-Treatment Sessions

You and your patient should also discuss a self-therapy plan. This can be implemented during the weeks between the two relapse prevention sessions, so your patient gains practice before treatment ends. If your patient meets with you at four o'clock on Monday afternoons, the patient can now use this time for self-therapy sessions. Using the same time slot may increase the likelihood that your patient remembers to engage in a self-session. Encourage your patient to schedule self-sessions and mark them on the calendar. At the end of treatment, suggest starting with weekly self-sessions, then tapering to twice a month, once a month, once a season, and finally, once a year. You should also review the advantages and disadvantages of doing self-sessions. For example, doing self-sessions helps your patient remember which techniques to use when they are needed and may prevent relapse. A disadvantage might be that it takes time. The Self-Coaching Session Form handout may serve as a useful guide in planning these sessions. You can also encourage your patient to reread relevant CT notes during these sessions and at times of stress.

Medication

Determine your patient's general plans regarding medication changes, if any. If your patient is considering reducing current medications, warn that if he or she reduces them too quickly, it may precipitate a relapse or an episode of depression. In most cases where clear benefit from CT is evident, recommend that current medications be continued for another six months, with a gradual tapering thereafter under the psychiatrist's supervision. With your patient's written permission, verify this recommendation by a phone consult with his or her psychiatrist before the end of treatment.

Support Groups

Provide your patient with information about support groups in the local area, as well as newsletters, self-help books, or other resources for maintaining treatment gains. Arrange for follow-up assessments, as appropriate to your patient's need.

ASSIGN HOMEWORK

After the first relapse prevention session, you might want to assign some homework to help your patient plan for the final session and beyond.

- Ask your patient to review all personal session forms to select the strategies that seemed to work best and to list all of them on a new summary form. Alternatively, you can recommend that your patient review the List of Cognitive Therapy Techniques handout and select those that have worked best during the therapy.

- Review the List of Cognitive Errors and Types of OCD Beliefs handouts to identify the specific types of thoughts and beliefs that have improved and others that need further work after treatment ends.

- Review the patient's cognitive model to determine how treatment has influenced the patient's beliefs and their relationship to OCD symptoms.

- Assign a review of all previous behavioral experiment forms and ask the patient to identify other experiments to be conducted before the final session and after treatment ends.

- Ask your patient to complete one or more core beliefs records to evaluate beliefs that continue to be somewhat problematic.

- Assign a problem-solving task using the Problem-Solving Worksheet to resolve one or more specific concerns pertinent to preventing relapse.

- Provide the Self-Coaching Session Form and ask your patient to try this out before the final session in preparation for using it after treatment ends.

- Ask your patient to attend a support group to determine whether it seems to be a good fit.

SUMMARY AND FEEDBACK

As in previous sessions, ask your patient to summarize the major points and to add any comments and questions about what he or she learned. In the final session, ask your patient to reflect over the entire course of therapy to describe what he or she has learned about him- or herself. Comment especially on progress and reinforce your patient for his or her work and learning during treatment. Ask for feedback about the treatment in general and invite comments about your own style. Finally, express honest feedback: "It was great working with you," "I'll miss working with you," "I'm so glad our work together helped," "I have a lot of confidence in you."

Appendix

OBSESSIVE COMPULSIVE SYMPTOMS RATING SCALE

Name: _____ Date: _____

My current treatment (please circle whatever is applicable): _____

1. Behavior Therapy
2. Cognitive Therapy
3. Medication
4. Other _____
5. Behavior Therapy & Cognitive Therapy
6. Behavior Therapy & Medication
7. Cognitive Therapy & Medication
8. Behavior Therapy, Cognitive Therapy, & Medication
9. None of the above

Each box below contains several thoughts or behaviors you may have experienced recently. Please circle all the symptoms in each box that you have had in the past week. Then rate the severity of these symptoms on the scale to the right of each box.

Example:

Forbidden or perverse sexual thoughts or images Forbidden or perverse sexual impulses about others Obsessions about homosexuality Sexual obsessions that involve children or incest Obsessions about aggressive sexual behavior towards others.	If you circled any symptoms in the box on the left, please mark the overall severity of these symptoms during the past week on the following scale: 0 1 2 3 4 5 6 7 8 9 10 no moderately very problem severe severe

Look at the example above. This person indicated having obsessions about homosexuality and aggressive sexual behavior towards others by circling those symptoms. Then the person rated the severity of the two symptoms combined as "very severe" by marking 10 on the rating scale.

1. Fear I might harm myself. 2. Fear I might harm other people. 3. I fear violent or horrific images in my mind. 4. I fear blurting out obscenities or insults 5. I fear doing something else embarrassing. 6. I fear I will act on an unwanted impulse (like stabbing a friend). 7. I fear I will steal things. 8. I fear I will be responsible for something else terrible happening (ie: fire, burglary). 9. I fear I will harm others because I'm not careful enough.	**10.** If you circled any symptoms in the box on the left, please mark the overall severity of these symptoms during the past week on the following scale: 0 1 2 3 4 5 6 7 8 9 10 no moderately very problem severe severe

11. I am concerned or disgusted with bodily waste or secretions (ie: urine, feces, saliva).	**19.** If you circled any symptoms in the box on the left, please mark the overall severity of these symptoms during the past week on the following scale:
12. I am concerned with dirt or germs.	
13. I am excessively concerned with environmental contaminants (ie: asbestos, radiation, toxic waste).	
14. I am excessively concerned with household chemicals (ie: cleaners, solvents).	0 1 2 3 4 5 6 7 8 9 10
15. I am excessively concerned with animals or insects.	no moderately very problem severe severe
16. I am bothered by sticky substances or residues.	
17. I am concerned that I will get ill because of contamination.	
18. I am concerned that I will get other ill because of contamination.	

20. I have forbidden or perverse sexual thoughts or images.	**25.** If you circled any symptoms in the box on the left, please mark the overall severity of these symptoms during the past week on the following scale:
21. I have forbidden or perverse sexual impulses about others.	
22. I have obsessions about homosexuality.	
23. I have sexual obsessions that involve children or incest.	0 1 2 3 4 5 6 7 8 9 10
24. I have obsessions about aggressive sexual behavior towards others.	no moderately very problem severe severe

26. I have an urge to save things.	**28.** If you circled any symptoms in the box on the left, please mark the overall severity of these symptoms during the past week on the following scale:
27. I have obsessions that if I don't save something, I'll make a mistake.	
	0 1 2 3 4 5 6 7 8 9 10
	no moderately very problem severe severe

29. I am concerned with sacrilege and blasphemy. 30. I have excess concern with right/wrong or morality.	**31.** If you circled any symptoms in the box on the left, please mark the overall severity of these symptoms during the past week on the following scale: 0 1 2 3 4 5 6 7 8 9 10 no moderately very problem severe severe
32. I am concerned about symmetry or exactness.	**33.** If you circled any symptoms in the box on the left, please mark the overall severity of these symptoms during the past week on the following scale: 0 1 2 3 4 5 6 7 8 9 10 no moderately very problem severe severe
34. I am concerned with a need to know or remember. 35. I have a fear of losing things.	**36.** If you circled any symptoms in the box on the left, please mark the overall severity of these symptoms during the past week on the following scale: 0 1 2 3 4 5 6 7 8 9 10 no moderately very problem severe severe
37. I have a fear of saying certain things. 38. I have a fear of not saying the right thing.	**39.** If you circled any symptoms in the box on the left, please mark the overall severity of these symptoms during the past week on the following scale: 0 1 2 3 4 5 6 7 8 9 10 no moderately very problem severe severe

40. I have superstitious ideas about lucky/unlucky numbers. 41. I have superstitious ideas about certain colors.	**42.** If you circled any symptoms in the box on the left, please mark the overall severity of these symptoms during the past week on the following scale: 0 1 2 3 4 5 6 7 8 9 10 no moderately very problem severe severe
43. I am concerned with getting an illness or disease.	**44.** If you circled any symptoms in the box on the left, please mark the overall severity of these symptoms during the past week on the following scale: 0 1 2 3 4 5 6 7 8 9 10 no moderately very problem severe severe
45. I experience intrusive (neutral, not horrific) images. 46. I experience intrusive nonsense sounds, words or music. 47. I am bothered by certain sounds or noises.	**48.** If you circled any symptoms in the box on the left, please mark the overall severity of these symptoms during the past week on the following scale: 0 1 2 3 4 5 6 7 8 9 10 no moderately very problem severe severe
49. I wash my hands excessively or in a ritualized way. 50. I have excessive showering, bathing, toothbrushing, grooming, or toilet routines. 51. I clean household items or other inanimate objects excessively. 52. I do other things to prevent or remove contact with contaminants.	**53.** If you circled any symptoms in the box on the left, please mark the overall severity of these symptoms during the past week on the following scale: 0 1 2 3 4 5 6 7 8 9 10 no moderately very problem severe severe

54. I check that I did not/will not harm others. 55. I check that I did not/will not harm myself. 56. I check that nothing terrible happened. 57. I check that I did not make a mistake. 58. I check some aspects of my physical condition or body.	**59.** If you circled any symptoms in the box on the left, please mark the overall severity of these symptoms during the past week on the following scale: 0 1 2 3 4 5 6 7 8 9 10 no moderately very problem severe severe
60. I reread or rewrite things. 61. I need to repeat routine activities (ie: going in or out doors, getting up or down from chairs	**62.** If you circled any symptoms in the box on the left, please mark the overall severity of these symptoms during the past week on the following scale: 0 1 2 3 4 5 6 7 8 9 10 no moderately very problem severe severe
63. I have counting compulsions.	**64.** If you circled any symptoms in the box on the left, please mark the overall severity of these symptoms during the past week on the following scale: 0 1 2 3 4 5 6 7 8 9 10 no moderately very problem severe severe
65. I have hoarding/collecting compulsions.	**66.** If you circled any symptoms in the box on the left, please mark the overall severity of these symptoms during the past week on the following scale: 0 1 2 3 4 5 6 7 8 9 10 no moderately very problem severe severe

67. I put things in order or arrange things.	**68.** If you circled any symptoms in the box on the left, please mark the overall severity of these symptoms during the past week on the following scale: 0 1 2 3 4 5 6 7 8 9 10 no moderately very problem severe severe

69. I need to touch, tap, or rub something. **70.** I have rituals involving blinking and staring.	**71.** If you circled any symptoms in the box on the left, please mark the overall severity of these symptoms during the past week on the following scale: 0 1 2 3 4 5 6 7 8 9 10 no moderately very problem severe severe

72. I pull my hair out. **73.** I pick at my skin. **74.** I carry out other self-damaging or self-mutilating behaviors.	**75.** If you circled any symptoms in the box on the left, please mark the overall severity of these symptoms during the past week on the following scale: 0 1 2 3 4 5 6 7 8 9 10 no moderately very problem severe severe

| 76. I do things mentally (other than checking/counting) to prevent harm to myself.

77. I do things mentally (other than checking/counting) to prevent harm to others.

78. I do things mentally (other than checking/counting) to prevent terrible consequences.

79. I pray to prevent harm to myself.

80. I pray to prevent harm to others.

81. I pray to prevent terrible consequences.

82. I mentally review events to prevent harm to myself.

83. I mentally review events to prevent harm to others.

84. I mentally review events to prevent terrible consequences. | **85.**

If you circled any symptoms in the box on the left, please mark the overall severity of these symptoms during the past week on the following scale:

0 1 2 3 4 5 6 7 8 9 10

no   moderately   very
problem   severe   severe |

| 86. I need to tell, ask, or confess things to obtain reassurance. | **87.**

If you circled any symptoms in the box on the left, please mark the overall severity of these symptoms during the past week on the following scale:

0 1 2 3 4 5 6 7 8 9 10

no   moderately   very
problem   severe   severe |

| 88. I engage in superstitious behaviors. | **89.**

If you circled any symptoms in the box on the left, please mark the overall severity of these symptoms during the past week on the following scale:

0 1 2 3 4 5 6 7 8 9 10

no   moderately   very
problem   severe   severe |

OBSESSIVE BELIEFS QUESTIONNAIRE—
EXTENDED (OBQ-EXT)

Patient's Name: _____ Date: _____

This inventory lists different attitudes or beliefs that people sometimes hold. Read each statement carefully and decide how much you agree or disagree with it. For each of the statements, choose the number on the rating scale matching the answer *that best describes how you think*. Because people are different, there are no right or wrong answers. To decide whether a given statement is typical of your way of looking at things, simply keep in mind what you are like *most of the time*.

OBQ Score Key
The following is a scoring key for the first six domains of this instrument. The numbers in parentheses identify the statements pertaining to each domain.

U=Tolerance for Uncertainty (3, 10, 26, 32, 35, 53, 57, 60, 63, 70, 73, 85, 87)

T=Threat Estimation (6, 9, 16, 30, 39, 40, 50, 52, 61, 68, 72, 79, 80, 82)

C=Control of Thoughts (2, 5, 8, 12, 15, 17, 29, 37, 44, 54, 59, 69, 75, 86)

I=Importance of Thoughts (1, 14, 18, 24, 34, 46, 48, 49, 55, 58, 64, 66, 76, 83)

R=Responsibility (4, 7, 20, 21, 23, 25, 27, 38, 41, 43, 47, 62, 67, 71, 77, 81)

P=Perfectionism (11, 13, 19, 22, 28, 31, 33, 36, 42, 45, 51, 56, 65, 74, 78, 84)

Use the following scale:

1	2	3	4	5	6	7
disagree very much	disagree moderately	disagree a little	neither agree nor disagree	agree a little	agree moderately	agree very much

As you use this scale, try to avoid using the middle point (4), but rather indicate whether you usually disagree or agree with the statements about your own beliefs and attitudes.

1.	Having bad thoughts or urges means I'm likely to act on them.	1 2 3 4 5 6 7
2.	Having control over my thoughts is a sign of good character.	1 2 3 4 5 6 7
3.	If I am uncertain, there is something wrong with me.	1 2 3 4 5 6 7
4.	If I imagine something bad happening, then I am responsible for making sure that it doesn't happen.	1 2 3 4 5 6 7

5.	If I don't control my unwanted thoughts, something bad is bound to happen.	1 2 3 4 5 6 7
6.	I often think things around me are unsafe.	1 2 3 4 5 6 7
7.	When I hear about a tragedy, I can't stop wondering if I am responsible in some way.	1 2 3 4 5 6 7
8.	Whenever I lose control of my thoughts, I must struggle to regain control.	1 2 3 4 5 6 7
9.	I am much more likely to be punished than are others.	1 2 3 4 5 6 7
10.	If I'm not absolutely sure of something, I'm bound to make a mistake.	1 2 3 4 5 6 7
11.	There is only one right way to do things.	1 2 3 4 5 6 7
12.	I would be a better person if I gained more control over my thoughts.	1 2 3 4 5 6 7
13.	Things should be perfect according to my own standards.	1 2 3 4 5 6 7
14.	The more distressing my thoughts are, the greater the risk that they will come true.	1 2 3 4 5 6 7
15.	I can have no peace of mind as long as I have intrusive thoughts.	1 2 3 4 5 6 7
16.	Things that are minor annoyances for most people seem like disasters for me.	1 2 3 4 5 6 7
17.	I must know what is going on in my mind at all times so I can control my thoughts.	1 2 3 4 5 6 7
18.	The more I think of something horrible, the greater the risk it will come true.	1 2 3 4 5 6 7
19.	In order to be a worthwhile person, I must be perfect at everything I do.	1 2 3 4 5 6 7
20.	When I see any opportunity to do so, I must act to prevent bad things from happening.	1 2 3 4 5 6 7
21.	It is ultimately my responsibility to ensure that everything is in order.	1 2 3 4 5 6 7
22.	If I fail at something, I am a failure as a person.	1 2 3 4 5 6 7
23.	Even if harm is very unlikely, I should try to prevent it at any cost.	1 2 3 4 5 6 7
24.	For me, having bad urges is as bad as actually carrying them out.	1 2 3 4 5 6 7
25.	I must think through the consequences of even my smallest actions.	1 2 3 4 5 6 7
26.	If an unexpected change occurs in my daily life, something bad will happen.	1 2 3 4 5 6 7

27.	If I don't react when I foresee danger, then I am to blame for any consequences.	1 2 3 4 5 6 7
28.	If I can't do something perfectly, I shouldn't do it at all.	1 2 3 4 5 6 7
29.	I must be ready to regain control of my thinking whenever an intrusive thought or image occurs.	1 2 3 4 5 6 7
30.	Bad things are more likely to happen to me than to other people.	1 2 3 4 5 6 7
31.	I must work to my full potential at all times.	1 2 3 4 5 6 7
32.	It is essential for me to consider all possible outcomes of a situation.	1 2 3 4 5 6 7
33.	Even minor mistakes mean a job is not complete.	1 2 3 4 5 6 7
34.	If I have aggressive thoughts or impulses about my loved ones, this means I may secretly want to hurt them.	1 2 3 4 5 6 7
35.	I must be certain of my decisions.	1 2 3 4 5 6 7
36.	If someone does a task better than I do, that means I failed the whole task.	1 2 3 4 5 6 7
37.	If I have an intrusive thought while I'm doing something, what I'm doing will be ruined.	1 2 3 4 5 6 7
38.	In all kinds of daily situations, failing to prevent harm is just as bad as deliberately causing harm.	1 2 3 4 5 6 7
39.	Avoiding serious problems (for example, illness or accidents) requires constant effort on my part.	1 2 3 4 5 6 7
40.	Small problems always seem to turn into big ones in my life.	1 2 3 4 5 6 7
41.	For me, not preventing harm is as bad as causing harm.	1 2 3 4 5 6 7
42.	I should be upset if I make a mistake.	1 2 3 4 5 6 7
43.	I should make sure others are protected from any negative consequences of my decisions or actions.	1 2 3 4 5 6 7
44.	If I exercise enough willpower, I should be able to gain complete control over my mind.	1 2 3 4 5 6 7
45.	For me, things are not right if they are not perfect.	1 2 3 4 5 6 7
46.	Having nasty thoughts means I am a terrible person.	1 2 3 4 5 6 7
47.	I often believe I am responsible for things that other people don't think are my fault.	1 2 3 4 5 6 7
48.	If an intrusive thought pops into my mind, it must be important.	1 2 3 4 5 6 7
49.	Thinking about a good thing happening can prevent it from happening.	1 2 3 4 5 6 7
50.	If I do not take extra precautions, I am more likely than others to have or cause a serious disaster.	1 2 3 4 5 6 7

51.	If I don't do as well as other people, that means I am an inferior person.	1 2 3 4 5 6 7
52.	I believe that the world is a dangerous place.	1 2 3 4 5 6 7
53.	In order to feel safe, I have to be as prepared as possible for anything that could go wrong.	1 2 3 4 5 6 7
54.	To avoid disasters, I need to control all the thoughts or images that pop into my mind.	1 2 3 4 5 6 7
55.	I should not have bizarre or disgusting thoughts.	1 2 3 4 5 6 7
56.	For me, making a mistake is as bad as failing completely.	1 2 3 4 5 6 7
57.	It is essential for everything to be clear-cut, even in minor matters.	1 2 3 4 5 6 7
58.	Having a blasphemous thought is as sinful as committing a sacrilegious act.	1 2 3 4 5 6 7
59.	I should be able to rid my mind of unwanted thoughts.	1 2 3 4 5 6 7
60.	I should be 100 percent certain that everything around me is safe.	1 2 3 4 5 6 7
61.	I am more likely than other people to accidentally cause harm to myself or to others.	1 2 3 4 5 6 7
62.	For me, even slight carelessness is inexcusable when it might affect other people.	1 2 3 4 5 6 7
63.	If something unexpected happens, I will not be able to cope with it.	1 2 3 4 5 6 7
64.	Having bad thoughts means I am weird or abnormal.	1 2 3 4 5 6 7
65.	I must be the best at things that are important to me.	1 2 3 4 5 6 7
66.	Having an unwanted sexual thought or image means I really want to do it.	1 2 3 4 5 6 7
67.	If my actions could have even a small effect on a potential misfortune, I am responsible for the outcome.	1 2 3 4 5 6 7
68.	Even when I am careful, I often think that bad things will happen.	1 2 3 4 5 6 7
69.	Having intrusive thoughts means I'm out of control.	1 2 3 4 5 6 7
70.	It is terrible to be surprised.	1 2 3 4 5 6 7
71.	Even if I think harm is very unlikely, I should still try to prevent it.	1 2 3 4 5 6 7
72.	Harmful events will happen unless I am very careful.	1 2 3 4 5 6 7
73.	I should go to great lengths to get all the relevant information before I make a decision.	1 2 3 4 5 6 7
74.	I must keep working at something until it's done exactly right.	1 2 3 4 5 6 7

75.	Being unable to control unwanted thoughts will make me physically ill.	1 2 3 4 5 6 7
76.	Having violent thoughts means I will lose control and become violent.	1 2 3 4 5 6 7
77.	To me, failing to prevent a disaster is as bad as causing it.	1 2 3 4 5 6 7
78.	If I don't do a job perfectly, people won't respect me.	1 2 3 4 5 6 7
79.	Even ordinary experiences in my life are full of risk.	1 2 3 4 5 6 7
80.	When things go too well for me, something bad will follow.	1 2 3 4 5 6 7
81.	If I take sufficient care, I can prevent any harmful accident from occurring.	1 2 3 4 5 6 7
82.	When anything goes wrong in my life, it is likely to have terrible effects.	1 2 3 4 5 6 7
83.	Having a bad thought is morally no different than doing a bad deed.	1 2 3 4 5 6 7
84.	No matter what I do, it won't be good enough.	1 2 3 4 5 6 7
85.	I often think that I will be overwhelmed by unforeseen events.	1 2 3 4 5 6 7
86.	If I don't control my thoughts, I'll be punished.	1 2 3 4 5 6 7
87.	I need the people around me to behave in a predictable way.	1 2 3 4 5 6 7

Reprinted from the Obsessive Compulsive Cognitions Working Group. First printed in *Cognitive Approaches to Obsessions and Compulsions: Theory, Assessment and Treatment* (477-488), edited by Randy Frost and Gail Steketee (2002). Kidlington, Oxford, UK: Elsevier Science Ltd. Reprinted with permission. Copyright 2002 by Elsevier.

OBQ Addendum		
Fear of Positive Experiences		
1.	For me, good things are always followed by bad ones.	1 2 3 4 5 6 7
2.	If I start to feel good, something will ruin it.	1 2 3 4 5 6 7
3.	I don't deserve to feel good.	1 2 3 4 5 6 7
4.	I should avoid pleasure because it might trigger bad thoughts.	1 2 3 4 5 6 7
5.	If I start to make progress, I won't be able to maintain my gains.	1 2 3 4 5 6 7
6.	Good feelings are always replaced by bad ones.	1 2 3 4 5 6 7
7.	I'll be punished for having a good time.	1 2 3 4 5 6 7
8.	If I become too confident, I will fail.	1 2 3 4 5 6 7
9.	If someone trusts me, eventually I'll let them down.	1 2 3 4 5 6 7

10.	When someone has confidence in me, eventually they'll be disappointed.	1 2 3 4 5 6 7
11.	If I am too successful, surely I'll fail.	1 2 3 4 5 6 7
12.	If I do well in treatment, eventually I'll relapse.	1 2 3 4 5 6 7
13.	If I get better, I won't be able to handle all of the expectations placed on me.	1 2 3 4 5 6 7
14.	I'd rather keep things the way they are than try something new.	1 2 3 4 5 6 7

Consequences of Anxiety

15.	It's important for me to control anxiety.	1 2 3 4 5 6 7
16.	I'm often afraid that I'll be overwhelmed by anxiety.	1 2 3 4 5 6 7
17.	If I get highly anxious, I could lose control of myself.	1 2 3 4 5 6 7
18.	If the worst happens, I won't be able to cope with it.	1 2 3 4 5 6 7
19.	I can't tolerate feeling nervous or tense.	1 2 3 4 5 6 7
20.	Anxiety will never go away.	1 2 3 4 5 6 7
21.	Too much tension could lead me to explode.	1 2 3 4 5 6 7
22.	Whenever I feel anxious, it must mean that danger is lurking about.	1 2 3 4 5 6 7
23.	If I get very anxious, I won't be able to manage it.	1 2 3 4 5 6 7
24.	When I cannot keep my mind on a task, I worry that I might be going crazy.	1 2 3 4 5 6 7
25.	I like to be in control of my emotions.	1 2 3 4 5 6 7
26.	When I feel nervous, I'm afraid I might be mentally ill.	1 2 3 4 5 6 7
27.	High anxiety is harmful.	1 2 3 4 5 6 7
28.	I'm not confident that I can control my anxiety.	1 2 3 4 5 6 7
29.	Once I get nervous, I think my anxiety might get out of hand.	1 2 3 4 5 6 7

OCD ASSESSMENT FORM

Patient's Name: _____ **Date:** _____

Before conducting this interview with the patient, refer to the pretreatment diagnostic interview for information about comorbid conditions (see chapter 2), and review the results of self-report questionnaires such as the YBOCS, OCRS, or BDI-II. Spend about forty-five minutes on this interview, and do not get caught up in details, as this is just the first step in conceptualizing the OCD symptoms.

Current OCD Symptoms

1. Can you tell me more about your OCD symptoms? What kind of thoughts, images, or impulses do you have that make you feel anxious or guilty? What triggers them? Are there any other types of intrusive thoughts that bother you?

2. What situations do you avoid because of your OCD?

3. What kind of compulsions do you do? Do you ask others for reassurance about things you have or have not done? Do you do any compulsions that other people cannot see, such as undoing one thought with another, praying, or saying "stop" in your mind? [Get examples of behavioral rituals like washing and checking, as well as examples of mental rituals.]

4. What triggers your compulsions? Do they only occur in certain situations? Do they sometimes occur just in response to a thought?

5.   What is the worst thing that would happen if you didn't avoid _____? What is the worst thing that would happen if you didn't do your rituals? [These questions get at catastrophic fears (e.g., hurting a loved one, going to jail, getting AIDS, dying, going to hell) that provoke OCD symptoms. Some patients may fear only that "it wouldn't feel right." If your patient reports forced consequences, ask the next follow-up question.]

6.   How likely do you think it is that this will really happen? Use a scale from 0 (not likely at all) to 100 (very likely, certain). [If you suspect a difference between a patient's gut versus rational estimate, ask for both, and then ask for an explanation of the difference between the two estimates. If insight seems to be a problem, ask what other people would say and why this differs from the patient's own views.]

History of OCD

7.   When did your obsessions and compulsions first begin? What do you remember about that time? Have your symptoms changed much since then? [Briefly discuss all current and past symptoms checked on the YBOCS or OCRS.]

8.   Has the severity of your symptoms fluctuated? If so, why, do you think?

9.   What's your theory about why your OCD symptoms began when they did? [Based on previous therapy, family explanations, or other sources, the patient's own theory may be genetic, biological (chemical imbalance, brain structures), family-based, or associated with historical experiences or traumas.]

10.   How have your OCD symptoms interfered with your life?

11. Do other members of your family have OCD? Have they had any other significant psychiatric problems?

Treatment History/Medications

12. Are you currently taking any medications? What kind and what dosage? Do they help your OCD?

13. What medications have you tried in the past? What kind and what dosage? Did they help? [Determine whether pharmacotherapy was adequate, including the patient's perception of benefits and problems.]

14. What sort of psychotherapy have you received up until now? What type and how much? Did it help? Why/why not?

15. Have you tried any other things to get rid of or control your symptoms? [Ask about other providers, diet, homeopathic remedies, etc., and treatment outcomes, as well as your patient's attitudes.]

Comorbid Conditions

16. Your interview indicated that you also have some problems with _____. Can you tell me about this? Do these symptoms affect your OCD symptoms? How?

17.   I understand you have had some traumatic experiences. Can you tell me about that?

Current Context

18.   Tell me a little about what your life is like now. What is your daily routine? How about your family life? Do you see friends often? How do you feel about your work?

19.   Were you raised in a particular religion? What was that like? What religion do you practice now, if any?

COGNITIVE THERAPY SESSION REPORT

Patient's Name: _____ Date: _____

Session No.: _____

Mood and symptom check:

Agenda:

Homework report and percent of homework completed:

Session focus:

    Cognitive domains and beliefs addressed:

    Cognitive strategies used:

Homework assigned:

Patient summary and feedback:

Goals for next or future sessions:

WHAT IS OCD?

People with OCD suffer from frequent obsessions and/or compulsions that cause marked distress or interfere with work or school, relationships, and everyday activities.

What Are Obsessions?

Obsessions are recurrent unwanted, intrusive thoughts, images, ideas, and urges or impulses that recurrently run through a person's mind. Frequently the obsessions don't make sense, are unpleasant, or repugnant. Typical obsessions include impulses to harm someone, including family members; sexual thoughts; fears about dirt, germs, contamination, infection, and contagion; recurrent thoughts that something has been done incorrectly; blasphemous thoughts; fear of losing something important; or concerns about symmetry and order. Obsessive thoughts, images, impulses, or urges provoke unpleasant feelings, such as anxiety, disgust, depression, and guilt. These feelings lead to strong urges to get rid of or neutralize the obsessions and/or avoid situations associated with them. Often the person develops rituals and avoidance behavior.

What Are Compulsions and What Is Avoidance Behavior?

Compulsions are usually done to reduce the distress caused by an obsession. However, the compulsive behavior is excessive, and often compulsions must be performed in a certain manner or even according to certain self-prescribed rules. Compulsions are maintained because they reduce tension, discomfort, depression, anxiety, or guilt associated with obsessions. Most sufferers recognize that their compulsions are excessive. Common compulsions include excessive hand washing, showering, cleaning, checking locks or appliances, superstitious behaviors, placing things in a certain order, and seeking reassurance about whether something has or has not happened. Many people have mental rituals to neutralize obsessive concerns. These can include praying silently, making lists, and mentally undoing, changing, or redoing a thought or image. In addition, people often develop other coping strategies to deal with OCD symptoms. For example, they avoid anything that triggers their OCD symptoms. Typical avoidance behaviors include not going to public restrooms, touching sharp objects, or using appliances.

These compulsive behaviors, mental rituals, and avoidance behaviors temporarily reduce the distress generated by obsessions. Because they help somewhat, these strategies are used over and over again. Because people always engage in these maladaptive coping strategies, they don't learn that the their obsessive fears and predictions wouldn't have come true anyway, even without rituals or avoidance. Unfortunately, this means that their obsessive fears never get disconfirmed. Just as obsessions vary in their frequency and intensity, compulsions may occur only rarely or they may consume many hours each day.

How Severe is OCD?

The severity of OCD can range from mild to severe. Some people have a minor problem that goes unnoticed by others. Some people on the severe end of the continuum perform compulsions for several hours per day and are completely housebound.

How common is OCD?

About two in one hundred people have OCD. This means that most of us probably know several people with OCD (although most sufferers are somewhat secretive about their problem and therefore we might not necessarily be aware that they have OCD).

What Is the Typical Course of OCD?

OCD usually begins in adolescence or early adulthood, but it can begin in childhood. For females the mean age of onset is twenty-two to twenty-three years old, and for males it is sixteen to seventeen years old. If OCD is not treated, the course is usually chronic, with waxing and waning of symptoms.

Sex Ratio

Both women and men develop OCD with about equal frequency.

What Are the Best Treatments for OCD?

In recent years, OCD treatments have dramatically improved. At present, about 70 percent of people with OCD benefit from the available treatments. Various approaches are used in the treatment of OCD, including medications that affect the serotonin system, exposure and response prevention (i.e., behavior therapy), and cognitive therapy. These methods are about equally effective in providing relief for OCD symptoms and may be used alone or in combination.

Cognitive Therapy. Research has shown that over 90 percent of people have intrusive thoughts that are similar to those experienced by people who have OCD. Nevertheless, most people don't develop OCD. One important difference between people who develop OCD and those who don't is how they react to their intrusive thoughts, images, or impulses. People who don't suffer from OCD realize that occasionally they have unusual thoughts, but these thoughts are unimportant and have no significant meaning. So, they don't pay any attention to these types of thoughts.

On the other hand, people who have OCD respond to their intrusive thoughts as if they were meaningful and important. Therefore the intrusive thoughts cause emotional discomfort (e.g., anxiety). The discomfort is then reduced by compulsions or avoidance behavior. Cognitive therapy focuses on developing alternative explanations for intrusive thoughts that are less anxiety provoking. After developing these alternative explanations, the therapy uses a variety of strategies to examine the explanations.

Although cognitive therapy is relatively new, published research studies suggest that it is as effective as other forms of treatment, including exposure and response prevention. Most of these studies have been conducted with people in individual outpatient treatment. While most people improve substantially with cognitive therapy, it's rare that symptoms disappear completely. Nevertheless, the severity and frequency of OCD symptoms are usually much improved by the end of treatment. Also, most people continue to improve after treatment ends if they continue to apply the strategies they learned during treatment.

Adapted with permission from an unpublished manuscript by Söchting, Whittal, and McLean (1996).

PERSONAL SESSION FORM

Patient's Name: _____ Date: _____

Session No.: _____

Agenda:

Main points:

Homework:

To discuss next time:

INTRUSIONS REPORTED BY ORDINARY PEOPLE

1. Causing intentional physical harm to self through impulsive actions
- Thought of jumping out of high-story window
- Thought of jumping through a closed window
- Thought of jumping off a cliff or tall building
- Thought of throwing myself down stairs
- Thought of jumping off bridge onto highway below
- Thought of deliberately crashing car into tree
- Thought of accelerating the car on the freeway without steering and seeing how fast I can go before I crash
- Thought of driving into a truck
- Thought of jumping in front of a car
- Thought of running car off the road or onto oncoming traffic
- Image of stepping in front of oncoming traffic
- Thought of cutting my leg with a knife
- Thought of poking something into my eyes
- Thought of cutting my stomach off
- Thought of slicing own throat
- Impulse to jump in front of train
- Impulse to jump on train tracks as the train comes into station

2. Causing intentional physical harm to others
- Impulse to attack certain persons
- Image of killing a loved one
- Idea of hurting someone I love
- Idea of doing something mean toward incapable person
- Thought of harming a sibling
- Thought of harming someone who does not deserve it
- Thought of pushing someone in front of train
- Thought of grabbing someone's head and smashing it against a wall
- Thought of wishing that a person would die
- Image of firing a rifle at someone or something
- Image of taking a meat cleaver and threatening someone in the family

- Thought of killing the parking officer
- Thought of hitting people whose views I strongly oppose
- Thought of beating up a stranger
- Sudden urge to kick a baby
- Thought of dropping a baby
- Thought of running over an animal
- Impulse to be violent toward children, especially smaller ones
- Impulse to throw a child out of a bus
- Impulse to violently attack and kill someone
- Impulse to run over a pedestrian who walks too slowly
- Impulse to slap someone who talks too much
- Thought of leaving the cat in the fridge
- Thought of putting the cat in the microwave
- Wishing someone would disappear off the face of the earth
- Wishing someone close was hurt or harmed
- Wishing spouse would die

3. Causing nonintentional harm to self or others
- Thought of causing an accident
- Thought of misjudging the speed of other cars and having a car accident
- Worrying that something goes wrong because of my own error
- Getting into an accident while driving with children
- Thought of accidentally hitting someone at a crossing
- Thought that someone leaving the house might die if I never said goodbye
- Thought that something terrible will happen because I'm not careful

4. Thoughts of physical harm or death to others
- Image of loved one being injured or killed
- Image of death or murder of family members
- Thought of receiving news of death of husband
- Image of wife in car accident
- Image of friend killed in accident
- Image of mother dying of cancer
- Image of father dying

- Thought of best friend committing suicide
- Image of best friend dead
- Image of best friend falling off a building and dying
- Image of my funeral or someone's I love
- Image of my grandparents dead
- Imagining what it would be like if my brother died
- Image of my family being tortured in front of me
- Image of my family being killed in car crash
- Image of parents dying in earthquake
- Image of my son in an avalanche
- Thought of my boyfriend in a car accident
- Thought of my boyfriend being in a hospital
- Image of my sister being raped
- Thought of my sister being murdered by her boyfriend
- Thought that my family will die
- Thought that my friends will die
- Thought of my children being abducted
- Image of baby being thrown down stairs
- Thought of plane crashing with friends in it
- Image of my cat being ripped apart by a dog
- Image that my dog had to get put down or died
- Thought that probability of my plane crashing would be minimized if a relative had such an accident
- Fear of harm to husband and child through exposure to asbestos
- Thinking that loved one will die because I've thought about what I'd do if they did
- Idea that thinking of horrible things happening to a child will cause it to happen
- Thought that something terrible will happen to family member if I ignore her

5. Thoughts of physical harm or death to self
- Thinking of dying and then going to funeral to see who would attend
- Thought of the effect of my death on others around me
- Thought of being murdered
- Thought of being raped
- Image of being eaten by shark

- Thought of being poked in eye by an umbrella
- Image of objects flying into my eye
- Thought of someone following me at night
- Image that I got run over
- Thought of having a car accident
- Thought of someone attacking me while I'm walking alone
- Thought of being attacked at night
- Thought of knives slitting my throat
- Thought of myself dying suddenly
- Thought of being trapped in a car under water
- Thought of car bursting into flames while I am driving
- Thought of suffocating from sheets falling down on me
- Image of tripping at top of steps and falling
- Thought of being in a car accident with brothers
- Thought of being attacked by stranger
- Thought of plane I'm on crashing
- Thought of getting strangled

6. Being contaminated
- Thought of catching a disease from public pools
- Thought of catching diseases from various places
- Thought of having a disease
- Thought that use of public bathrooms will cause me harm
- Thoughts I may have caught a disease from touching toilet seat
- Thought of dirt that is always on my hand
- Thought of contracting a disease from contact with a sick person
- Thought of hands being contaminated after using toilet
- Thought of harm to self through exposure to asbestos

7. Causing social difficulties through impulsive actions
- Idea of insulting/abusing family/friends
- Urge to insult friend for no apparent reason
- Thought of saying something rude/insulting
- Thought of being rude in front of friends

- Thought of swearing rudely at my family
- Image of screaming at my relatives
- Impulse to say something hurtful
- Thought of swearing/yelling at my boss
- Thought I might have ruined a relationship with a friend
- Impulse to call my girlfriend and break up
- Thoughts of doing something embarrassing in public by accident, like forgetting to wear a top
- Impulse to say something nasty and damning to someone
- Impulse to push people away in a crowd
- Impulse to shout at and abuse someone
- Impulse to say rude things to people
- Impulse to say inappropriate things
- Impulse to do something shameful or terrible
- Idea of blaming coworker for my own mistakes

8. Doubts about safety at home and in car

- Thought that I left door unlocked
- Thought that I haven't locked the house up properly
- Thought of my house getting broken into while I'm not home
- Thought that I left appliance on and caused a fire
- Thought that I left iron on
- Thought of leaving my crimper on the carpet and forgetting to pull out plug
- Thought of electrical appliances catching fire while I'm not home
- Thought of having left heater and stove on and causing a fire
- Thought that my house has burned down and I've lost everything I own
- Thoughts that I didn't correctly put out an open fire
- Thoughts I've left something on or unlocked
- Thought that I have left the electric blanket on
- Thought that I have left car unlocked
- Thought that I haven't put my hand brake on properly and my car will crash into traffic while I'm away
- Thought that I lost my car key and caused the car to get stolen
- Thought that I forgot to pay for parking
- Thought that someone will break in and hurt self or family
- Thought that I left car lights on

9. Deviation from moral codes (intentional or nonintentional)

- Thought of doing something bad
- Thought contrary to my moral beliefs
- Thoughts which are contrary to religious beliefs
- Being thoughtless about others
- Idea of not being nice all the time to everyone
- Thought of intense anger toward someone, related to a past experience
- Hoping someone doesn't succeed
- Thinking I'm better than other people
- Thought of turning my back on a friend

10. Losing control or acting out of character

- Thought of being on a swing and not being able to mentally control it; it goes around instead of backwards and forwards
- Image of myself singing at friend's funeral
- Impulse to do something out of character
- Thought that I'll get out of control
- Thoughts of smashing a table full of crafts made of glass
- Thought of doing something dramatic like robbing a bank

11. Doubts about memory

- Thoughts that I have forgotten something I need when I already checked
- Thought that I've forgotten something once I've left home
- Thought of locking my keys inside my house
- Thought that I've forgotten something important
- Thought that I don't have my bus money when I know I do
- Thought that I haven't got any money when it's time to pay for something

12. Impulse to leave

- Impulse to just keep driving and never tell anyone I was leaving
- Impulse to pack my bags, go overseas, and cut off all ties
- Image of running away from home
- Impulse to drop everything and lead a different life

13. General negative thoughts and thoughts about failure

- Thought of my father losing everything he has worked for
- Thoughts of being alone with no one
- Thought that I will leave everything to the last minute and fail the university year
- Thought of past embarrassment, humiliation, or failure
- Thought of upsetting incident
- Thought of disappointing friends
- Thought of losing all my hair
- Thought of myself becoming a worthless person
- Thought of becoming homeless/a derelict

14. Sexual thoughts

- Thoughts of acts of violence in sex
- Sexual impulse toward attractive females, known and unknown
- Thought of "unnatural" sexual acts
- Impulse to sexually assault a female, known and unknown
- Impulse to engage in sexual practices that involve pain to the partner
- Image involving sex with inappropriate partners
- Image of penis
- Image of sex with the ugly people on the bus
- Unwanted sexual urge/image
- Thought of sex with stepsister
- Image of sex with a teacher
- Image of cheating on partner
- Thought of sleeping with someone I don't like
- Image of sex with opposite-sex friend

15. Symmetry/exactness/rightness thoughts

- Thought about objects not arranged perfectly

Compiled with permission from Kyrios (personal communication, 2000), Thordarson (personal communication, 1999), and Rachman and de Silva (1978).

RITUALS AND NEUTRALIZATION STRATEGIES

The following are examples of compulsive rituals and strategies for neutralizing or undoing obsessive thoughts, images, and impulses.

Overt Behaviors

- Checking
- Staring at something
- Seeking information excessively (e.g., on the Internet)
- Repeating or redoing an action
- Repeating questions or statements
- Confessing
- Washing
- Cleaning
- Counting aloud
- Collecting or saving things
- Arranging things in order
- Making a list
- Engaging in distracting activities
- Saying a prayer aloud
- Saying "stop" aloud

Mental Activities

- Praying silently
- Mentally reviewing events or procedures
- Reassuring yourself
- Making a mental list
- Counting in your mind
- Performing a mental activity to remove a thought
- Repeatedly thinking an activity through logically
- Replacing one thought or image with another
- Suppressing or stopping thoughts

COGNITIVE TRIANGLE

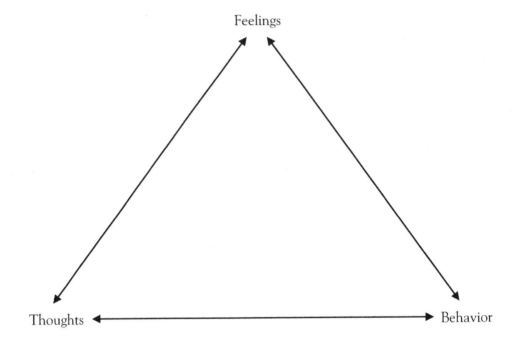

COGNITIVE MODEL OF OCD

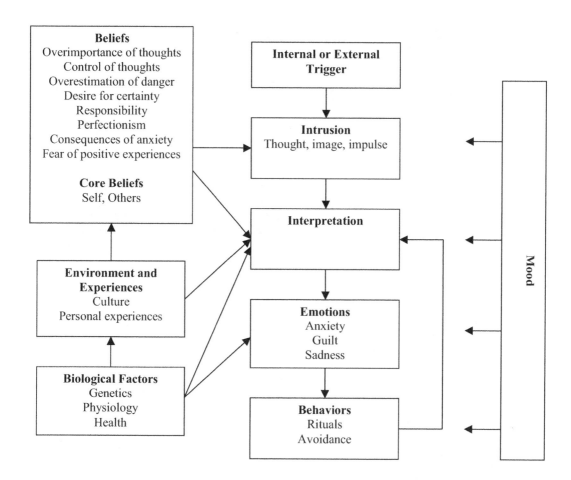

COGNITIVE MODEL OF OCD—BLANK FORM

Patient's Name: _____   Date: _____

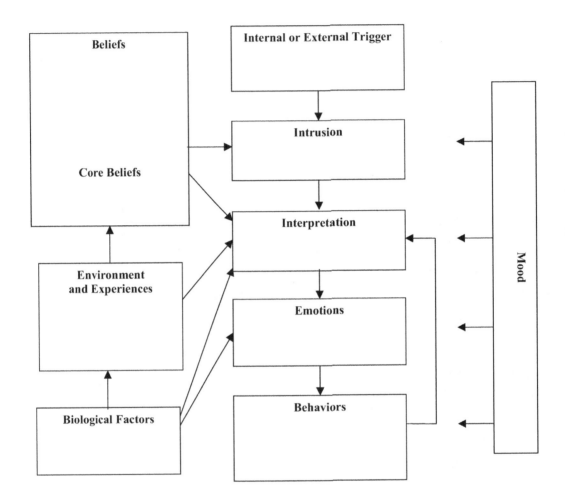

GRAPH OF PROGRESS IN THERAPY

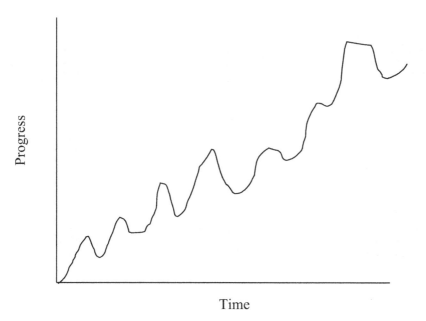

This graph is adapted from *Cognitive Therapy: Basics and Beyond* (p. 270), by J. Beck, 1995, New York: Guilford Press. Copyright 1995 by Guilford Press. Adapted with permission.

TREATMENT CONTRACT

Patient: I agree to work toward a goal of learning to identify and correct my interpretations of intrusive thinking and associated actions to relieve OCD symptoms. To accomplish this goal, I agree to work deliberately and regularly with my therapist on the following tasks:

1. Attend therapy sessions as mutually scheduled by us

2. Set the agenda for each session

3. Learn to identify my interpretations of obsessive ideas and compulsive behaviors

4. Learn to evaluate the usefulness and validity of these interpretations

5. Learn techniques to help change these interpretations and beliefs

6. Decide on and complete cognitive homework as agreed with my therapist

7. Give my therapist feedback

8. Plan strategies for maintaining benefits of therapy with my therapist

9. Not start any medication without notifying my therapist

10. Complete all assessments in a timely manner

I agree to the above-described treatment plan.

Signature: _____ Date: _____

Therapist: I agree to assist _____ in working toward the goal of learning to identify, evaluate, and correct interpretations about obsessive ideas and compulsions to reduce OCD symptoms. To accomplish this goal, I agree to:

1. Attend sessions of treatment as mutually scheduled by us

2. Determine the plan for each session in consultation with my patient

3. Assist my patient in identifying interpretations of obsessive ideas and compulsive behavior

4. Assist my patient in developing alternative thinking patterns and in reducing obsessive and compulsive symptoms.

5. Assign homework in consultation with my patient

6. Review assigned homework from the previous session

7. Review the progress with my patient and determine the next steps in treatment

8. Plan strategies with my patient to maintain benefits of therapy

I agree to the above-described treatment plan.

Signature: _____ Date: _____

TYPES OF OCD BELIEFS

Overimportance of thoughts. Some individuals attach too much importance to particular kinds of thoughts, mistakenly believing that normal people don't have these thoughts. They may also experience thought-action fusion or the almost magical idea that simply having a thought or urge increases the likelihood that it will come true ("Thinking about stabbing someone makes me more likely to do it").

Control of thoughts. Beliefs about the overimportance of thoughts lead naturally to beliefs about the necessity of controlling them and also to the need to control your actions. Moreover, efforts to control particular thoughts usually result in a rebound effect; trying to suppress or block thoughts actually makes them recur more frequently.

Overestimation of danger. OCD sufferers often overestimate the likelihood of danger and of making mistakes and presume the worst outcomes. In contrast to most people who presume they are safe unless there is clear evidence of danger, OCD patients appear to assume the reverse; that is, a situation is dangerous unless proven safe. This is a difficult problem, for guarantees of safety are nearly impossible to obtain. Rituals to achieve this guarantee require extensive repetition, since there is always room for error, even for the most careful people. Individuals with OCD may also employ unusual methods for estimating the likelihood of harm, relying more heavily on recent salient events (a newspaper article; something someone told them) to make predictions rather than taking into account the objective frequency of events over time.

Desire for certainty. Because they overestimate threat, OCD patients have difficulty tolerating ambiguous situations and tend to doubt the adequacy of their decisions and actions. Related to this problem are beliefs that it is important to be certain about things. The patient might believe that he or she lacks the capacity to cope with change and will not be able to function in situations that are inherently ambiguous.

Responsibility. Responsibility refers to the belief that you possess pivotal power to cause or prevent particular unwanted outcomes, often with moral overtones. People with OCD are often as concerned about failing to prevent a bad outcome (sins of omission) as about directly causing it to happen (sins of commission). They may view responsibility for feared outcomes as exclusively theirs, rather than being shared with others. Excessive assumption of responsibility produces guilt, which compulsions are often used to relieve.

Perfectionism. Perfectionistic attitudes presume that it is both possible and desirable to find an exact solution to every problem. People may believe that even minor mistakes will have serious consequences. Early experiences with rigid teachings might lead them to be more vulnerable to perfectionistic standards and fears of failing. Perfectionism has been linked to checking, cleaning, repeating and ordering rituals, and may be an important feature of obsessions and compulsions about needing to know, "just right" phenomena, and the need for symmetry.

Consequences of anxiety. Irrational beliefs about being unable to tolerate anxiety or emotional discomfort may play a role in the development and maintenance of OCD. Extreme variants of these beliefs include fears that the person will lose control and "go crazy" or become mentally ill, although there is no evidence to support such fears. Other variants include fears that anxiety will render the person nonfunctional or cause unusual embarrassment. Susceptible individuals may view rituals and avoidance as their only available coping strategy to prevent anxiety from causing one of these outcomes.

Fear of positive experiences. As they make progress in treatment, some people with OCD express concern that they do not deserve or will not be able to sustain the positive experiences they have briefly experienced. Although sometimes merely superstitious ("good events will be followed by bad ones"), these doubts often take on a moral character, as people believe they are unworthy of having guilt-free or anxiety-free enjoyment of life.

LIST OF COGNITIVE ERRORS

1. **Polarized, or all-or-nothing thinking** (also called black and white or dichotomous thinking): You see things in only two categories and there is no middle
   ground (e.g., matters are either good or bad, safe or toxic, clean or
   contaminated).

2. **Labeling:** Labeling is a version of all-or-nothing thinking. Instead of saying, "This
   didn't go well. I misunderstood," attach a global negative label to yourself: "I'm a
   failure."

3. **Overgeneralization:** You interpret one isolated current situation as a sequence of
   bad events by using words like "always" or "never" when you describe it or think
   about it.

4. **Mental filter (also called filtering or selective abstraction):** You focus on an
   isolated negative detail and selectively attend to it, so that ultimately your interpretation of everything that's happening becomes distorted.

5. **Discounting the positive:** You disqualify positive events and assume that they
   don't matter. If you accomplish something you could be proud of, you tell yourself
   that it wasn't that important, or that anyone could have done it.

6. **Mind reading:** You automatically assume that others are reacting negatively to
   you without having any evidence for it.

7. **Fortune-telling (also called catastrophizing):** You automatically assume that
   things will turn out terribly before they even start and without having any
   evidence for this prediction.

8. **Magnification:** You blow out of proportion your shortcomings and problems
   (usually this is goes along with minimizing or discounting all your positive
   qualities).

9. **Emotional reasoning:** You assume that your feelings reflect the way things really
   are. "I feel guilty, so I must have done something wrong. I feel anxious, therefore
   the situation must be dangerous."

10. **"Should" and "must" statements (also called imperatives):** You expect that
    things should be the way you want them to be. If they are not, you feel guilty. "I
    shouldn't have made so many mistakes."

This list is adapted from *Cognitive Therapy: Basics and Beyond* (p. 119), by J. Beck, 1995, New
York: Guilford Press (and from A. Beck). Copyright 1995 by Guilford Press. Adapted with
permission.

THOUGHT RECORD AND GUIDE—FIVE COLUMN

Patient's Name: _____   Date: _____

Situation/Trigger Describe what led to the intrusive thought and unpleasant emotion.	Intrusion Describe unwanted thought, image, or impulse.	Interpretation a) Write interpretation. b) Rate belief in interpretation, 0 to 100 percent.	Emotion a) Specify emotions. b) Rate strength of emotion, 0 to 100 percent.	Compulsions/Avoidance a) Rate urge to neutralize or avoid, 0 to 100 percent b) Specify rituals or avoidance.

This table is adapted from *Cognitive Therapy: Basics and Beyond* (p. 126), by J. Beck, 1995, New York: Guilford Press. Copyright 1995 by J. Beck. Adapted with permission.

Instructions:

1. **Situation/trigger.** Describe the actual situation that caused the unpleasant emotion, or describe the flow of thoughts, the daydream, or the recollection that led to the intrusion and unpleasant emotion.

2. **Intrusion.** Describe the unwanted thought, image, or impulse that is unpleasant and difficult to get rid of.

3. **Interpretation.** This is your immediate reaction to the intrusion or the meaning you think it has. Write your interpretation of the intrusive thought. How strongly do you believe this thought, 0 to 100 percent?

4. **Emotion.** Describe what emotion(s) you had. How strong is this emotion, 0 to 100 percent?

5. **Compulsions/avoidance.** Rate your urge to engage in rituals, neutralization, or avoidance, 0 to 100 percent. If you engaged in rituals, neutralization, or avoidance, indicate what you did.

THOUGHT RECORD AND GUIDE—SEVEN COLUMN

Patient's Name: _____   Date: _____

Situation/ Trigger Describe what led to the intrusive thought and unpleasant emotion.	Intrusion Describe unwanted thought, image, or impulse.	Interpretation a) Write interpretation. b) Rate belief in interpretation, 0 to 100 percent.	Emotion a) Specify emotions. b) Rate strength of emotion, 0 to 100 percent.	Maladaptive Coping Strategies a) Rate urge to neutralize or avoid, 0 to 100 percent. b) Specify rituals or avoidance.	Rational Response a) Write rational response to interpretation. b) Rate belief in rational response, 0 to 100 percent.	Outcome a) Rerate interpretation, 0 to 100 percent. b) Specify and rate subsequent emotions, 0 to 100 percent.

This table is adapted from *Cognitive Therapy: Basics and Beyond* (p. 126), by J. Beck, 1995, New York: Guilford Press. Copyright 1995 by J. Beck. Adapted with permission.

Instructions:

1. **Situation/trigger.** Describe the actual situation that caused the unpleasant emotion, or describe the thoughts, ideas, or recollections that led to the unpleasant emotion.

2. **Intrusion.** Describe the unwanted thought, image, or impulse that is unpleasant and difficult to get rid of.

3. **Interpretation.** This is the immediate reaction that you have to the intrusion. Write your interpretation of the intrusive thought. How strongly do you believe this thought, 0 to 100 percent?

4. **Emotion.** Describe your emotion. How strong is this emotion, 0 to 100 percent?

5. **Maladaptive coping strategies.** Rate your urge to engage in maladaptive coping strategies, 0 to 100 percent. If you engaged in maladaptive neutralizing, rituals, coping, or avoidance, indicate what you did here.

Now, evaluate the interpretation by using strategies you have discussed with your therapist or by using the following questions:

- What is the evidence for and against the specific interpretation?

- Are my interpretations logical?

- Have I confused a thought with a fact?

- Are my interpretations of the situation realistic?

- What would be a more rational way of looking at that?

- Am I using all-or-nothing thinking?

- Am I confusing certainties with possibilities?

- Is my judgment based on the way I feel instead of facts?

- Have I emphasized the irrelevant factors?

- What would I tell a friend who told me this?

- What would a friend say to me?

- What could I tell myself?

- What are the advantages and disadvantages of this type of thinking?
  These questions are adapted from *Cognitive Therapy: Basics and Beyond* (p. 126), by J. Beck, 1995, New York: Guilford Press. Copyright 1995 by J. Beck. Adapted with permission.

6. **Rational response.** Write down your rational response to the interpretation. How strongly do you believe this thought, 0 to 100 percent?

7. **Outcome.** How credible is the original interpretation now, 0 to 100 percent? Which emotions does it cause and how strong are these, 0 to 100 percent?

STATES OF MIND DIAGRAM

Patient's Name: _____   Date: _____

Rational
Mind

Emotional
Mind

Wise
Mind

Rational thoughts   **Emotional thoughts**

_____   _____

_____   _____

_____   _____

_____   _____

Wise thoughts

_____

_____

_____

This diagram is adapted from the *Skills Training Manual for Treating Borderline Personality Disorder* (p. 109), by M. Linehan, 1993, New York: Guilford Press. Copyright 1993 by Guilford Press. Adapted with permission.

BEHAVIORAL EXPERIMENT FORM

Patient's Name: _____ **Date:** _____

1. Behavioral experiment to be completed:

   _____

   _____

2. Feared consequences (what you predict will happen):

   _____

   _____

3. Rate strength of belief in the feared consequences (from 0 to 100 percent):

   _____

4. Rate your discomfort (from 0 to 100 percent) at the beginning of the behavioral experiment: _____

5. How could you challenge your feared consequence/predictions? What alternative prediction could you make?

   _____

   _____

6. Rate your discomfort (from 0 to 100 percent) at the end of the behavioral experiment: _____

7. Actual consequences:

   _____

   _____

8. Did your predictions come true?

   _____

   _____

9. Was challenging the thought helpful? (If not, why not?)

   _____

   _____

Adapted with permission from an unpublished manuscript by Söchting, Whittal, and McLean (1996).

DOWNWARD ARROW FORM

Patient's Name: _____ Date: _____

Interpretation

1.

⬇ If that were true, what would that mean? *

2.

⬇ If that were true, what would that mean? *

3.

⬇ If that were true, what would that mean? *

4.

⬇ If that were true, what would that mean? *

5.

⬇ If that were true, what would that mean? *

6.

*Alternate wording for questions:

"What would it mean about you?"

"What's so bad about that?"

"What's the worst about that?"

THOUGHT-SUPPRESSION GRAPH

Patient's Name: _____ Date: _____

Number of intrusions

100 80 60 40 20

Day 1   Day 2   Day 3   Day 4   Day 5   Day 6   Day 7

CORE BELIEF FILTER

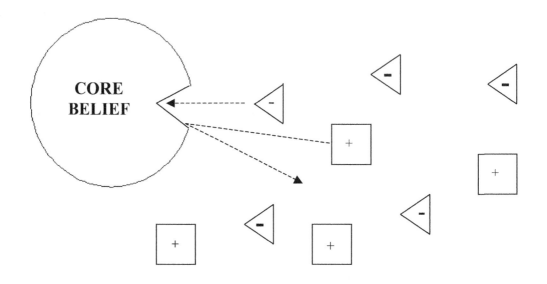

Negatively perceived information (triangles) is readily incorporated.

Positive information (squares) is deflected.

CORE BELIEFS RECORD

Patient's Name: _____ Date: _____

Old core belief 1: _____

How much do you believe this right now in your gut? (0 to 100 percent) _____

How much do you believe this right now rationally? (0 to 100 percent) _____

Alternative belief 1: _____

How much do you believe this right now in your gut? (0 to 100 percent) _____

How much do you believe this right now rationally? (0 to 100 percent) _____

Evidence that contradicts old core belief and supports new belief: _____

_____

Evidence that supports old core belief with a reframe (yes ..., but ...): _____

_____

Old core belief 2: _____

How much do you believe this right now in your gut? (0 to 100 percent) _____

How much do you believe this right now rationally? (0 to 100 percent) _____

Alternative belief 2: _____

How much do you believe this right now in your gut? (0 to 100 percent) _____

How much do you believe this right now rationally? (0 to 100 percent) _____

Evidence that contradicts old core belief and supports new belief: _____

_____

Evidence that supports old core belief with a reframe (yes ..., but ...): _____

_____

SELF-COACHING SESSION FORM

Name: _____   Date of session: _____

Mood check:

Important changes in symptoms:

Homework check: (How did I do on homework I set for myself last week? What got in my way? How can I learn from this experience for next time?)

What skills have I been practicing well?

Where am I still having troubles and what should I do about this?

What are my treatment goals for the coming week?

What homework assignment will help me meet these goals?

Date for next session:

(Don't forget to call my support person or coach if I have a problem.)

LIST OF COGNITIVE THERAPY TECHNIQUES

- ☐ Socratic questioning—thinking like a scientist or detective
- ☐ Identifying cognitive errors
- ☐ Using thought records to evaluate interpretations
- ☐ Review of the CT model
- ☐ Wise mind = rational + emotional thinking
- ☐ Courtroom technique
- ☐ Downward arrow
- ☐ Behavioral experiments
- ☐ Consulting an expert
- ☐ Double-standard technique
- ☐ Continuum technique
- ☐ Advantages and disadvantages
- ☐ Thought-suppression experiment
- ☐ Calculating the probability of harm/danger
- ☐ Betting money
- ☐ Conducting a survey
- ☐ Fill-in-the-blanks
- ☐ Pie chart
- ☐ Taking another's perspective
- ☐ Making extreme contrasts
- ☐ Retrospective review of the evidence
- ☐ Core belief filter
- ☐ Core beliefs record—developing alternative beliefs
- ☐ Reframing the evidence
- ☐ Restructuring early memories
- ☐ Historical testing of core beliefs
- ☐ Problem solving
- ☐ Psychoeducation
- ☐ Role-play

PROBLEM-SOLVING WORKSHEET

Patient's Name: _____ Date: _____

1. What is the problem?

2. What is the special meaning of this problem? What interpretations or beliefs does the problem provoke?

3. Rational response to the special meaning:

4. What possible solutions to the problem can you think of? Be creative and think of as many as possible.

5. Which solution is most likely to work best?

6. How and when will you try this solution?

7. What happened when you tried this solution?

8. If this solution didn't work well enough, what other solution from Step 4 should be tried?

References

Abramowitz, J. S. (1997). Effectiveness of psychological and pharmacological treatments for obsessive-compulsive disorder: A quantitative review. *Journal of Consulting and Clinical Psychology, 65,* 44-52.

Abramowitz, J. S. (2001). Treatment of scrupulous obsessions and compulsions using exposure and response prevention: A case report. *Cognitive and Behavioral Practice, 8,* 79-85.

Abramowitz, J. S. (2002). Treatment of obsessive thoughts and cognitive rituals using exposure and response prevention: A case study. *Clinical Case Studies, 1,* 6-24.

Abramowitz, J. S., & Foa, E. B. (1998). Worries and obsessions in individuals with obsessive-compulsive disorder with and without comorbid generalized anxiety disorder. *Behaviour Research and Therapy, 36,* 695-700.

Abramowitz, J. S., Franklin, M. E., Schwartz, S. A., & Furr, J. M. (2003). Symptom presentation and outcome of cognitive-behavioral therapy for obsessive-compulsive disorder. *Journal of Consulting and Clinical Psychology, 71,* 1049-1057.

American Psychiatric Association. (1994). *Diagnostic and statistical manual of mental disorders* (4th ed.). Washington, DC: Author.

Arntz, A., Rauner, M., & van den Hout, M. (1995). "If I feel anxious, there must be danger": Ex-consequentia reasoning in inferring danger in anxiety disorders. *Behaviour Research and Therapy, 33,* 917-925.

Baer, L. (1994). Factor analysis of symptom subtypes of obsessive compulsive disorder and their relation to personality and tic disorders. *Journal of Clinical Psychiatry, 55*(Suppl.), 18-23.

Basoglu, M., Lax, T., Kasvikis, Y., & Marks, I. M. (1988). Predictors of improvement in obsessive compulsive disorder. *Journal of Anxiety Disorders, 2,* 299-317.

Baxter, L. R., Schwartz, J. M., Bergman, K. S., Szuba, M. P., Guze, B. H., Mazziotta, J. C., et al. (1992). Caudate glucose metabolic rate changes with both drug and behavior therapy for obsessive-compulsive disorder. *Archives of General Psychiatry, 49*, 681-689.

Beck, A. T. (1976). *Cognitive therapy and emotional disorders*. New York: International Universities Press.

Beck, A. T., Steer, R. A., & Brown, G. K. (1996). *Beck Depression Inventory–second edition: Manual*. San Antonio, TX: Psychological Corporation.

Beck, J. (2005). *Cognitive therapy for challenging problems: What to do when the basics don't work*. New York: Guilford Press.

Beck, J. (1995). *Cognitive therapy: Basics and beyond*. New York: Guilford Press.

Bell, A. (1997). *The mind and heart in human sexual behavior: Owning and sharing our personal truths*. Northvale, NJ: Jason Aronson.

Bellodi, L., Scuito, G., Diaferia, G., Ronchi, P., & Smeraldi, E. (1992). Psychiatric disorders in the families of patients with obsessive-compulsive disorder. *Psychiatry Research, 42*, 111-20

Black, D. W., Monahan, P., Gable, J., Blum, N., Clancy, G., & Baker, P. (1998). Hoarding and treatment response in 38 nondepressed subjects with obsessive-compulsive disorder. *Journal of Clinical Psychiatry, 59*, 420-425.

Burns, D. D. (1980). *Feeling good: The new mood therapy*. New York: New American Library.

Burns, D. D. (1989). *Feeling good handbook*. New York: Morrow.

Calamari, J. E., Wiegartz, P. S., & Janeck, A. S. (1999). Obsessive-compulsive disorder subgroups: A symptom-based clustering approach. *Behaviour Research and Therapy, 37*(2), 113-125.

Carr, A. T. (1974). Compulsive neurosis: A review of the literature. *Psychological Bulletin, 81*, 311-318.

Chambless, D. L., & Steketee, G. (1999). Unpublished data, available from Gail Steketee, Boston University School of Social Work, 264 Bay State Rd., Boston, MA 02215.

Christensen, H., Hadzi-Pavlovic, D., Andrews, G., & Mattick, R. (1987). Behavior therapy and tricyclic medication in the treatment of obsessive-compulsive disorder: A quantitative review. *Journal of Consulting and Clinical Psychology, 55*, 701-711.

Ciarrocci, J. (1995) *The Doubting Disease: Help for Scrupulosity and Religious Compulsions*. New Jersey: Paulist Press International.

Clark, D. A., & Purdon, C. (1993). New perspectives for a cognitive theory of obsessions. *Australian Psychologist, 28*, 161-167.

Cordioli, A. V., Heldt, E., Bochi, D. B., Margis, R., de Sousa, M. B., Tonello, J. F., et al. (2003). Cognitive-behavioral group therapy in obsessive-compulsive disorder: A randomized clinical trial. *Psychotherapy and Psychosomatics, 72*, 211-216.

Cottraux, J., Mollard, E., Bouvard, M., Marks, I., Sluys, M., Nury, A. M., et al. (1990). A controlled study of fluvoxamine and exposure in obsessive compulsive disorder. *International Clinical Psychopharmacology, 5*, 17-30.

Cottraux, J., Note, I., Yao, S. N., Lafont, S., Note, B., Mollard, E., et al. (2001). A randomized controlled trial of cognitive therapy versus intensive behavior therapy in obsessive compulsive disorder. *Psychotherapy and Psychosomatics, 70*, 288-297.

de Silva, P., & Marks, M. (1999). The role of traumatic experiences in the genesis of obsessive-compulsive disorder. *Behaviour Research and Therapy, 37*, 941-951.

Di Nardo, P. A., Brown, T. A., & Barlow, D. H. (1994). *Anxiety disorders interview schedule for DSM-IV: Lifetime version (ADIS-IV-L)*. San Antonio, TX: Psychological Corporation.

Eisen, J. L., Goodman, W. K., Keller, M. B., Warshaw, M. G., DeMarco, L. M., Luce, D., et al. (1999). Patterns of remission and relapse in obsessive-compulsive disorder: A two-year prospective study. *Journal of Clinical Psychiatry, 60,* 346-351.

Eisen, J. L., & Rasmussen, S. A. (1993). Obsessive compulsive disorder with psychotic features. *Journal of Clinical Psychiatry, 54,* 373-379.

Ellis, A. (1962). *Reason and emotion in psychotherapy.* New York: Lyle Stuart.

Emmelkamp, P. M. G., & Beens, H. (1991). Cognitive therapy with obsessive-compulsive disorder: A comparative evaluation. *Behaviour Research and Therapy, 29,* 293-300.

Emmelkamp, P. M. G., Visser, S., & Hoekstra, R. (1988). Cognitive therapy vs. exposure in vivo in the treatment of obsessive-compulsives. *Cognitive Therapy and Research, 12,* 103-114.

First, M. B., Spitzer, R. L., Gibbon, M., & Williams, J. B. W. (1995). *Structured clinical interview for DSM-IV axis I disorders–patient edition.* New York: Biometrics Research Department, New York Psychiatric Institute.

Foa, E. B. (1979). Failure in treating obsessive compulsives. *Behaviour Research and Therapy, 17,* 169-176.

Foa, E. B., Franklin, M. E., & Kozak, M. J. (1998). Psychosocial treatments for obsessive-compulsive disorder: Literature review. In R. P. Swinson, M. M. Antony, S. Rachman, & M. A. Richter (Eds.), *Obsessive compulsive disorder: Theory, research and treatment* (pp. 258-276). New York: Guilford Press.

Foa, E. B., & Kozak, M. J. (1986). Emotional processing of fear: Exposure to corrective information. *Psychological Bulletin, 99,* 20-35.

Foa, E. B., & Kozak, M. J. (1993). Pathological anxiety: Meaning and the structure of fear. In N. Bierbaumer & A. Ohman (Eds.), *The structure of emotion: Physiological, cognitive, and clinical aspects* (pp.110-121). Seattle, WA: Hogrefe and Huber.

Freeston, M. H., & Ladouceur, R. (1997). *The cognitive behavioral treatment of obsessions: A treatment manual.* Unpublished manuscript, École de psychologie, Université Laval, Canada.

Freeston, M. H., Ladouceur, R., Gagnon, F., Thibodeau, N., Rhéaume, J. Letarte, H., et al. (1997). Cognitive-behavioral treatment of obsessive thoughts: A controlled study. *Journal of Consulting and Clinical Psychology, 65,* 405-413.

Freeston, M. H., Ladouceur, R., Thibodeau, N., & Gagnon, F. (1991). Cognitive intrusions in a non-clinical population: Response style, subjective experience, and appraisal. *Behaviour Research and Therapy, 29,* 585-597.

Freeston, M. H., Rhéaume, J., & Ladouceur, R. (1996). Correcting faulty appraisals of obsessional thoughts. *Behavior Research and Therapy, 34,* 433-446.

Friday, N. (1998). *My secret garden.* New York: Simon & Schuster.

Frost, R. O., & Steketee, G. (1997). Perfectionism in obsessive-compulsive disorder patients. *Behaviour Research and Therapy, 35,* 291-296.

Gershuny, B. S., & Sher, K. J. (1995). Compulsive checking and anxiety in a nonclinical sample: Differences in cognition, behavior, personality, and affect. *Journal of Psychopathology and Behavioral Assessment, 32,* 19-38.

Goodman, W. K., Price, L. H., Rasmussen, S. A., Mazure, C., Fleischman, R. L., Hill, C. L., et al. (1989). The Yale-Brown obsessive compulsive scale. I. Development, use, reliability. *Archives of General Psychiatry, 46,* 1006-1011.

Guenbeger, D., & Padesky C. A. (1995). *Mind over Mood: Change How You Feel by Changing the Way You Think.* New York: Guilford Press.

Guidano, V. F., & Liotti, G. (1983). *Cognitive processes and emotional disorders.* New York: Guilford Press.

Hartl, T. L., & Frost, R. O. (1999). Cognitive-behavioral treatment of compulsive hoarding: A multiple baseline experimental case study. *Behaviour Research and Therapy, 37,* 451-461.

Helzer, J. E., Robins, L. N., & McEvoy, L. (1987). Post-traumatic stress disorder in the general population. Findings of the epidemiologic catchment area survey. *New England Journal of Medicine, 317,* 1630-1634.

Hiss, H., Foa, E. B., & Kozak, M. J. (1994). Relapse prevention program for treatment of obsessive-compulsive disorder. *Journal of Consulting and Clinical Psychology, 62,* 801-808.

Horowitz, M. J. (1975). Intrusive and repetitive thoughts after experimental stress: A summary. *Archives of General Psychiatry, 32,* 1457-1463.

Jones, M. K., & Menzies, R. G. (1997). The cognitive mediation of obsessive-compulsive handwashing. *Behaviour Research and Therapy, 35,* 843-850.

Kolada, J. L., Bland, R. C., & Newman, S. C. (1994). Obsessive-compulsive disorder. *Acta Psychiatrica Scandinavica, 89*(Suppl.), 24-35.

Kozak, M. J., & Foa, E. B. (1994). Obsessions, overvalued ideas, and delusions in obsessive compulsive disorder. *Behavior Research and Therapy, 32,* 343-353.

Kozak, M. J., & Foa, E. B. (1997). *Mastery of obsessive-compulsive disorder: A cognitive behavioral approach.* San Antonio, TX: Psychological Corporation.

Kozak, M. J., Foa, E. B., & McCarthy, P. R. (1988). Assessment of obsessive-compulsive disorder. In C. Last & M. Hersen (Eds.), *Handbook of anxiety disorders* (pp. 87-108). New York: Pergamon Press, Inc.

Kozak, M. J., Liebowitz, M. R., & Foa, E. B. (2000). Cognitive behavior therapy and pharmacotherapy for obsessive-compulsive disorder: The NIMH-sponsored collaborative study. In W. K. Goodman, M. V. Rudorfer, & J. D. Maser (Eds.), *Obsessive-compulsive disorder: Contemporary issues in treatment.* (pp. 501-530). Mahwah, NJ: Lawrence Erlbaum Associates.

Leckman, J. F., Grice, D. E., Boardman, J., Zhang, H., Vitale, A., Bondi, C., et al. (1997). Symptoms of obsessive-compulsive disorder. *American Journal of Psychiatry, 154,* 911-7.

Linehan, M. M. (1993). *Skills training manual for borderline personality disorder.* New York: Guilford Press.

Lucey, J. V., Butcher, G., Clare, A. W., & Dinan, T. G. (1994). The clinical characteristics of patients with obsessive-compulsive disorder: A descriptive study of an Irish sample. *Irish Journal of Psychological Medicine, 11,* 11-14.

March, J., Frances, A., Carpenter, D., & Kahn, D. (1997). Expert consensus guidelines: Treatment of obsessive compulsive disorder. *Journal of Clinical Psychology, 58,* 1-72.

Mataix-Cols, D., Marks, I. M., Greist, J. H., Kobak, K. A., & Baer, L. (2002). Obsessive-compulsive symptom dimensions as predictors of compliance with and response to behaviour therapy: Results from a controlled trial. *Psychotherapy and Psychosomatics, 71,* 255-262.

Mataix-Cols, D., Rauch, S. L., Manzo, P. A., Jenike, M. A., & Baer, L. (1999). Use of factor-analyzed symptom dimensions to predict outcome with serotonin reuptake inhibitors and placebo in the treatment of obsessive-compulsive disorder. *American Journal of Psychiatry, 156,* 1409-1416.

McCarthy, B., & McCarthy, E. (1998). *Male sexual awareness.* New York: Carroll & Graf.

McFall, M. E., & Wollersheim, J. P. (1979). Obsessive-compulsive neurosis: A cognitive-behavioral formulation and approach to treatment. *Cognitive Therapy and Research, 3,* 333-348.

McLean, P. D., Whittal, M. L., Thordarson, D. S., Taylor, S., Söchting, I., Koch, W. J., et al. (2001). Cognitive versus behavior therapy in the group treatment of obsessive-compulsive disorder. *Journal of Consulting and Clinical Psychology, 69,* 205-214.

Minichiello, W. E., Baer, L., & Jenike, M. A. (1987). Schizotypal personality disorder: A poor prognostic indicator for behavior therapy in the treatment of obsessive-compulsive disorder. *Journal of Anxiety Disorders, 1,* 273-276.

Obsessive Compulsive Cognitions Working Group (1997). Cognitive assessment of obsessive-compulsive disorder. *Behaviour Research and Therapy, 35,* 667-681.

O'Sullivan, G., Noshirvani, H., Marks, I., Monteiro, W., & Lelliott, P. (1991). Six-year follow-up after exposure and clomipramine therapy for obsessive-compulsive disorder. *Journal of Clinical Psychiatry, 52,* 150-155.

Otto, M. W. (2000). Stories and metaphors in cognitive-behavior therapy. *Cognitive and Behavioral Practice, 7,* 166-172.

Parkinson, L., & Rachman, S. J. (1981). Are intrusive thoughts subject to habituation? *Behaviour Research and Therapy, 18,* 409-418.

Pato, M. T., Zohar-Kadouch, R., Zohar, J., & Murphy, D. L. (1988). Return of symptoms after discontinuation of clomipramine in patients with obsessive-compulsive disorder. *American Journal of Psychiatry, 145,* 1521-1525.

Persons, J. B., & Foa, E. B. (1984). Processing of fearful and neutral information by obsessive-compulsives. *Behaviour Research and Therapy, 22,* 259-265.

Pigott, T. A., & Seay, S. M. (1999). A review of the efficacy of selective serotonin reuptake inhibitors in obsessive-compulsive disorder. *Journal of Clinical Psychiatry, 60,* 101-106.

Purdon, C. (1999). Thought suppression and psychopathology. *Behaviour Research and Therapy, 37,* 1029-1054.

Rachman, S. (1993). Obsessions, responsibility, and guilt. *Behaviour Research and Therapy, 31,* 149-154.

Rachman, S. (1997). A cognitive theory of obsessions. *Behaviour Research and Therapy, 35,* 793-802.

Rachman, S., & de Silva, P. (1978). Abnormal and normal obsessions. *Behaviour Research and Therapy, 16,* 233-248.

Rachman, S., & Hodgson, R. (1980). *Obsessions and compulsions.* Englewood Cliffs, NJ: Prentice Hall.

Rasmussen, S. A., & Eisen, J. L. (1990). Epidemiology and clinical features of obsessive-compulsive disorder. In M. A. Jenike, L. Baer, & W. E. Minichiello (Eds.), *Obsessive-compulsive disorders: Theory and management* (2nd ed., pp. 10-29). Chicago: Year Book Medical Publishers.

Rasmussen, S. A., & Eisen, J. L. (1992). The epidemiology and clinical features of obsessive compulsive disorder. *Psychiatric Clinics of North America, 15,* 743-758.

Rasmussen, S. A., & Tsuang, M. T. (1986). Clinical characteristics and family history in DSM-III obsessive-compulsive disorder. *American Journal of Psychiatry, 143*(3), 317-322.

Reed, G. F. (1985). *Obsessional experience and compulsive behaviour: A cognitive-structural approach.* Orlando, FL: Academic Press.

Rhéaume, J., Freeston, M. H., Léger, E., & Ladouceur, R. (1998). Bad luck: An underestimated factor in the development of obsessive-compulsive disorder. *Clinical Psychology and Psychotherapy, 5,* 1-12.

Riggs, D. S., & Foa, E. B. (1993). Obsessive compulsive disorder. In D. H. Barlow (Ed.), *Clinical handbook of psychological disorders: A step-by-step treatment manual* (2nd ed., pp. 189-239). New York: Guilford Press.

Salkovskis, P. M. (1985). Obsessional-compulsive problems: A cognitive-behavioral analysis. *Behaviour Research and Therapy, 23,* 571-584.

Salkovskis, P. M. (1989). Cognitive-behavioural factors and the persistence of intrusive thoughts in obsessional problems. *Behaviour Research and Therapy, 27,* 677-682.

Salkovskis, P. M., & Campbell, P. (1994). Thought suppression induces intrusion in naturally occurring negative intrusive thoughts. *Behaviour Research and Therapy, 32,* 1-8.

Salkovskis, P., & Harrison, J. (1984). Abnormal and normal obsessions: A replication. *Behaviour Research and Therapy, 22,* 549-552.

Salkovskis, P., Shafran, R., Rachman, S., & Freeston, M. H. (1999). Multiple pathways to inflated responsibility beliefs in obsessional problems: Possible origins and implications for therapy and research. *Behaviour Research and Therapy, 37,* 1055-1072.

Savage, C. R., Baer, L., Keuthen, N. J., Brown, H. D., Rauch, S. L., & Jenike, M. A. (1999). Organizational strategies mediate nonverbal memory impairment in obsessive-compulsive disorder. *Biological Psychiatry, 45,* 905-916.

Schwartz, J. M., Stoessel, P. W., Baxter, L. R., Jr., Martin, K. M., & Phelps, M. E. (1996). Systematic changes in cerebral glucose metabolic rate after successful behavior modification treatment of obsessive-compulsive disorder. *Archives of General Psychiatry, 53,* 109-113.

Shafran, R., Thordarson, D. S., & Rachman, S. (1996). Thought-action fusion in obsessive compulsive disorder. *Journal of Anxiety Disorders 10,* 379-391.

Skoog, G., & Skoog, I. (1999). A 40-year follow-up of patients with obsessive-compulsive disorder. *Archives of General Psychiatry, 56,* 121-127.

Söchting, I., Whittal, M. L., & McLean, P. D. (1996). *Group cognitive behavior therapy (GCBT) treatment manual for obsessive compulsive disorder (OCD).* Unpublished manuscript, University of British Columbia, Canada.

Sookman, D., Pinard, G., & Beck, A. T. (2001). Vulnerability schemas in obsessive-compulsive disorder. *Journal of Cognitive Psychotherapy: An International Quarterly, 15,* 109-130.

Steketee, G. (1999). *Overcoming obsessive-compulsive disorder: A behavioral and cognitive protocol for the treatment of OCD.* Oakland, CA: New Harbinger Publications.

Steketee, G., & Barlow, D. H. (2002). Obsessive-compulsive disorder. In D. H. Barlow (Ed.), *Anxiety and its disorders: The nature and treatment of anxiety and panic* (2nd ed., pp. 516-550). New York: Guilford Press.

Steketee, G., Chambless, D. L., & Tran, G. (2001). Effects of Axis I and II comorbidity on behavior therapy outcome for obsessive compulsive disorder and agoraphobia. *Comprehensive Psychiatry, 42,* 76-86.

Steketee, G., & Frost, R. O. (1998). Cost-effective behavior therapy for obsessive compulsive disorder. In E. Sanavio (Ed.), *Behavior and cognitive therapy today: Essays in honor of Hans J. Eysenck* (pp. 289-304). Oxford, England: Elsevier.

Steketee, G., & Frost, R. O. (in press). *Compulsive hoarding: Therapist guide.* Oxford, England: Oxford University Press.

Steketee, G., Frost, R. O., Wincze, J., Greene, K. A. I., & Douglass, H. (2000). Group and individual treatment of compulsive hoarding: A pilot study. *Behavioural and Cognitive Psychotherapy, 28,* 259-268.

Steketee, G., Henninger, N. J., & Pollard, C. A. (2000). Predicting treatment outcomes for obsessive-compulsive disorder: Effects of comorbidity. In W. K. Goodman, M. V. Rudorfer, & J. D. Maser (Eds.), *Obsessive-compulsive disorder: Contemporary issues in treatment* (pp. 257-274). Mahwah, NJ: Lawrence Erlbaum Associates.

Steketee, G., & Shapiro, L. J. (1995). Predicting behavioral treatment outcome for agoraphobia and obsessive-compulsive disorder. *Clinical Psychology Review, 15,* 317-346.

Summerfeldt, L. J., Richter, M. A., Antony, M. M., & Swinson, R. P. (1999). Symptom structure in obsessive-compulsive disorder: A confirmatory factor-analytic study. *Behaviour Research and Therapy, 37,* 297-311.

Tallis, F. (1996). Compulsive washing in the absence of phobic and illness anxiety. *Behaviour Research and Therapy, 33,* 361-362.

van Balkom, A. J. L. M., de Haan, E., van Oppen, P., Spinhoven, P., Hoogduin, K. A. L., & van Dyck, R. (1998). Cognitive and behavioral therapies alone versus in combination with fluvoxamine in the treatment of obsessive compulsive disorder. *Journal of Nervous and Mental Disease, 186,* 492-499.

van Balkom, A. J. L. M., van Oppen, P., Vermeulen, A. W. A., van Dyck, R., Nauta, M. C. E., & Vorst, H. C. M. (1994). A meta-analysis on the treatment of obsessive-compulsive disorder: A comparison of antidepressants, behavior, and cognitive therapy. *Clinical Psychology Review, 14,* 359-381.

van Oppen, P., & Arntz, A. (1994). Cognitive therapy for obsessive-compulsive disorder. *Behavior Research and Therapy, 32,* 79-87.

van Oppen, P., de Haan, E., van Balkom, A. J. L. M., Spinhoven, P., Hoogduin, K., & van Dyck, R. (1995). Cognitive therapy and exposure in vivo in the treatment of obsessive-compulsive disorder. *Behaviour Research and Therapy, 33,* 379-390.

Wegner, D. M. (1989). *White bears and other unwanted thoughts.* New York: Viking.

Weissman, M. M., Bland, R. C., Canino, G. J., Greenwald, S., Hwo, H. G., Lee, C. K., et al. (1994). The cross national epidemiology of obsessive compulsive disorder. *Journal of Clinical Psychiatry, 55,* 5-10.

Welner, A., Reich, T., Robins, E., Fishman, R., & VanDoren, T. (1976). Obsessive neurosis: Record, follow-up, and family studies. I. Inpatient record study. *Comprehensive Psychiatry, 17,* 527-539.

Whittal, M. L., Thordarson, D. S., & McLean, P. D. (in press). Treatment of obsessive-compulsive disorder: Cognitive behavior therapy vs. exposure and response prevention. *Behaviour Research and Therapy.*

Wilhelm, S. (2000). Cognitive therapy for obsessive compulsive disorder. *Journal of Cognitive Psychotherapy, 14,* 245-259.

Wilhelm, S., Steketee, G., Fama, J. M., & Golan, E. (2003, November). A controlled trial investigating cognitive therapy for OCD: Treatment outcome, acceptability, and mechanisms of improvement. In S. Wilhelm (Chair), *Mechanisms and predictors of effective OCD treatment.* Symposium conducted at the meeting of the Association for Advancement of Behavior Therapy, Boston.

Wilhelm, S., Steketee, G., Reilly-Harrington, N., Deckersbach, T., Buhlmann, U., & Baer, L. (in press). Effectiveness of cognitive therapy for obsessive-compulsive disorder: An open trial. *Journal of Cognitive Psychotherapy.*

Wilhelm, S., Steketee, G., & Yovel, I. (2004, July). *Multi-site study of predictors of treatment outcome for OCD.* Paper presented at the annual conference of the Obsessive Compulsive Foundation, Chicago.

Wilhelm, S., Yovel, I., Gershuny, B., Steketee, G., Buhlmann, U., Mitchell, J., et al. (2005). *The obsessive-compulsive symptoms rating scale: Development and psychometric analysis.* Manuscript submitted for publication (2005).

Wisner, K. L., Peindl, K. S., Gigliotti, T., & Hanusa, B. H. (1999). Obsessions and compulsions in women with postpartum depression. *Journal of Clinical Psychiatry, 60,* 176-180.

Yaryura-Tobias, J. A., Grunes, M. S., & Todaro, J. (2000). Nosological insertion of axis I disorders in the etiology of obsessive-compulsive disorder. *Journal of Anxiety Disorders, 14,* 19-30.

Index

Male Sexual Awareness (McCarthy and
McCarthy), 78
McCarthy, Barry and Emily, 78
McKay, Matthew, 38
measures, symptom. *See* symptom measures
medications, 15, 177-178
metaphors, 41; control of thoughts and, 94;
core beliefs and, 167 overestimation of
danger and, 108; overimportance of
thoughts and, 79-80 perfectionism and,
140-141
Mind and Heart in Human Sexual Behavior, The
(Bell), 78
money, betting, 44, 108-109
mood: beliefs and, 11-12; checking with
patients about, 50; stressors and, 6-7
mood disorders, 5
My Secret Garden (Friday), 78

N

negative core beliefs, 27, 39, 161
neutralizing thoughts/behaviors, 2
notebooks, 50

O

obsessions vs. normal intrusions, 5-6, 55-56
Obsessive Beliefs Questionnaire–Extended
(OBQ-Ext), 24, 35; sample of, 189-194
Obsessive Compulsive Cognitions Working
Group (OCCWG), 8
obsessive compulsive disorder (OCD): assessing
symptoms of, 37 characteristics of, 1-2;
cognitive models of, 7-13; cognitive
therapy for, 15-19; comorbid conditions
with, 5, 12, 22-23; defining for patients,
51 diagnosis of, 22-23; etiology of, 6-7, 32;
insight/recognition of, 3 normal intrusions
and, 5-6, 55-56; prevalence of, 4; severity
assessment, 23-24; symptoms of, 1-2, 3-4,
18-19; treatments for, 13-15, 23; types of
beliefs in, 8-11, 64-65
Obsessive Compulsive Symptoms Rating Scale
(OCSRS), 23-24, 35; sample of, 181-188
OCD Assessment Form, 36, 37, 52; sample of,
195-198
Otto, Michael, 79, 140
overestimation of danger, 9-10, 101-109;
agenda overview, 102; CT techniques,
103-109; handouts and forms, 101-102;
homework assignments, 102-103, 109
session summary/feedback, 109
overimportance of thoughts, 9, 73-90; agenda
overview, 74; CT techniques, 76-89;
handouts and forms, 73-74; homework
assignments, 75-76, 90 session
summary/feedback, 90

P

panic disorder, 5
perfectionism, 10-11, 133-142; agenda
overview, 134; CT techniques, 134-141
handouts and forms, 133-134; homework
assignments, 124, 141; importance of
flexibility with, 34; session
summary/feedback, 142
Personal Session Form, 50, 55, 63, 68; sample
of, 203
perspective taking, 45, 137-138
pharmacological treatments, 15, 177-178
pie chart technique, 45, 125-127
positive core beliefs, 160-161
positive experiences, fear of, 11, 151-157
positive reinforcement, 34
pregnancy, 7
pretreatment assessment, 21-24
preventing relapses. *See* relapse prevention
probability of harm, 44, 104-106
problem-solving methods, 46, 176-177
Problem-Solving Worksheet, 232
pros and cons technique. *See* advantages and
disadvantages technique
psychoeducation: overimportance of thoughts
and, 78-79; perfectionism and, 141

R

rational thinking, 43, 77-78
reassuring patients, 34
reframing the evidence, 167
relapse prevention, 27, 46, 171-179; agenda
overview, 172; coping with stressors,
175-176; crediting patient progress,
174-175; handouts and forms, 171-172;
healthy behaviors and, 177; homework
assignments, 173, 178; medications and,
177-178; orienting patients to, 175;
problem- solving methods and, 176-177;
reviewing CT techniques for, 173-174;
self- treatment sessions and, 177; session
summary/feedback, 179; support groups
and, 178; termination concerns and, 173
religious beliefs, 31-32; control of thoughts
and, 95-96; overimportance of thoughts
and, 78-79
responsibility concerns, 121-131; agenda
overview, 122; beliefs about, 7-8, 10; CT
techniques, 122-130; handouts and forms,
121-122; homework assignments, 122,
130-131; session summary/feedback, 131
retrospective review of the evidence, 45-46;
anxiety avoidance and, 147-148 fear of
positive experiences and, 155

Sabine Wilhelm, Ph.D., is associate professor of psychology at the Harvard Medical School. She directs the Cognitive Behavior Therapy Program, the Body Dysmorphic Disorder Clinic and is clinical director of the Obsessive-Compulsive Disorder Clinic, at Massachusetts General Hospital. A graduate of Marburg University in Germany, she completed her internship and post-doctoral fellowship at Massachusetts General Hospital/Harvard Medical School. Dr. Wilhelm's pioneering research on OCD and related disorders is funded by the National Institute of Mental Health and by private foundations. She has lectured internationally and has published numerous articles and book chapters on OCD and related disorders. Dr. Wilhelm serves on several editorial boards and on the Scientific Advisory Board of the Obsessive-Compulsive Foundation. Her current research projects focus on understanding the nature of, OCD, body dysmorphic disorder and Tourette's syndrome and on developing new treatments for those disorders.

Gail Steketee, Ph.D., is professor and dean ad interim of the School of Social Work at Boston University. A graduate of Harvard University and Bryn Mawr College's Graduate School of Social Work and Social Research, Dr. Steketee has conducted research on the psychopathology and treatment of anxiety disorders, especially OCD and related conditions such as hoarding. She has published numerous articles and chapters on OCD and related anxiety disorders, as well as four books on OCD for clinicians and researchers and for sufferers and their families. She is principal investigator of 2 NIMH-funded studies of compulsive hoarding and together with Dr. Wilhelm has conducted an NIMH-funded study to develop and test a cognitive therapy for OCD. She serves on the Scientific Advisory Board for the Obsessive Compulsive Foundation and co-chairs a group of international researchers, the Obsessive-Compulsive Cognitions Working Group, who have developed and tested cognitive assessment strategies for OCD using multi-site research methods.

Some Other
New Harbinger Titles

The End of-life Handbook, Item 5112 $15.95

The Mindfulness and Acceptance Workbook for Anxiety, Item 4993 $21.95

A Cancer Patient's Guide to Overcoming Depression and Anxiety, Item 5044 $19.95

Handbook of Clinical Psychopharmacology for Therapists, 5th edition, Item 5358 $55.95

Disarming the Narcissist, Item 5198 $14.95

The ABCs of Human Behavior, Item 5389 $49.95

Rage, Item 4627 $14.95

10 Simple Solutions to Chronic Pain, Item 4825 $12.95

The Estrogen-Depression Connection, Item 4832 $16.95

Helping Your Socially Vulnerable Child, Item 4580 $15.95

Life Planning for Adults with Developmental Disabilities, Item 4511 $19.95

Overcoming Fear of Heights, Item 4566 $14.95

Acceptance & Commitment Therapy for the Treatment of Post-Traumatic Stress Disorder & Trauma-Related Problems, Item 4726 $58.95

But I Didn't Mean That!, Item 4887 $14.95

Calming Your Anxious Mind, 2nd edition, Item 4870 $14.95

10 Simple Solutions for Building Self-Esteem, Item 4955 $12.95

The Dialectical Behavior Therapy Skills Workbook, Item 5136 $21.95

The Family Intervention Guide to Mental Illness, Item 5068 $17.95

Finding Life Beyond Trauma, Item 4979 $19.95

Five Good Minutes at Work, Item 4900 $14.95

It's So Hard to Love You, Item 4962 $14.95

Energy Tapping for Trauma, Item 5013 $17.95

Thoughts & Feelings, 3rd edition, Item 5105 $19.95

Transforming Depression, Item 4917 $12.95

Helping A Child with Nonverbal Learning Disorder, 2nd edition, Item 5266 $15.95

Leave Your Mind Behind, Item 5341 $14.95

Learning ACT, Item 4986 $44.95

ACT for Depression, Item 5099 $42.95

Integrative Treatment for Adult ADHD, Item 5211 $49.95

Freeing the Angry Mind, Item 4380 $14.95

Living Beyond Your Pain, Item 4097 $19.95

Call **toll free, 1-800-748-6273,** or log on to our online bookstore at **www.newharbinger.com** to order. Have your Visa or Mastercard number ready. Or send a check for the titles you want to New Harbinger Publications, Inc., 5674 Shattuck Ave., Oakland, CA 94609. Include $4.50 for the first book and 75¢ for each additional book, to cover shipping and handling. (California residents please include appropriate sales tax.) Allow two to five weeks for delivery.

Prices subject to change without notice.

Made in the USA
Monee, IL
04 November 2021